365 DAYS
OF NATURE AND DISCOVERY

Illustrated by Jane Reynolds

Text by Phil Gates
and Gaden Robinson

Harry N. Abrams, Inc., Publishers

For Ella whose idea inspired this book

Library of Congress Catalog Card Number: 94–70820

ISBN 0–8109–3876–6

Published in 1994 by Harry N. Abrams, Incorporated, New York
A Times Mirror Company

Designed and produced by Bellew Publishing Company Limited, London

Printed and bound in Italy

INTRODUCTION

Many scientists now believe there may be as many as 30 million different living organisms, and some calculate that this figure should be closer to 100 million. If there are 30 million species, we would need another 3.25 km/2 mi. of shelf space containing 81,250 books like this one in order to represent the whole of life on earth.

No one will ever write all those books because organisms are becoming extinct at such a rapid rate that many will have vanished before they can be collected, named and described. During this century, the destruction of forests, pollution of land and the oceans, drainage of wetlands, the spread of intensive farming and changes in the atmosphere have brought levels of extinction unparalleled since the great geological upheavals of the remote past, millions of years ago.

Conserving the diversity of life on the planet is now one of the most important tasks for mankind. Most people would agree that we have a moral duty to protect the organisms that share the planet with us.

Undiscovered species on Earth are not only microscopic forms of life. Recently a goat-sized mammal, the Vu Quang ox, that is completely new to science, has been discovered in the Vietnamese jungle. In the darkness of the deep ocean floor whole ecosystems of giant tubeworms, crabs and mollusks that live on sulfur have been located and described for the first time in the last 25 years. Scientists have had to invent new taxonomic terms for them because they are so different from any other organism that we know of. The megamouth shark was only discovered in 1976 and a mere handful have been seen since. The oceans are so vast and inaccessible that it is certain that there are many more unknown animals lurking in their depths.

Our knowledge of the intimate details of the lives of most of the 1,413,000 species that have been named is minimal; for many of them it would literally be possible to write all that is known about them on the back of a postage stamp. Modern biological science has generated powerful techniques for probing the secrets of DNA, the molecule that contains the genetic code for all of the characteristics of living animals. For a few organisms this has allowed biologists to unravel their secrets, gene by gene, molecule by molecule, cell by cell, so we can follow their development from the moment of conception, when sperm fertilizes the egg, and we can even change the pattern of development at will.

We should never forget just how little we know about the simplest details of the day to day lives of the vast majority of organisms on the planet. This book is full of facts, but it is what we don't know about our fellow life forms that is the most telling indictment of the way in which we treat them. The destruction of species that have taken millions of years to evolve, without gaining even the simplest knowledge of their biology is, quite simply, uncivilized.

It is the task of natural historians to observe and interpret the diversity of life on Earth. Often, this requires little more than a well-developed sense of curiosity, a generous measure of patience, and keen and meticulous observation. These are exciting and turbulent times for anyone who cares about the planet Earth. We hope that this book will encourage readers to go out and explore it for themselves.

THE DAYS

This book is designed to be used day by day and cross references appear on every page. Additional information, including safety instruction (p. 368), scientific classification, experiments and a comprehensive index including Latin names can be found between pages 366 to 394.

SHARK DAY

A shark has up to 3,000 teeth, arranged in between 6 and 20 rows, which move forward as if on a conveyor belt. Worn front rows are replaced every few days and a shark uses about 20,000 teeth in a lifetime. The bite of a shark is 300 times more powerful than that of a human.

The Hollywood image of the great white shark, as a savage man-eater, ignores the fact that it is one of the most beautifully adapted carnivores in the ocean, with exceptionally well-developed sensory systems. There are about 370 shark species and only a handful are known to attack swimmers, mistaking them for seals and other natural prey. Most species are fish-eaters.

A finely tuned sense of smell, which can detect one drop of blood in over 100 litres/25 gallons of water, helps sharks to locate injured prey. Their snouts are also equipped with a sensitive system for detecting electric charges emitted by other animals, which can perceive one millionth of a volt.

Most sharks are ovoviviparous, with eggs hatching in their wombs, so that young are born alive. They have a cartilaginous, rather than bony, skeleton and their streamlined, muscular bodies, with a large, asymmetric tail fin, are perfectly designed for fast swimming. The mako shark is probably the fastest fish in the world, capable of swimming at 95 kph/60 mph.

☛ 52 RAY; 119 KILLER WHALE.

SEAL DAY

Seals are aquatic mammals whose closest relatives are the Carnivora (cat-, dog- and bear-like mammals). They are highly adapted to life in cold seas (although a few of the 32 species occur in fresh water). Streamlined, their limbs are reduced to webbed paddles and their hair is short and dense. They spend most of their lives in water but breed on land or on ice floes.

Mating male hooded seals display a repulsive-looking red bladder from their noses – the nostril lining.

Thick waterproof fur and a deep layer of fat (blubber) below the skin insulate seals so effectively that they can swim happily in water so cold that a human would die within a few minutes of immersion.

The largest seals, bull elephant seals (above) weighing up to 4 tons, battle for dominance and a harem of cows on beaches on the subantarctic islands.

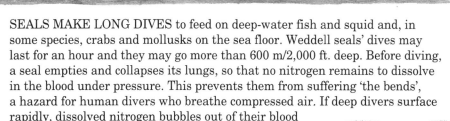

SEALS MAKE LONG DIVES to feed on deep-water fish and squid and, in some species, crabs and mollusks on the sea floor. Weddell seals' dives may last for an hour and they may go more than 600 m/2,000 ft. deep. Before diving, a seal empties and collapses its lungs, so that no nitrogen remains to dissolve in the blood under pressure. This prevents them from suffering 'the bends', a hazard for human divers who breathe compressed air. If deep divers surface rapidly, dissolved nitrogen bubbles out of their blood and becomes trapped in the heart or brain, often with fatal results.

☛ 26 WALRUS.

PIG DAY

Wild boar, which are the ancestors of today's farmyard pigs, were first domesticated by neolithic people in the Middle East and North Africa. Even now, domestic pig populations that escape into the wild tend to revert to characteristics that are typical of their wild ancestors, such as striped camouflage patterns in piglets.

Pigs give birth to between eight and twelve young and have a short breeding cycle.

Wild boar are equipped with dangerous tusks and readily attack when confronted. Domestic boars retain some of this natural aggression and boars and sows can deliver painful bites.

Numerous local races of pig have been selected over the centuries. In Britain, striped saddlebacks, Tamworths, Gloucester old spots and large whites are four of the best known varieties.

IN THE AMERICAS pigs are represented by peccaries, which look similar but live in closely knit groups that defend territories against competitors. Old World wild pigs lack territorial aggression, which makes them more suitable for domestication in herds.

Unlike cattle and sheep, pigs display the high levels of intelligence that are more often associated with dogs. They can be trained to find truffles and sniff out drugs.

☛ *172 CATTLE; 144 SHEEP.*

3

FROG AND TOAD DAY

The 3,400 species of frogs and toads – the Anura – represent about 90 percent of amphibian species. They have no tails, except during the larval (tadpole) stages. Adults are equipped with long hind legs that often give them the ability to jump. Their protruding eyes, mounted high on the head, allow 360 degree vision. Some toads have tongues that can be flicked out instantaneously, to capture prey.

Many frogs and toads are highly vocal animals, producing mating calls with inflated vocal sacs.

Darwin's frog, from South America, lives on the forest floor and carries its tadpoles in its mouth, in an enlarged vocal sac.

The Cameroon toad (right) is well disguised, with a dorsal surface that mimics a leaf. Until it moves, it is almost invisible.

Aneurid species diversity is highest in humid tropical rainforests, where the small poison dart frogs (above, left) are common. Frog and toad populations are declining worldwide and pesticide pollution, acid rain, viral diseases and climate change are all possible causes.

Many frog species, including the red-eyed frog (above) are arboreal. Their long, prehensile toes make them agile climbers. Other species, like the narrow-mouthed burrowing rain frog (above, center) survive drought in arid areas by remaining dormant underground until rains return.

Tropical aneurans, like the golden toad (left) and painted reed frog (below), are often brilliantly colored. Striped skins disrupt outlines and provide camouflage, while the bright colors of poison dart frogs (bottom, left and right) serve as a warning; a single individual of one of these species can produce enough batrachotoxin to kill 1,500 people.

Frogs generally have longer legs, more slender bodies and smoother skins than warty toads. Neither group is confined to permanently wet habitats and many species can live and breed well away from standing water.

Many of the smaller tropical frogs produce few eggs and guard them during development. Some poison dart frogs carry their tadpoles on their backs (below).

Ground-living, semi-aquatic species like the leopard frog (left) have webbed hind toes and muscular hind legs, adapted for swimming and leaping.

THE DEVELOPMENT OF FROG AND TOAD SPAWN can be studied in an aquarium, but only a few eggs should be collected. Tadpoles feed on algae and water weeds in the early stages, but once legs appear they switch to an animal diet and should be transferred to a pond. Frogs and toads lose their gills and become air-breathing once the tail begins to shrink; unless they are able to climb out of the water, they will drown. Frogs will happily breed in garden ponds, feeding on slugs and other garden pests.

☛ 8 NEWT; 349 SALAMANDER; 56 POND.

PINEAPPLE DAY

Pineapple belongs to a tropical plant family called the Bromeliaceae. Its fruit is composed of an aggregate of up to 200 flowers on a short stem, which swell to form the familiar pineapple (right). The long, sharp leaves produce tough fibers which are used to produce a lustrous textile in the Philippines.

The decorative flowers and foliage of several bromeliad species makes them popular houseplants.

Many bromeliads are tropical epiphytes, growing on branches in the tree canopy. They have poorly developed root systems and their overlapping leaf bases accumulate and absorb rainwater. These aerial mini-ponds become colonized by a wide variety of animals; terrestrial crabs, mosquitoes, damselflies and frogs (bottom left) all breed in them. Such miniature aquatic ecosystems in plants are known as phytotelmata.

RIPE PINEAPPLE contains powerful protein-digesting enzymes called proteases, which can dissolve proteins like gelatin. Buy a gelatin in a supermarket and dissolve it in hot water, then leave it to cool and set. When it has solidified cut a slice of fresh pineapple and lay pieces in a pattern on the gelatin surface in a warm room overnight. By morning the fruit protease enzymes will have dissolved parts of the gelatin, leaving clear impressions etched in the surface.

☛ 237 EXOTIC FRUITS; 125 BANANA.

BAOBAB DAY

A*dansonia digitata*, the baobab, rarely grows more than 12 m/40 ft. tall but its trunk may have an equal diameter. The tree sometimes lives for 2,000 years. Its stumpy branches look like roots; bushmen believe that God found his creation so ugly that He ripped it from the ground and left it upside down. Baobab is a multipurpose tree and cloth, rope, food, fuel, medicines and glue are extracted from various parts. Its commodious trunk is sometimes hollowed out and made into a room; some baobab trunks have been adapted as jails, bus shelters and lavatories.

☞ 227 OAK; 78–9 DESERT; 174 KILLER SNAKES.

Baobabs survive long droughts, thanks to a widespread root system that captures rainfall efficiently. Thousands of gallons of water are stored in old hollow trees, which provide natural drinking reservoirs for bushmen in arid areas. Elephants gouge out the pulpy bark when water is scarce.

Baobab is a 'wildlife hotel', home to bushbabies, boomslangs, hornbills, weaver birds, geckos, mantids, moths and bees. Bats pollinate its white, bell-shaped flowers; its fruit, known as 'monkey bread', is the favorite food of baboons.

NEWT DAY

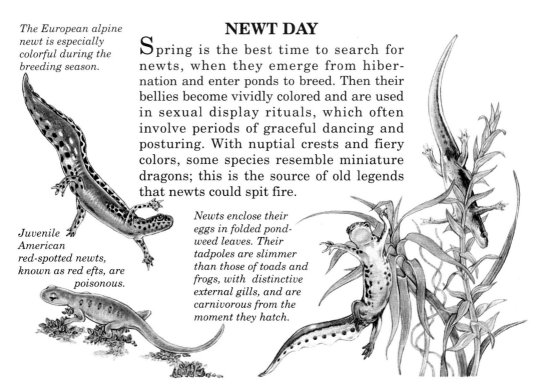

The European alpine newt is especially colorful during the breeding season.

Spring is the best time to search for newts, when they emerge from hibernation and enter ponds to breed. Then their bellies become vividly colored and are used in sexual display rituals, which often involve periods of graceful dancing and posturing. With nuptial crests and fiery colors, some species resemble miniature dragons; this is the source of old legends that newts could spit fire.

Juvenile American red-spotted newts, known as red efts, are poisonous.

Newts enclose their eggs in folded pond-weed leaves. Their tadpoles are slimmer than those of toads and frogs, with distinctive external gills, and are carnivorous from the moment they hatch.

THE MATING DANCES OF NEWTS are easy to watch in an aquarium. Like all amphibians they breathe air, and so must be able to climb out of the water, otherwise they soon become exhausted and drown. Outside of the breeding season they can be kept for short periods in a vivarium. The great crested newt is a protected, declining species in Britain and should not be taken from ponds. Outside the breeding season newts can often be found in moist habitats under logs and stones. They feed on small slugs, insects and other invertebrates.

☛ *4–5 FROG AND TOAD.*

MAYFLY DAY

Mayflies are aquatic insects whose larvae live in ponds, streams and rivers. They are remarkable for the adult has two forms. The first, the subimago, emerges on dry land from the last molt of a nymph that has crawled ashore. It dries its wings then flies but within a few hours molts again into a fully developed imago or adult.

Flattened, feathery gills on either side of the abdomen act exactly like a fish's gills, absorbing oxygen from the water and releasing carbon dioxide.

Pond-dwelling mayfly nymphs are rounded, but those from fast-flowing rivers are flattened so that they can cling to stones without being swept away.

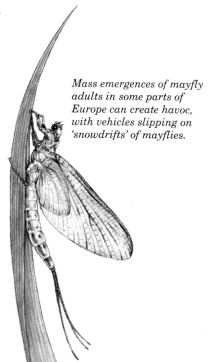

Mass emergences of mayfly adults in some parts of Europe can create havoc, with vehicles slipping on 'snowdrifts' of mayflies.

MAYFLY NYMPHS are common in clean streams and rivers and easy to find just by lifting a stone and examining the surface. You will be able to see the nymphs more clearly by brushing the stone in a shallow white dish containing a little water. Most mayfly nymphs have three 'tails' (cerci), as do the adults.

☞ *329 RIVERBANK; 56 POND; 45 TROUT; 36 LACEWING; 72 DRAGONFLY.*

FLIGHTLESS BIRD DAY

Birds lose the power of flight for, apparently, only one reason, and that is the absence or irrelevance of predators. So flightlessness has evolved in bird species in isolated habitats such as remote islands where there are no predators, or in birds too big to be bothered by hunters. Extinct flightless species include the 3-m/10-ft. tall moa from New Zealand.

South African ostriches are farmed for feathers, meat and leather.

Cassowaries of northern Australia and New Guinea defend themselves by slashing with their sharply spined feet which can kill a man.

Shy kiwis survive in the deep forests of New Zealand, using their slender beaks to probe for worms and grubs.

New Zealand's takahe, long thought extinct, was rediscovered in a hidden valley in 1948.

MANY FLIGHTLESS BIRDS have become extinct since man became seafaring. The dodo, a giant flightless pigeon, survived on the island of Mauritius only until 1680. Hunting by sailors and theft of its eggs by introduced pigs and monkeys drove it to extinction. The last surviving examples of the Wake Island rail were eaten by the starving Japanese garrison during World War II. Over 30 species of flightless rail on oceanic islands have been exterminated by rats and cats introduced by passing ships.

☛ 242 OSTRICH; 51 EMU.

FUNGI DAY

Take a mushroom and slice it carefully lengthwise with a sharp knife to show a section as in the picture on the left. The top of the mushroom is the cap – it may have irregular scales on its surface, like the fly agaric (below). Hanging below the cap are the radiating gills which produce the dusty spores when the mushroom is mature.

The volva forms an often torn thin cup around the base of the stem.

Button mushrooms (above) are immature – the cap is not fully opened.

A third of the way down the stem is the ring. Absent in some species, it may be anything from a faint scar to a conspicuous loose skirt around the stem.

In puffballs the cap completely encloses the developing spores.

THE RING AND VOLVA are remnants of the veils that protect the immature mushroom when it emerges from the soil. When present, their shape may help in identification.

☛ *14 FUNGI AND MOULD; 286 BIOLUMINESCENCE.*

11

HYENA DAY

The cry of hyenas, resembling the howling wind or a chattering laugh, is one of the most spine-tingling sounds of the African night. It used to be thought that they were merely scavengers, sharing with the vultures the remnants of a lion's kills after the hunter had moved on. Recent research shows that they are hunters too, assembling in packs at night and bringing down zebra, wildebeest and antelope.

Aardwolves resemble small striped hyenas. They feed on termites and have weak jaws, defending themselves by ejecting an evil-smelling fluid from anal glands.

There are three species of hyena – the spotted, striped and brown – and all are similar, with longer front than hind legs, which gives them a skulking appearance. Hyenas are between 1 and 1.4 m / 3 and 5 ft. long and despite their dog-like features they are more closely related to cats.

HYENAS HAVE a bony skull crest which serves as an attachment for strong muscles, that give them one of the strongest bites of any carnivore – an essential adaptation for an animal that eats sinews and crushes tough bones that larger predators reject. They can digest almost all parts of a carcass, except hooves and antlers, which are regurgitated as pellets. Hyena packs have been reported to attack humans and they have been credited with imitating a man's voice – probably a figment of the imagination of frightened travelers, surrounded by strange sounds in tropical darkness.

☛ 46 AARDVARK; 160 WILD DOG; 266 VULTURE.

AROMATIC PLANTS DAY

Scented plants have always been important to civilization. Egyptian pharaohs were mummified with aromatic plant extracts and resins. Medieval castle floors were strewn with scented herbs to mask the unpleasant smells that developed in these insanitary dwellings.

Balm of Gilead is another scented resin, used to make incense. It comes from the tree Commiphora gileadensis, *which grows beside the Red Sea.*

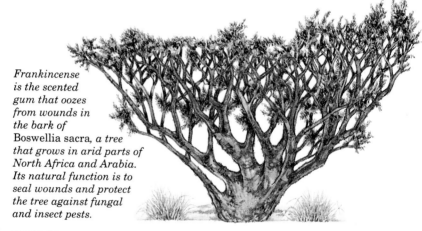

Frankincense is the scented gum that oozes from wounds in the bark of Boswellia sacra, *a tree that grows in arid parts of North Africa and Arabia. Its natural function is to seal wounds and protect the tree against fungal and insect pests.*

EXPLORE THE NATURAL SCENTS of plants by crushing leaves and fruits. Pine needles, black currant, chrysanthemum and lavender leaves all have distinctive aromas.

☛ *344 ALOE.*

*Many herbs contain aromatic compounds, and sweet cicely (*Myrrhis odorata*), which grows throughout Europe, has a strong aniseed aroma when crushed. It was used to sweeten puddings before sugar became widely available.*

13

FUNGI AND MOLD DAY

The mycelium ('roots') of a fungus form its feeding mechanism. Most fungi are saprophytic – their mycelia secrete enzymes to dissolve dead or dying plant and animal matter so that it can be absorbed, providing food for the fungus. Some fungi are parasites, attacking living organisms; some root fungi are symbionts, providing essential nutrients to tree seedlings.

Fungi are especially important as decomposers, recycling the materials needed for new life. They are beneficial in other ways – yeasts are used in bread-making and fermentation, and blue mold flavors and matures cheese.

Ink caps, themselves fungi, decay through the action of smaller saprophytic fungi and bacteria.

Fungi are also pests – dry rot attacks woodwork, athlete's foot and other pathogenic fungi attack man, and mildew attacks plants (bottom right).

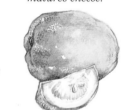

IT IS EASY TO GROW MOLD on stale bread. Dampen the bread and leave it to stand overnight. Fungal spores in the air will settle and begin to grow. Put the bread in an airtight container and keep it warm and slightly damp. The mold mycelium will spread from the spore and be visible within two to three days. The mold will eventually produce black spores, visible under a magnifying glass.

☛ *248 POISONOUS FUNGI; 342 ASCOMYCETE AND BASIDIOMYCETE FUNGI; 11 FUNGI; 166 CEREALS; 285 EPIDEMIC.*

SPARROW DAY

Seven thousand years ago, when neolithic people migrated across Europe from the Middle East, house sparrows probably followed close behind. They are always associated with human settlements, except during a brief period in autumn when they move on to arable fields to feed. House sparrows were introduced into the New World and Australia by European settlers.

House sparrows are finches, with broad powerful beaks for crushing seeds

HOUSE SPARROWS have a very patchy distribution and their close association with man gives an exaggerated impression of their abundance. Large areas are devoid of sparrows. Use a map to make a survey of sparrow populations in your area. Mark the locations of house sparrow flocks; you will find that they coincide with places like parks, wasteland, gardens and farms, where food is easily obtained.

☛ *35 PIGEON; 18 TANAGER.*

SEA SQUIRT DAY

Some sea squirt species are attached to their substrate with a stalk. Others are free-floating and live in the plankton.

Sea squirts, also known as tunicates or ascidians, are the most primitive living relatives of humans and all other animals with a backbone.

Their larvae have a 'notochord' – a stiff but flexible rod which gives internal strength to their tail – and they also possess a nerve chord and a rudimentary brain.

The tadpole-like sea squirt larvae are called oikopleura and swim in the plankton before settling on a rock or seaweed and becoming an adult gelatinous 'blob'.

Sea squirts are unique in the animal kingdom because their outer 'tunic' (hence 'tunicates') contains cellulose, a substance only otherwise found in plant cells. This is just one of many unusual features; another is that their direction of blood flow reverses after every 30 heartbeats. They also have an unusual propensity to accumulate heavy metals, including gold, from seawater.

SEARCH FOR SEA SQUIRTS under rocks and among seaweed at extreme low tide on the seashore. Many species look like shapeless lumps of jelly, but close examination reveals inhalent and exhalent water siphons and a gentle squeeze will send jets of water from these – hence the name 'sea squirt'.

☛ 254 PLANKTON.

CORAL DAY

Coral atolls form around the peaks of volcanoes which are slowly sinking below the sea surface, while barrier reefs grow along the edges of continents that are slowly sinking. The Great Barrier Reef, formed on the gently rolling hills of the submerged Queensland plateau, is the largest animal construction on earth and is visible from outer space.

Crevices, bored into the coral by sponges and other coral feeders, provide a lair for some of the fiercer predators, like moray eels.

An exceptionally diverse array of animals live in and on reefs, which are often referred to as 'the rainforests of the oceans'.

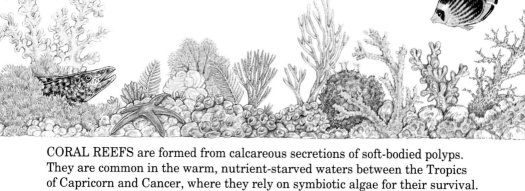

CORAL REEFS are formed from calcareous secretions of soft-bodied polyps. They are common in the warm, nutrient-starved waters between the Tropics of Capricorn and Cancer, where they rely on symbiotic algae for their survival. Red and green algae live within the polyps, photosynthesizing and providing a carbohydrate supply for their hosts. Blue-green algae live on the surface of the reef and supply essential nitrogen compounds. Coral reefs only form in shallow water, where sunlight can penetrate and provide the energy source for algal photosynthesis.

☛ 113 GIANT CLAM; 315 ROCK POOL; 134 BUTTERFLY FISH.

TANAGER DAY

There are 248 species of tanager belonging to the Emberizidae, a family which also includes buntings and cardinals. Many buntings from Old World temperate regions have drab, streaked plumage but the tropical and subtropical cardinals and tanagers of the New World are noted for their vibrant red, blue, yellow or black feathers.

Many of the tanager species of Mexico and South America form noisy flocks that move through the undergrowth, feeding on seeds, fruits and insects. Fruit-eating tanagers are important seed dispersers in the tropics.

The ant tanagers follow columns of army ants, feeding on the insects that are stirred up in their wake. Palm tanagers search the crowns of palm trees for insects.

The thick-billed euphonia is a tanager that mimics other birds' calls. When predators approach it imitates alarm calls of other species, which are attracted by the ruse and congregate to harass the intruder.

THE SCARLET TANAGER spends the summer in the deciduous forests of the central and southeastern United States, then migrates south, to tropical South America, during the winter. In the autumn the brilliant scarlet feathers of the males are molted and replaced with green and yellow plumage, so that they become hard to distinguish from females throughout the winter. Survey the birds in your area and identify those that develop distinctive breeding plumage.

☞ *118 MIGRATION; 180–1 SEED DISPERSAL.*

WILD SHEEP DAY

Domestication of sheep and goats began early in the Neolithic period, between 9000 and 6000 BC, but it is doubtful whether any existing wild sheep, which all have hairy rather than woolly coats, are direct descendants. Thirty-seven wild sheep species survive, including the Tibetan bharal or blue sheep (left), whose straight horns are almost a 1 m/3 ft. long.

Bighorn or Rocky Mountain sheep of North America and Siberia are extremely agile climbers and jumpers that are perfectly at home on narrow mountain ledges, safe from wolves and pumas.

The protagonists escape brain damage because their horns are attached to a tough structure called an ossicone, which dissipates the force of the collisions.

Like all male sheep, they compete for females by head-butting. These bruising encounters end in one animal establishing dominance.

VISIT A SHEEPDOG TRIAL and watch the skilled way in which shepherds use dogs to control a flock. Wild sheep have a natural tendency to scatter when they are threatened, whereas most domestic sheep have been bred to huddle together in a flock when approached by carnivores.

Domesticated sheep can be aggressive, and will sometimes charge and head-butt intruders who appear to threaten their lambs.

☛ 144 SHEEP; 313 GOAT.

STICK INSECT DAY

Successful camouflage in animals depends on a combination of external features, like shape and color, and behavior patterns. Stick insects hold their thin, twig-shaped bodies perfectly motionless for hours and are almost invisible amongst foliage. If camouflage fails some tropical stick insects release a repulsive vapor which deters ant predators.

Stick insects belong to an insect order known as phasmids, noted for their unusual reproductive behavior. Many species reproduce by virgin birth, or parthenogenesis, when females lay viable eggs without being fertilized by a male. Males are completely absent in some species and rare in many others.

The females scatter large numbers of eggs on the ground, where many are eaten by other animals. Some species lay eggs that mimic plant seeds and may remain dormant for up to two years before hatching.

Phasmids range in size from about 2.5 cm/ 1 in. long to the 33 cm/13 in. giant stick insect of Indonesia, which is the world's longest insect.

KEEP A FEW STICK INSECTS as pets. Most exotic species can be fed on bramble or privet leaves. When they are handled they occasionally shed legs. This phenomenon is known as autotomy and allows them to escape from the jaws of a predator. A new leg is regenerated at the next molt.

☛ *330 CAMOUFLAGE; 293 MIMICRY.*

TORTOISE DAY

*The giant tortoises of the Galapagos Islands (*Testudo elephantopus) *and Indian Ocean islands (*T. gigantia) *grow to 1.5 m / 5 ft. long and are large enough for a person to ride.*

The tortoise's armored dome is formed from enlarged reptilian scales, fused with underlying bony scales of a kind found in extinct reptiles. The shell is joined to the animal's ribs and underbody shield (the plastron), so the head, legs and tail can be retracted for complete protection. Tortoises crush vegetable food in horny, toothless, beaked jaws. Aldabran giant tortoises have a nasal valve that allows them to drink through their nostrils.

There are three species of southern European tortoise: Hermann's, the spur-thighed and the marginated tortoise. All are declining through overcollecting as pets, deaths on roads and scrub fires.

TORTOISES ON DIFFERENT Galapagos Islands have local variations in shell shape and pattern that are specific to each island. Charles Darwin used these characteristics to support his theory that isolated populations of organisms evolve different characters that enhance their adaptation to their particular environments. One Galapagos tortoise shell type has a front recess, allowing its occupant to stretch its neck upward to feed on tall cacti. Such small adaptations are the raw material of evolutionary advance.

☛ *217 MARINE TURTLE; 156 DARWIN'S FINCHES.*

HARVEST MOUSE DAY

Prehensile tails, fleshy pads for grasping on the forefeet, and gripping toes on the hind feet are all adaptations which make harvest mice skilled and acrobatic climbers. With a body length of about 6 cm/ 2.5 in. and unusually light skeletons, they can climb through fragile, swaying grass stems with sure-footed agility. The tail also serves as a balancing organ when the mouse perches on grass stalks. They are active day and night, feeding on a diet of seeds.

A harvest mouse's nest is a beautifully interwoven, 8-cm/3-in. ball of dried grass suspended between grass stems. Several litters, of between four and nine young, are produced each year but each litter is usually produced in a new nest. The young are born blind.

Harvest mice breed in cereal fields, grassland beside roads, railways and in reed beds above water; they are good swimmers, tucking their forelimbs under their chins and paddling with their hind legs.

THE HARVEST MOUSE was first described in England in 1767 by Gilbert White, a great naturalist who kept detailed diaries of his wildlife observations around his home in Selborne. There is still much to be discovered about plants and animals, and carefully recorded observations by amateur naturalists can have real scientific value. Even simple lists of the flora and fauna of specific locations can provide records of the changing wildlife in towns and the countryside that might be of real value in the future. See the end of the book for advice on keeping a natural history diary.

☛ *184 RAT.*

DOLPHIN DAY

Dolphins use a wide range of sounds – whistles, clucks, barks and squeals – to communicate with each other. They make special high-pitched clicks to locate objects underwater, including the fish on which they feed, by bouncing the sound off them. This is called echo location.

Dolphins form secure and protective family groups, swimming, feeding and playing together.

During the birth of a dolphin, 'aunts' assist the mother. One becomes a permanent helper for the first few months of the young dolphin's life.

Being mammals, dolphins must breathe. When they sleep they must float or rise regularly to the surface to breathe through the blow-hole on top of their head.

Dolphins jump when swimming fast. This helps them to breathe, reduces water resistance, and throws off skin parasites.

TRY BOUNCING SOUND off a door. Stand 1 m/3 ft. away and shout – a quick, sharp shout. Now open the door and do it again. Not nearly as much sound will come back at you.

You can measure distance by the time taken for an echo to return. Sound travels about 1 km/0.6 mi. every 3 seconds. A six-second echo from a valley-side means it's about 1 km/0.6 mi. away. Judge the distance of a lightning flash by counting the seconds between flash and thunder: divide by three for the distance in kilometers (five for the distance in miles).

☛ 119 KILLER WHALE.

EGRET DAY

Egrets are members of the heron family and their name comes from the French term 'aigrette' used to describe their filamentous breeding plumes. In the 19th century egrets were slaughtered in vast numbers for their feathers, to satisfy a demand from fashionable society ladies for extravagant decorations for fancy hats.

Cattle egrets are a common sight on tropical farmland.

Egrets are members of the heron family, which also includes bitterns, ibises, storks and spoonbills. Most members of the family have long beaks and legs, and are wading birds, feeding along the margins of lakes and rivers.

Long necks and dagger-shaped bills are common to many members of the heron family. In flight and at rest the neck is drawn into the shoulders.

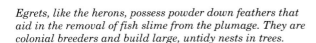

Egrets, like the herons, possess powder down feathers that aid in the removal of fish slime from the plumage. They are colonial breeders and build large, untidy nests in trees.

CATTLE EGRETS ride on the backs of buffaloes, rhinos and cattle, catching insects that are disturbed by their host's feet. Watch a flock of gulls following a tractor that is ploughing farmland in autumn. Egrets follow ploughs drawn by oxen in tropical climates. Both birds are exploiting human agricultural activity, which uncovers a rich supply of worms and other soil animals.

☛ 65 GULL; 246 HERON.

SALMON DAY

Journeying upstream, salmon must avoid many dangers. Here a grizzly bear tries to snatch chinook salmon weighing up to 40 kg/90 lbs. as they jump a waterfall.

Adult salmon leave the sea in autumn, swim into rivers and head upstream. In gravel beds at the head of the river the male uses his tail to dig a trench in which the female lays several thousand eggs. The male fertilizes the eggs, covers them with gravel, and the adults return to the sea. The young salmon hatch and feed on insect larvae. After two years they migrate to the sea and feed for at least another year before returning to the river as adults to breed.

All seven salmon species are native to North America or northwest Asia; only this one, the Atlantic salmon, also occurs in Europe.

SALMON ARE POWERFUL enough to leap waterfalls 3–4 m/10–13 ft. high. Ask a parent to help you examine a fish or a piece of one. Find the backbone and see how it is formed from short sections of bone with gristle (properly called cartilage) between. The cartilage is flexible: cut out a section of backbone and see how it can be flexed from side to side. It won't move easily up and down, nor can it be pushed shorter. The 'meat' on either side is muscle. Salmon and other fish swim by shortening (contracting) the muscles on either side of the backbone to make it, and thus the whole body, flex.

☛ 45 TROUT; 362 EEL.

WALRUS DAY

The long tusks of male and female walruses allow them to dig in the ooze on the sea floor in search of buried bivalve mollusks, which are the main items in their diet. Digging stirs up a cloud of sediment, but their moustache of highly sensitive whiskers allows them to locate their food in the murky water.

Walruses are excellent swimmers but are clumsy on land.

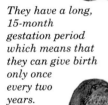

They have a long, 15-month gestation period which means that they can give birth only once every two years.

Walruses breed in noisy colonies around the Arctic ice sheet. Their pharynx has elastic walls and can be inflated as a buoyancy bag, but it also acts as a resonance chamber, giving their calls a bell-like quality that echoes over their breeding beaches.

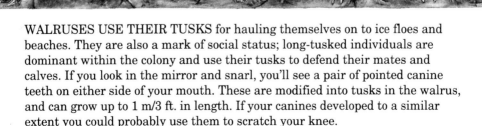

WALRUSES USE THEIR TUSKS for hauling themselves on to ice floes and beaches. They are also a mark of social status; long-tusked individuals are dominant within the colony and use their tusks to defend their mates and calves. If you look in the mirror and snarl, you'll see a pair of pointed canine teeth on either side of your mouth. These are modified into tusks in the walrus, and can grow up to 1 m/3 ft. in length. If your canines developed to a similar extent you could probably use them to scratch your knee.

☛ *153 BIVALVE MOLLUSKS.*

DONKEY DAY

The donkey is the domesticated form of the African wild ass, a shy animal that is now rare in desert regions of Ethiopia and surrounding countries. Horses and asses are grazing mammals that evolved the ability to run on the tips of their toes across the dry, grassy plains that developed 20 million years ago, as the climate became more arid.

Donkeys have become indispensable beasts of burden on almost every continent. Feral descendents of donkeys used by prospectors in the Californian gold rush now live wild in Death Valley and the Grand Canyon. All horses and asses in America have been introduced by man; wild populations became extinct there at the end of the Pleistocene Ice Ages, 12,000 years ago.

Asses, horses, tapirs and rhinoceroses are all hoofed animals (ungulates) with odd numbers of toes on each foot.

HORSES AND ASSES are sometimes interbred, producing offspring that are more surefooted and have greater powers of endurance. When the horse is the female parent the offspring is called a mule; when a donkey is a female parent the result is a hinny. In either case, the offspring is sterile. Biologists consider that the inability of two species to form a fertile hybrid is a good test of their status as distinct species. This is known as the biological species concept, and is regarded as a better criterion for defining species than merely looking for differences in external appearance, which can vary enormously within a single species.

☛ 310 RHINOCEROS; 218 TAPIR.

MOUNTAIN DAY

Despite long winters and short summers, many animals are adapted to life in this harsh environment. European alpine salamanders (left) are common below the tree line, but agile mountain goats (right) live in the highest and most inaccessible mountains in the western United States.

The plumage of willow grouse and ptarmigan turns white in winter, even covering their toes. They feed by digging heather shoots from the snow.

Marmots – ground squirrels that occur across Asia and as far west as Poland – are highly social animals that live in colonies amongst broken rock scree (left).

The snow leopard of the high mountains of Central Asia rarely ventures below 1,000 m/ 3,250 ft., and is so well camouflaged against its frozen environment that it is sometimes called the phantom cat. Surefooted and capable of leaping 8 m/25 ft. ravines, it is a superb predator of the hares, marmots, ibex and mountain goats that graze on mountain pastures in summer and descend to the tree line in winter.

A small number of bird species, like the mountain bluebird of the western United States (below, left), are adapted to seasonal breeding at altitudes of up to 4,000 m / 13,000 ft. Most alpine birds feed their broods on insects during the short summer, when mountain grasshoppers (left) and the alpine butterflies (right) appear in large numbers.

Thick fur is an essential insulation against heat loss at high altitude. South American vicuna rarely venture below 4,000 m / 13,000 ft. and their wool is finer than that of the best merino sheep. These small relatives of the camel were herded by the Incas, to provide wool for cloth. Vicuna have sharp teeth, with long lower incisors that grow continuously to compensate for the wear imposed by chewing tough bunch grasses, that stand up above the snow.

Fur of many alpine mammals, including the mountain hare, often becomes white in winter, to provide camouflage.

Carrion feeders, like the bearded vulture, congregate around sick animals and the kills of mountain predators; they smash bones by dropping them from a height onto rocks, then eat the marrow.

TEST THE HARDINESS of a variety of plants by putting 20-cm/8-in. shoots in the freezer for four hours. Then trim a further 2 cm/0.75 in. from the cut end and immediately transfer the shoots to a vase of water, to thaw. Many will be killed by ice crystals that burst their cells and air bubbles that choke their conducting tissues; antifreeze systems in alpine plants prevent this internal ice damage.

☛ 43 SNOW.

OCTOPUS DAY

Adventure movies have given the octopus a formidable reputation but it is more likely to grip divers out of curiosity than aggression. Its suckers are sensory organs, used to investigate its surroundings, and it catches crabs and other seabed-living creatures with its muscular tentacles, which draw the prey toward its horny beak.

The largest European octopus grows to about 1 m / 3 ft. long.

Octopuses undergo frequent color changes, which they use as a form of communication, to signify aggression and other emotions. They have excellent eyesight, but are color blind.

Octopuses are advanced mollusks and have the best eyes and highest brain-to-body weight ratio of any invertebrate. They brains are proportionately larger than those of many fish, reptiles and mammals.

Giant octopuses live for about three years. The female stops eating while guarding her eggs, which are laid under a rock ledge, and starves to death before the baby octopuses leave the den.

EUROPEAN OCTOPUS SPECIES usually move by crawling over rocks, using their suction disks as anchors. The giant octopus of the North Pacific, sometimes known as the devil fish, is a more active swimmer. Octopuses swim using jet propulsion, forcing water in the muscular sac out through short siphons on either side of the head. Fill a balloon with water and release it under water in the bathtub, where it will shoot forward. The octopus propulsion system works in exactly the same way.

☞ *228 CUTTLEFISH AND SQUID; 113 GIANT CLAM.*

TERMITE DAY

Termites play a vital role in the ecology of the tropics, consuming waste vegetable matter, but they are also major pests. The concerted gnawing of millions of worker termites can quickly reduce wooden structures to dust.

Termite nests can be up to 7 m / 23 ft. high. They are made from a mixture of mud, saliva and excrement, which is so hard that it can often only be destroyed with explosives. Each nest is divided into numerous chambers and has an air circulation system which keeps the millions of inhabitants at an even temperature.

Termites are related to cockroaches but are classified in an insect order of their own, the Isoptera. They do not have a larval form, but hatch from an egg and continue to grow through a series of molts, or 'instars'.

Worker termites spend their lives foraging and building. The larger soldiers cannot feed themselves.

The king and queen are the largest members of the colony. The queen has a distended abdomen and is little more than an egg-laying machine.

A SYMBIOTIC PROTOZOAN called *Trichonympha* lives in the termite gut and digests the wood that it consumes. The more advanced termites cultivate fungus gardens, where edible fungi are grown on indigestible vegetable matter.

☛ 46 AARDVARK; 109 PANGOLIN.

PIRANHA DAY

Piranhas are the most feared freshwater predatory fish. A full-grown piranha is rarely longer than 60 cm/2 ft., but the fish hunt in shoals and each fish's razor-sharp, interlocking teeth can strip 1 cubic inch/ 15 cm³ of flesh with every bite. A shoal can strip the flesh from its prey in a matter of minutes. The presence of blood in the water is known to drive piranhas into a feeding frenzy and they occasionally attack bathers and domestic animals, but most species feed on other fish.

The Amazon, Orinoco and other South America rivers are the haunts of piranhas. There are 25 Amazonian species; the most dangerous is the red-bellied piranha, Serrasalmus nateri, *which is about 20 cm / 8 in. long. Shoals become concentrated in rivers when the water level drops in the dry season.*

Piranha are good to eat and can be caught with a rod and line, provided that a strong, bite-proof wire trace is used. Once caught, they must be handled with care: they can bite through leather gloves and shoes, and the flesh and bone inside.

ALTHOUGH THE BITE of a single piranha is dangerous, they do not develop feeding frenzy until they congregate in shoals of 20 or more. Their attacks are then so ferocious that the victim may have little chance of escape. An adult human has about 3,000 cubic inches (50,000 cm³) of flesh. If a piranha can strip 1 cubic inch (15 cm³) with every bite and can take five bites in a minute, how long would it take a shoal of 100 piranhas to reduce a human to a skeleton? (Answer at the end of the book.)

☛ 1 SHARK.

SUNFLOWER DAY

The pale yellow oil from sunflower seeds is used for cooking, margarine and paint, and the seed meal is used in animal feed. Sunflower crops are now grown over much of central and southern Europe, and in America where the crop originated.

The disk florets in the centre of the flower, and later the seeds, are arranged in precise spirals.

Hollow sunflower stems are packed with exceptionally light pith cells, which were once used to stuff sailors' life-jackets.

The flower heads face east in the morning and track the sun as it moves through the sky, until they face west at sunset.

Jerusalem artichokes are a species of sunflower which produces sweet tubers and rarely flowers. They have no connection with the city of Jerusalem; the name is probably a corruption of 'girasole', the Italian name for sunflower.

SUNFLOWER CROPS are usually short stemmed, but ornamental garden varieties are much taller. The record for the world's tallest sunflower is regularly broken, but currently stands at over 7 m/23 ft. Try to beat the record by raising seedlings in pots early in the year and then transplanting them to a warm, sheltered spot outside. A south-facing wall of a house is ideal. Feed and water the plant regularly.

☛ 47 DAISY; 260 DANDELION.

33

NUDIBRANCH DAY

The brilliant hues of sea slugs, or nudibranchs, serve as a warning to predators that they are poisonous, helping to compensate for their lack of a protective shell. Most nudibranchs are carnivores, feeding on sponges, corals and hydroids. Aeolis feeds on sea anemones, drawing the pigments of its prey into its own body and salvaging the anemones' stinging cells for its own protection.

Nudibranchs lack the gills of other marine mollusks, absorbing oxygen over their whole body surface or through the gill-like structures on their backs, called cerata.

The sea hare, a slug-like relative of the nudibranchs with a small internal shell, releases a purple dye into the water when it is threatened. This is reputed to have been used by the Minoans for dyeing cloth.

ONE OF THE LARGEST SEA SLUGS in temperate waters is the pale yellow, 7-cm/2.75-in. sea lemon, which mates in spring and lays a 15-cm/6-in. long egg ribbon that contains up to 500,000 eggs. Other species produce egg ribbons in neat spirals that can be found on the surfaces of rocks and seaweeds.

☛ 117 SHELL; 343 SLUG.

PIGEON DAY

Pigeons often feed in huge flocks and can become serious agricultural pests. In 1866 one flock of North American passenger pigeons was estimated to be 480 km/300 mi. long, 1.6 km/1 mi. wide and to contain 3 billion birds. This species was hunted to extinction and the last died in the Cincinnati Zoo in 1914.

Three-quarters of the 304 pigeon species live in tropical forests. African green pigeons eat tropical fruits and disperse their seeds in their droppings.

The common street pigeon of London and other major cities is a feral rock dove. Stone ledges of urban buildings make an excellent substitute for its natural cliff ledge nesting site.

Pigeons feed their nestlings on a thick, milky secretion from glands in their crops.

The world's largest species is the turkey-sized crowned pigeon of lowland New Guinea rainforests. Only males carry the magnificent crest.

THE SOPORIFIC 'COOING' of pigeons can be heard in parks and squares of major cities almost everywhere. Their tameness offers an easy opportunity to study bird behavior. Watch the way in which courting males puff up their throats and feathers, bowing and cooing to females to attract their attention.

☛ 180–1 SEED DISPERSAL; 321 DODOS AND EXTINCTION; 24 EGRET; 246 HERON.

LACEWING DAY

The fate of an aphid that meets a lacewing larva is particularly gruesome. Lacewing larvae have large, hollow jaws, with which they impale their prey and suck out their body fluids. Then, the withered corpse is entangled in hairs on the predator's back, where it serves as impromptu camouflage.

Lacewings belong to an ancient order of insects known as the Neuroptera, whose muslin-like wings show extensive cross-venation. Their origins can be traced back at least to the Permian, 250 million years ago.

Eggs, each on the end of a delicate stalk, are laid on the underside of leaves and stems.

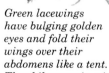

Green lacewings have bulging golden eyes and fold their wings over their abdomens like a tent. They hibernate in winter and re-emerge in spring to mate and lay eggs. Two generations are produced each year.

GREEN LACEWINGS have a weak, fluttering flight, are often attracted to lit windows at night and can be easily captured. Put one in an insect cage with some leaves infested with aphids and watch the effect of the predator on these sap-sucking pests. The aphids often drop off leaves to escape the jaws of the lacewing.

Lacewings are now being artificially bred in large numbers for mass release as aphid predators, replacing environmentally damaging chemical insecticides.

☛ 259 LADYBUG.

FISH PARTNERSHIP DAY

Sea anemone tentacles are armed with stinging cells called nematocysts, which fire microscopic poisoned harpoons when small fish brush against trigger hairs on their surface. The poison that is released paralyzes the prey, which is drawn into the hollow body cavity of the anemone and digested. Clown fish, covered with a protective slime, are immune to their host's lethal tentacles.

The sea anemones tentacles protect the clown fish from predators and provide it with a reliable supply of paralyzed food, which the fish can nibble while the anemone slowly draws its prey into its stomach.

The benefits to the anemone are less clear. One suggestion is that clown fish act as decoys, luring larger fish to their doom among the stinging tentacles and providing the anemone with a meal. It's a good theory, but so far no one has seen this decoy mechanism in action.

RELATIONSHIPS LIKE THIS, where two different organisms live together, are called symbiotic associations. There are many theories about the functions of relationships between living organisms, but scientific proof is often lacking. In studying natural history, try to develop the questioning, experimental attitude of a scientist. In this case, to prove the benefits of the clown fish/anemone symbiosis, it would be important to demonstrate that the animals were less successful separately than they were as a team.

☛ *139 SHRIMP; 326 PARTNERSHIP; 339 SEA ANEMONE.*

WILD ROSE DAY

There are about 100 species of wild rose. Most grow in the cool climates of northern temperate regions. Typical wild roses have a single ring of petals that surround the ovary wall; the exotic garden species with multiple rows of petals have been bred by crossing wild species and selecting mutants which have extra petals.

Rose hips, rich in vitamin C, were collected by school children during the World War II to produce rose hip syrup, as a vitamin supplement to a restricted wartime diet.

Most wild roses have a brief flowering period. Garden varieties with prolonged flowering were first produced in the 18th century, by hybridizing existing varieties with repeat-flowering China roses.

Many cultivated roses are grafted onto the more vigorous roots of wild roses, which produce stronger plants.

Hooked rose thorns help arching stems of dog rose to scramble through hedges. In the extremely spiny burnet rose they protect the plant against browsing animals.

GARDEN ROSES are often grafted onto wild rose roots, which are more vigorous. Make a bud graft by inserting a bud and a shield-shaped piece of surrounding tissue from a garden rose into a T-shaped cut in a wild rose stem. Bind the two together with raffia. If the living cambium cells of the two tissues unite, your graft will take and you will then have a rose with two types of flowers. Check gardening manuals for other types of grafts.

☛ 116 STRAWBERRY.

YAK DAY

Yaks (*Bos mutus*) are closely related to cattle (*Bos taurus*). Wild yaks still occur on the Tibetan plateau in Central Asia. But most yaks are domesticated and are used as pack-animals, milk producers, and for meat, hides and hair by the nomadic herdsmen of this, the highest and most bleak part of the inhabited world.

In summer yaks forage for food at heights of 6,000 m / 20,000 ft., feeding on sparse vegetation, moss and lichen.

Wild yaks are black and the tips of their horns turn outward. Domesticated yaks may be brown to black or even piebald, and the horn tips turn inwards.

At 6,000 m / 20,000 ft. there is permanent snow; the air is thin and temperatures drop to –40°C / –40°F. Large lungs allow yaks to breathe at high altitudes, and matted coats provide insulation.

YAKS ARE CRUCIAL to the survival of Tibetan nomads, providing many of their needs including the hides to make their tents. Yak milk is used to make yak butter, eaten with barley bread or spooned into tea in which it forms an often rancid pool of oil.

Milk is an emulsion of fat droplets. Make fresh butter by filling a large jar two-thirds full of whole milk. Screw the cap on tightly and shake vigorously for ten minutes. This knocks the fat droplets together, so they form lumps of butter, which can be strained off.

☞ 172 CATTLE.

BEE-EATER DAY

Bee-eaters feed on wasps and other insects as well as bees. But they are not popular with bee-keepers. The East African red-throated bee-eater removes a bee's sting and venom sac by rubbing and banging the bee against a branch of a tree before swallowing it whole.

Bee-eaters have some natural immunity to bee-stings but do occasionally get badly stung.

The African carmine bee-eater often sits on the back of kori bustards and eats insects flushed up by the bustard as it walks through the grass.

The white-throated bee-eater has adapted to life in oil-palm plantations. A squirrel raids the fruit and drops the skins; the bee-eater catches them in mid-air and eats them.

Bee-eaters nest in a tunnel excavated in sand and lay as many as 10 eggs which both parents incubate.

MANY INSECTIVOROUS BIRDS, like bee-eaters and flycatchers, catch their prey in flight, then perch before eating their food. Others, like swifts, swallows and martins, feed in flight, without landing. Some species remove indigestible wings and spiny legs before swallowing their prey.

Find a dead bee (they often become caught in car radiators) and press its abdomen to expose its sting. Pull it out with tweezers and examine it under a hand lens. You should find a venom sac hanging from the sting's base.

☛ *82 BUMBLEBEE.*

ANTEATER DAY

The true anteaters, Myrmecophagidae, comprise three species – the giant and two-toed (or dwarf) anteaters and the tamandua. They occur from southern Mexico to northern Argentina. All lack teeth, and their middle toes are armed with long powerful claws for breaking open ants' nests and termite mounds.

Australian echidnas are ant-eaters but unrelated to the American ones.

Tamanduas seek ants' nests in dead branches.

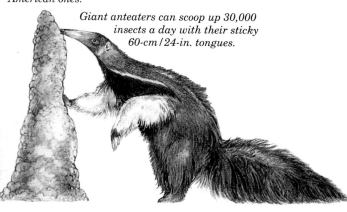

Giant anteaters can scoop up 30,000 insects a day with their sticky 60-cm / 24-in. tongues.

Anteaters have to walk on the knuckles and sides of their forefeet so that they don't trip over their claws.

APART FROM TRUE ANTEATERS, the pangolins, echidnas and aardvarks also eat ants and termites. All are adapted in the same way to deal with the problem of breaking into hard ant and termite nests and eating large numbers of small prey. They have powerful limbs and claws, long sticky tongues, and few or no teeth. Although they have evolved from very different ancestors, similar changes in structure have evolved in each of these groups to deal with a similar problem. This is called convergent evolution.

☛ *201 ANT; 31 TERMITE.*

PIKE DAY

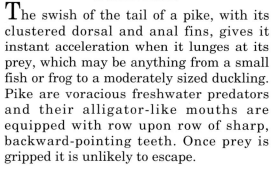

The swish of the tail of a pike, with its clustered dorsal and anal fins, gives it instant acceleration when it lunges at its prey, which may be anything from a small fish or frog to a moderately sized duckling. Pike are voracious freshwater predators and their alligator-like mouths are equipped with row upon row of sharp, backward-pointing teeth. Once prey is gripped it is unlikely to escape.

All pike are good game fish and put up a ferocious struggle when they are hooked. Many specimens weighing over 20 kg/45 lbs. have been landed and there are lurid stories, which are probably mythical, of monster specimens attacking dogs that have swum too close to their lairs.

There are five species of pike, including the North American muskellunge or muskie, which may weigh over 30 kg/65 lbs. and reach a length of 1.5 m/5 ft.

WEAR POLAROID SUNGLASSES to search for pike amongst the weeds in reservoirs and slow-moving rivers. Their mottled green markings match the pattern of sunlight and shadow in the weeds where they lurk, motionless, waiting for a careless fish to venture too close. Prey is grabbed sideways, then maneuvered into the mouth until it can be swallowed whole, head first. Pike are considered to be pests in salmon and trout fisheries, because of their appetite for these prized fish.

Large female pike can lay almost half a million eggs, but predators and cannabilism account for most of these.

☞ 45 TROUT; 66 BARRACUDA.

SNOW DAY

Polar and subpolar animals must adapt to seasonal changes in background, as well as temperature. During the long, white Arctic winter many animals change color to blend with the snowy background. This seasonal transformation is known as leukomism and should not be confused with albinism, which is caused by a genetic defect that prevents any pigment formation in fur and feathers and leaves animals with red eyes.

Stoats' winter fur is called ermine.

Snowy owls are almost invisible when they are perched on a rock in a white arctic landscape.

The brown summer coat of snowshoe or varying hares is replaced by gray fur in autumn, which molts again to reveal the underlying white winter coat.

Harp seal pups are born with an exceptionally thick, insulating coat called a lanugo, which is molted within a few weeks of birth.

Polar bears' heat insulation is so effective that they cannot be detected with an infrared camera.

Arctic foxes are farmed for their coats, which increase in thickness by up to 50 percent in winter.

SOME ANIMALS LIVE below the blanket of snow in winter. When a thaw sets in after a snowfall, search the grassland around hedges and woodlands for the network of mouse and vole tunnels, where they move in relative safety under the snow.

☞ 279 POLAR BEAR; 28–9 MOUNTAIN; 192 PIGMENTATION.

TEA DAY

Tea is a mild stimulant, due to the presence of alkaloids like caffeine.

Legend has it that tea drinking was invented by the Chinese Emperor Shen Nung in 2737 BC, when leaves from burning tea twigs blew upward from the fire and landed in his cauldron of boiling water. Tea was brought from China to Europe by the Dutch and British in about 1650. The British brew 180,000 tons of tea leaves annually – more than the rest of Europe and North America combined.

Green teas are made by steaming the leaves soon after they are picked, to prevent enzymes within the tissues oxidizing and blackening the leaf. Artificial drying caramelizes sugars and gives some teas a distinctive aroma.

Tea pickers collect two leaves and a bud from each shoot. The finest quality products are made from unexpanded leaves during the first flush of growth.

CAMOMILE TEA is made from the aromatic herb *Anthemis nobilis*, by making an infusion of the flowers, and is said to be a good sedative for restless children and a cure for nightmares. Try making some refreshing tea from peppermint leaves, which can be bought in health food shops.

☛ 99 COFFEE.

TROUT DAY

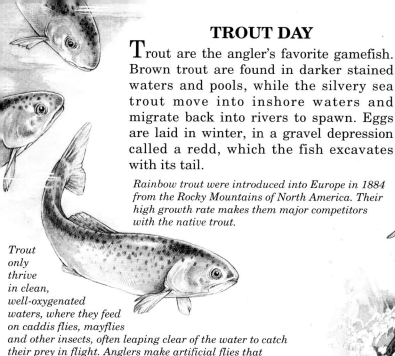

Trout are the angler's favorite gamefish. Brown trout are found in darker stained waters and pools, while the silvery sea trout move into inshore waters and migrate back into rivers to spawn. Eggs are laid in winter, in a gravel depression called a redd, which the fish excavates with its tail.

The age of trout can be calculated by counting rings on their scales. Most fish live for about 5 years, but 20-year-old specimens have been caught.

Rainbow trout were introduced into Europe in 1884 from the Rocky Mountains of North America. Their high growth rate makes them major competitors with the native trout.

Trout only thrive in clean, well-oxygenated waters, where they feed on caddis flies, mayflies and other insects, often leaping clear of the water to catch their prey in flight. Anglers make artificial flies that mimic natural prey, luring trout to their hooks by keeping the 'fly' constantly moving on the water surface.

RAINBOW TROUT are bred on trout farms. These are often open to visitors and offer an opportunity to see all stages in the growth of the fish. Eggs are stripped from a female (hen) fish by gently squeezing her flanks. The eggs hatch into alevins, which slowly absorb the yolk sac that remains attached to their body. Then they are fed on artificial pellets and quickly grow through the immature parr stage to become adult, saleable fish. Old rainbow trout have a distinctive, iridescent stripe along their flanks that gives them their common name. This marking is less evident on fast-grown, farmed fish.

☞ 25 SALMON.

AARDVARK DAY

'Aardvark' is Afrikaans for 'earth-pig' – an appropriate name for this secretive, nocturnal, burrowing southern African animal. Aardvarks are about 2 m/7 ft. long and weigh up to 80 kg/180 lbs. They dig rapidly and efficiently, using the blunt claws on their stocky forefeet to find food and make deep resting burrows.

The aardvark's long sticky tongue is used to scoop up termites and ants. Like other ant-eating mammals it has no front teeth but has 8–10 peg-like rootless back teeth for crushing termites.

Termite mounds are demolished rapidly and their inhabitants removed from galleries and tunnels by the aardvark's probing tongue. Its nostrils are surrounded by bristles and can be closed at will, preventing termites from entering.

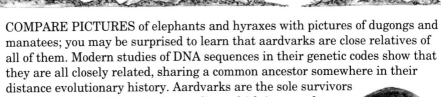

COMPARE PICTURES of elephants and hyraxes with pictures of dugongs and manatees; you may be surprised to learn that aardvarks are close relatives of all of them. Modern studies of DNA sequences in their genetic codes show that they are all closely related, sharing a common ancestor somewhere in their distance evolutionary history. Aardvarks are the sole survivors of their branch of this evolutionary line, which is more than 50 million years old.

☛ 12 HYENA.

DAISY DAY

Daisies belong to a large family of plants called the Compositae, which includes sunflowers, chicory and lettuce. They all share one characteristic – a flower head made up of large numbers of two different kinds of flowers. Ray florets, arranged in a ring around the edge, have a petal and their purpose is to attract insects. Tiny disc florets in the center have no petal, but do have pollen and stigmas, for seed production.

Rosettes of daisy leaves, pressed close to the soil, escape the mower blades that decapitate the flowers.

Ornamental varieties, with double flowers, are often cultivated. These carry a genetic mutation which converts all disk florets in ray florets, producing flower heads with dense masses of petals.

Bellis – the scientific name for daisy – is derived from the Latin word for 'beautiful'.

DAISY RAY FLORETS only open fully in bright sunshine and the flowers close up at night. On a sunny day, cover a patch of daisies on a lawn with a cardboard box for an hour. You will find that these flowers will close during their artificial night. The petals of many flowers fold up in dull, cloudy weather, to protect the pollen from rain.

☞ 33 SUNFLOWER.

FISH KISSING
AND COURTSHIP DAY

Siamese fighting fish are perciform or spiny-finned fishes. In fighting fish the fins are long and frilled and are used as symbols of dominance, in the same way that deer use antlers.

The study of animal behavior is known as ethology and reveals how individuals interact with their own and other species. Animals use threat displays to scare off rivals for mates or to defend their territories. Real fights, ending in injury, are rare. Aggressive poses and threatening behavior are usually enough to ensure that one or other rival establishes dominance.

Competing fish undergo long periods of confrontation and fin-waving. Wild fighting fish are generally dull red, but highly colored forms have been selectively bred for keeping in aquaria.

Siamese fighting fish and kissing gouramis are both species of freshwater fish that breathe atmospheric air, absorbing oxygen through a labyrinthine breathing organ. They drown if they cannot gulp air from the surface.

SET UP AN AQUARIUM and keep notes on the behavior of the fish that you keep. You will soon discover patterns of behavior when each animal has established its own territory.

☛ 134 BUTTERFLY FISH.

The kissing gourami, found in India and Malaysia, is a close relative of the Siamese fighting fish and its behavior appears at first to be affectionate. Individuals approach and appear to kiss. This is, however, a threat display, in the form of an eyeball-to-eyeball confrontation.

LICE DAY

Lice are insects which have lost their wings and become ectoparasites, attached to the outer surface of their hosts by hooked claws that grip hairs and feathers.

The 2,600 species of biting lice are parasites, feeding on fur, feathers and fatty skin secretions of mammals and birds. The largest are up to 6 mm/ 0.2 in. long and all have flat, oval bodies and gripping, clawed feet. Each type of biting louse only lives on one host species and soon dies if transferred to another.

The parasitic sucking lice, illustrated here, all live on mammals and siphon off their blood through hollow mouth parts, injecting saliva into blood vessels to prevent blood clotting. There are about 250 species, each with different hosts, which include elephants, pigs, cattle and man. Schoolchildren often become infested with human head lice, which glue their eggs ('nits') to individual hairs and must be removed with a fine-tooth comb.

Book lice are not parasites but live on leaves and trees. Some species infest libraries, where they emit a ticking noise as they chew mould from pages of damp books.

Human body lice live on parts of the human anatomy other than the head and transmit typhus, a dangerous disease.

LOOK FOR BOOK LICE in damp books. They are tiny, pale insects that race across the pages and can be picked up with a paintbrush moistened with denatured alcohol. Examine them under a microscope and notice their flattened, wingless bodies.

☞ *188 FLEA.*

BABOON DAY

Baboon troops are ruled by a dominant male using a series of complicated facial expressions and poses and considerable aggression. Communication involves young animals learning the different signals and the correct responses. Because they have still to learn, the black-furred young are immune from aggression. When they are weaned their color changes and they have to conform.

The baboon's brilliant hindquarters provide instant recognition of sex and, often, individual. The rump is displayed as an expression of confidence or submission.

The terrifying threat posture exposes razor-sharp teeth; a troop of baboons can mob and drive off a leopard.

Immunity of juveniles extends to those closest to them – males may grab and groom youngsters just to deter aggression from other males.

THE MEANING of the baboon's threat posture is clear. The higher primates have a variety of subtle expressions with meanings clear to other members of the troop. With the mouth not so open and the lips over the teeth, the message is less serious – 'Be very careful, my friend.' With the teeth almost together and the lips drawn back, the baboon means 'Forgive me, I'm harmless' – an expression of submission and appeasement. In the chimpanzee this 'fear grin' is a sign of friendliness; in humans it has become the smile.

☛ 225 CHIMPANZEE; 222 GIBBON.

EMU DAY

Rheas are large South American ratites that live on the pampas. Several females lay eggs in the same nest.

The emu is an Australian representative of a group called the ratites, large flightless birds which have developed powerful legs for walking and running.

Emus are omnivores, feeding on flowers, fruit, seeds, young shoots and insects. They live in pairs and lead a nomadic life, moving across the dry Australian interior in search of suitable food.

The birds store fat before the winter breeding season. The eggs are incubated by the male, who sits on them for eight weeks without eating, drinking or defecating, relying on his stored fat reserves for survival. Chicks are well covered with down when they hatch and can feed themselves and follow their father almost immediately. He guards them for seven months, while the female leaves to find a new mate.

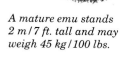

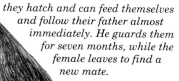

A mature emu stands 2 m / 7 ft. tall and may weigh 45 kg / 100 lbs.

EMUS ARE STILL COMMON, favoring coastal scrub, eucalypt woodland and saltbush plains, as well as farmland where bush still remains. Examine the breastbone of a cooked chicken. The vertical keel running down the center anchors the wing muscles but in flightless ratites, like the ostrich and the emu, this is missing and the breastbone is flat. Flightless birds have evolved many times in different groups from flying ancestors, almost always on islands where there are few natural terrestrial predators.

☞ 242 OSTRICH.

RAY DAY

The flattened, winglike bodies of rays, which are closely related to sharks, allow them to settle on the sea floor and lie hidden on the sandy bottom, where they are often superbly camouflaged. Most rays feed on bottom-living mollusks and crabs.

The manta ray of the Pacific is one of the largest sea creatures, measuring over 6 m / 20 ft. between the tips of its wing-like fins. Rhythmic beats of the 'wings' allow it to swim fast enough to leap clear of the water.

Rays grow and breed slowly, making them vulnerable to overfishing. It takes nine years for a spotted ray to reach maturity, when it lays only 70 eggs each year. These can take up to 15 months to hatch.

There are 200 species of ray, living in every ocean.

The elecric ray, which lives in the Atlantic, stuns its prey with an electric discharge.

Some species have a serrated, poisonous spine on their tail, which they use as a whip. Stingray wounds often become infected and are potentially dangerous if left untreated.

IF YOU VISIT YOUR LOCAL FISH MARKET you will find fish labeled 'skate'; this common name is given to several similar species of ray. At the seaside, search seaweeds and rock pools at low tide for ray egg cases, which are rectangular, leathery purses fixed to seaweeds by tough threads. If you hold one of these 'mermaids' purses' up to the light you may be lucky enough to see the young fish inside, attached to its yolk sac, which nourishes it during a development period which can last up to five months.

☛ 1 SHARK.

MARINE IGUANA DAY

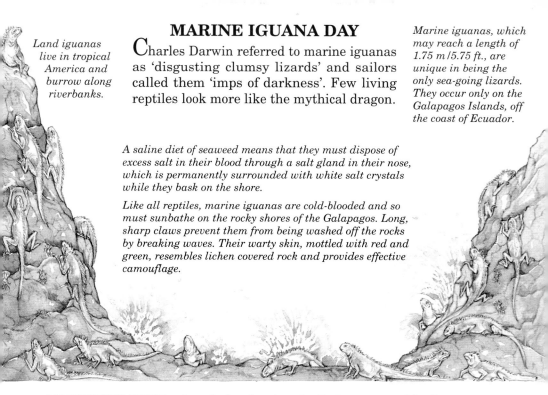

Land iguanas live in tropical America and burrow along riverbanks.

Charles Darwin referred to marine iguanas as 'disgusting clumsy lizards' and sailors called them 'imps of darkness'. Few living reptiles look more like the mythical dragon.

Marine iguanas, which may reach a length of 1.75 m /5.75 ft., are unique in being the only sea-going lizards. They occur only on the Galapagos Islands, off the coast of Ecuador.

A saline diet of seaweed means that they must dispose of excess salt in their blood through a salt gland in their nose, which is permanently surrounded with white salt crystals while they bask on the shore.

Like all reptiles, marine iguanas are cold-blooded and so must sunbathe on the rocky shores of the Galapagos. Long, sharp claws prevent them from being washed off the rocks by breaking waves. Their warty skin, mottled with red and green, resembles lichen covered rock and provides effective camouflage.

MARINE IGUANAS bask on dark volcanic rocks that are warmed by the sun. Take two identical empty bottles; coat one with aluminium foil and the other with mat black paint. Attach a thermometer in the neck of each with modeling clay and stand them on a sunny windowsill. Measure the rate of temperature increase in both. You will soon see why cold-blooded animals choose to bask on surfaces that absorb solar radiation.

☛ 199 LIZARD.

UNDERGROUND DAY

The upper layers of the Earth's surface provide a habitat for animals that live and breed in burrows and holes.

Natural underground caverns provide hibernating and roosting sites for horseshoe bats (left). Many mammals dig burrows. Social groups of prairie dogs (below), a North American form of ground squirrel, excavate massive networks of underground tunnels, which are a menace to horsemen.

The soil has a large insect population, and termite colonies extend outward over a wide area below their towering nests.

Wet sand is easy to tunnel into and mollusks, like pod razor shells, use their muscular feet to withdraw into a burrow where they filter food from seawater.

Piddocks are bivalve mollusks with rough shells which they use as drills for boring into soft rocks.

European little owls sometimes nest in rabbit holes. The burrowing owl, from the Americas, can excavate a tunnel but more often commandeers prairie-dog burrows.

Naked mole rats live in colonies in the dry savannas of East Africa. Uniquely among mammals, a single breeding female produces castes of workers and non-workers. Workers dig tunnels all their lives; nonworkers attend the breeding female and only breed if she dies. All members of the colony develop teats to feed the young.

Tadpole shrimps survive as eggs in the sand, which hatch rapidly after rainfall.

The barking gecko is one of many reptiles that burrow underground.

In southern Africa spring hares dig complex burrows in loose sandy soil, emerging at night to bound across the landscape like miniature kangaroos, to eat crops.

Quill worms build protective tubes of sand.

Badgers, like the North American badger, excavate large tunnel systems with several entrances. When surprised in the open, this species digs frantically, throwing a column of soil into the air.

FIND TUNNELS AND BURROWS in a hedge bank and test whether they are occupied by tying a fine thread of cotton across the entrance. If the thread is broken when you return, something lives inside.

☛ 153 BIVALVE MOLLUSKS; 31 TERMITE; 58 GECKO; 187 BURROWING OWL; 85 PLAINS.

Fennec foxes live in underground lairs.

POND DAY

Ponds are ideal habitats for studying food chains. Water plants are primary producers, using solar energy to convert water and carbon dioxide into sugars that they use for growth. Herbivores, like ramshorn snails (left), graze on plants. Carnivores, including water scorpions (right) and newts and sticklebacks (bottom), are the top predators. Freshwater shrimps scavenge on the detritus that falls to the bottom of the pond.

Pond skaters (top right) patrol the surface, ready to impale small insects that become trapped in the surface film. Dragonflies and damselflies (left) lay eggs in waterweeds by crawling backward down their stems until they are half submerged. Water scorpions use their tail siphons to replenish their air supplied from the surface, but water spiders (top left) carry bubbles of air like aqualungs down from the surface to an air-bubble diving bell trapped in the submerged vegetation.

EVERY GARDEN should have a pond, however small. Details of building a pond and maintaining a freshwater aquarium can be found at the end of the book.

☛ 72 DRAGONFLY; 92 WATER SURFACE; 8 NEWT.

RABBIT DAY

The breeding capacity of rabbits is legendary: one doe can produce thirty young in eight months. Although these are born blind and naked, they can breed within fourteen weeks.

Wild breeding colonies of rabbits now exist almost everywhere in the British Isles. They are classed as a major agricultural pest, damaging crops and pastures.

The Normans introduced rabbits into Britain from southern Europe, farming them in artificial warrens for meat and fur. Angora rabbits are still kept for their fine fur, which is spun like wool into garments.

Emigrants took rabbits from Britain to New Zealand and Australia. In Australia they devastated pastures and crops and, through competition for food, caused the near-extinction of some of the native marsupials.

Myxomatosis, a South American virus disease, almost wiped out British and Australian rabbits in the middle of the 20th century but virus-resistant populations are multiplying again.

WATCH DOMESTIC RABBITS CLOSELY. Notice that they eat their own droppings, a habit known as coprophagy. All rabbits must do this, because their intestines are too short to digest plant food during its first passage through their gut. Domestic rabbits retain the natural behavior patterns of wild rabbits and thump their cage floor when alarmed – a signal used by wild rabbits in their burrows to warn of approaching predators, like stoats and foxes.

☛ *182 HARE.*

GECKO DAY

There are 650 species of gecko throughout the warmer parts of the world and four of these occur in southern Europe. Most species are nocturnal and their large eyes make them effective predators in darkness.

The flying gecko can glide short distances, using its webbed feet and fringe of skin around its body as a parachute.

Geckos are supremely adapted to climbing smooth surfaces, thanks to adhesive pads on their toes. These are covered with fine branched hairs (setae), which cling to minute crevices and allow geckos to hang from ceilings.

Nocturnal squeaks and barks, and pattering feet on the ceiling, are a feature of many hotel rooms in the tropics, where geckos often take up residence. They hunt mosquitoes that are attracted to room lights.

Unlike lizards, geckos have vertical pupils in their eyes that in bright light close to a narrow slit perforated by four small holes.

Most species lay small numbers of hard-shelled eggs, often in crevices. Geckos can change color, becoming lighter or darker to tone with their surroundings.

EXAMINE A SMOOTH SURFACE with a powerful magnifying glass. You will find that even the shiniest surfaces often have minute holes and bumps; a gecko's claws and hairy foot pads can cling to these.

☛ 104–5 NOCTURNAL ANIMALS; 345 EYE.

DEER DAY

Deer are ruminants – mammals which chew and digest plant material. The moose is the largest living species, standing up to 2.5 m/8 ft. tall at the shoulder, but the extinct Irish elk was larger, with antlers that spanned 3 m/10 ft. and weighed 50 kg/110 lbs.

Antlers are sexual symbols, signaling to females that their owners are capable of fathering large, vigorous offspring. They are made of bone. Antlers begin to grow in one-month-old fawns and are covered in skin with a rich supply of blood vessels, which sloughs off when they mature. They are shed and regrow annually.

Male musk deer have a unique, apple-sized gland under their abdomen and are hunted for its contents, which are used in perfumery and folk medicine.

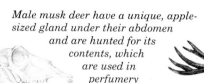

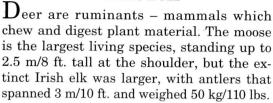

During the breeding (rutting) season red deer roar challenges to their rivals and antlers are used to settle disputes.

VISIT DEER PARKS to watch herds of these handsome animals at close quarters. Fawns of fallow and red deer are born in May and June and can stand within two hours of birth.

☛ *129 MOOSE.*

The most primitive deer are chevrotains, like the Indian meminna which are only 30 cm / 12 in. tall, and share many of the characteristics of pigs. They have no antlers, but defend territories with sharp, ever-growing canine teeth.

BIRDS' FEET DAY

Most birds' feet have four toes. In black-birds, three face forward and the hind toe curls around branches, gripping the perch. In woodpeckers (above, right) a pair of clawed toes faces in each direction, gripping bark when their muscles flex. Blackbirds hop, leaving paired footprints; crows walk, leaving a staggered line of tracks.

Sparrow hawks and other birds of prey are equipped with long, powerful talons, which grip and kill prey and are also used for carrying it back to the nest.

Ostriches are the only birds with two toes, an arrangement that favors fast running. The muscular leg and powerful claw makes its foot a potentially lethal weapon.

Ducks' toes are webbed to increase the surface area of the foot for efficient swimming. The toes close as the foot moves forward, then spread apart on the backstroke, levering the duck through the water.

LOOK FOR BIRD FOOTPRINTS in soft mud around a pond margin, where you should find tracks of ducks, waders and perching birds. Heavy birds, like swans and geese, have broad feet to spread their weight over a large area, allowing them to walk on sloppy mud. The long toes of a heron serve the same purpose, but also allow it to perch on branches in treetops, where it nests.

☛ *93 BEAK; 337 TRACKING.*

SOIL MITE DAY

Mites and ticks belong to an extremely large and varied order, known as the Acari. About 30,000 species of mite have been described but biologists estimate that between 500,000 and a million species exist.

Mites have eight legs, and so are arachnids, like spiders and scorpions. The front and rear parts of a spider's body are separated by a narrow waist; in mites the two sections are fused, giving the animals a bloated appearance. The feeding organs are carried on a small projection, called the capitulum. Most mites are 1 mm / 0.04 in. or less in length.

Soil mites are often the dominant animals in leaf litter and soil, where many feed on decaying plant matter, bacteria and fungi. Other species are predatory. Hundreds of individuals of several species can be found in a small sample of leaf mould from a tropical forest.

Eggs are laid in clusters, often amongst plant roots. When the larvae first hatch they have only six legs; after the first molt eight-legged nymphs develop until the adult stage is reached.

THE UPPER SOIL LAYERS provide a habitat for a large community of animals. Extract a sample by making a Tullgren funnel (see page 375). Your catch should include a substantial number of soil mites. Sample soils from different habitats, like woodland, agricultural land and roadsides, to see how species composition varies between habitats.

☛ 352 LEAF LITTER.

MOSS DAY

Mosses were one of the first types of plant to colonize land, over 400 million years ago. They still depend on water for sexual reproduction; their male sex cells swim in the surface film of water to fertilize eggs in flask-shaped structures called archegonia, hidden amongst the leaves of female plants. Fertilized archegonia then grow into elegant capsules, which release microscopic spores.

Mosses are unable to make woody tissue, so they are all small plants.

Mosses have no true roots and absorb water and mineral salts over their whole surface, so most of the 20,000 species are found in wet habitats.

EXAMINE THE CAPSULE of a moss with a hand lens. The membranous cap is the calyptra, which comes off easily. Below this is another lid – the operculum – which can be pulled off with fine forceps. Under this is a ring of peristome teeth, which curl outward as atmospheric humidity changes, allowing spores to escape. Spores germinate on wet soil into fine green threads called protonemata, which develop small buds that grow into new moss plants.

☛ *322 PEAT BOG; 114 FERN.*

LIONESS DAY

Although lionesses are 20 to 35 percent smaller than their mates, they are the hunters and killers in the lion family. Zebra and antelope are their favorite prey and they hunt in groups, fanning out and stalking their victims before catching them in a sudden ambush.

Lions are the most social of all the cats and live in groups called 'prides,' consisting of up to fifteen lionesses and their cubs and one to six adult males. African lion cubs are spotted for the first few months of life, an adaptation that camouflages them in the dry grass. They feed on kills made by the lioness until they are a year old, when they can hunt for themselves.

The mane of the lion is part of its sexual display. Although it gives males a fierce countenance, they do little actual hunting and spend up to 18 hours asleep each day.

LIONS ONCE OCCURRED throughout much of Asia and in southeastern Mediterranean countries, but are now only found south of the Sahara and in a small area of the Gir Forest in northwest India.

Big cats occupy an important place in the food chain and their rapid disappearence from many areas has serious ecological consequences. Without these predators, herbivores increase rapidly, resulting in overgrazing of grasslands.

☞ 261 TIGER; 316 CHEETAH.

LAMPREY DAY

Fossils show that there were many jaw-less fish in rivers during the Devonian era, 400 million years ago; today, only the lampreys and hagfishes feed without the use of hinged jaws.

Sea lampreys spend most of their lives in salt water and enter rivers to breed, constructing a circular stony nest where they spawn. The eggs hatch into burrowing larvae, called ammocoetes, which filter water and catch suspended food in sticky mucus. It may be seven years before ammocoetes mature into adult lampreys and make their way back to the sea, in search of fish to parasitize.

A lamprey looks like an eel, but its mouth is a sucking disk with a ring of horny teeth and it feeds as a parasite on other fish, attaching itself to the body of its prey and rasping the flesh. They are voracious feeders and the cutting of a canal between Lake Erie and Lake Ontario in 1828 allowed sea lampreys to travel from the latter into all the Great Lakes, decimating the fishing industry there.

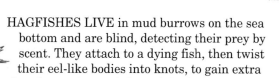

HAGFISHES LIVE in mud burrows on the sea bottom and are blind, detecting their prey by scent. They attach to a dying fish, then twist their eel-like bodies into knots, to gain extra leverage so that they can tunnel through its body and feed inside. They have few enemies and defend themselves by secreting vast amounts of thick slime, which they wipe off by sliding through their knotted bodies and sneezing, to blow the mucous from their nasal passage.

☛ 179 ABYSSAL FISH.

GULL DAY

The bright red spot on a herring gull's beak is used for communication between parents and chicks. Adults regurgitate food when a nestling pecks at the spot. The chicks' behavior is instinctive and they will peck at red spots painted on cardboard model beaks.

The greater black-backed gull is a determined hunter and feeds on other seabirds and their chicks, or chases smaller gulls and terns until they drop or disgorge food. Its long, sharp beak can also administer painful wounds to animals that venture too close to its nest site.

Black-headed gulls move inland in the breeding season, to nest in noisy colonies on moorlands. They are scavengers and often assemble in thousands on municipal rubbish heaps. In autumn they follow plows, feeding on earthworms.

SEA GULLS ARE EASY TO APPROACH and offer good opportunities to study the subtleties of bird flight. Their long wings are ideal for gliding over oceans and soaring on updrafts along cliff edges. Watch a gull soaring and you will see the ruffling of the small feathers on the top of the wing, lifted by low pressure over its curved surface. When gulls hover to pick up food from the water surface they exercise precise control, with the splayed tail acting as an air brake and rudder and short, rapid wing beats lowering the bird to the surface.

☛ *24 EGRET; 74 PUFFIN.*

BARRACUDA DAY

Their needle-sharp teeth, aggressive nature and a tendency to hunt in shoals ensure that divers maintain a respectful distance from barracudas. In the West Indies they are more feared than sharks.

Barracudas feed on other fish and will hunt cooperatively, herding a shoal of prey to make them easier to catch. They often congregate over reefs, where food is plentiful.

A streamlined body and a large tail fin allow the barracuda to swim rapidly and its barred markings provide camouflage in the dappled sunlight of shallow reef waters. Large specimens can reach over 35 kg/80 lbs., but this is small compared with the closely related groupers. The Queensland grouper weighs almost half a ton and has a habit of stalking pearl and shell divers as they swim over reefs.

LIKE THE CLOSELY RELATED mackerels and tunas, barracudas are good to eat – but not without the risk of a form of fish poisoning called ciguatera. Occasionally they accumulate toxins from other fish in their diet, and can themselves become poisonous. The toxins start life in poisonous algae that live on reef seaweeds, which are then concentrated and passed up the food chain via herbivores to the reef carnivores – a process known as bioaccumulation.

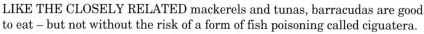

☞ *1 SHARK.*

PANDA DAY

Red pandas are nocturnal and spend most of their lives in the branches of trees. They are slow-moving and awkward on the ground.

Appearances can be deceptive. Although red pandas resemble cats and giant pandas look like bears, their internal anatomy shows that both are closely related to the raccoons of the New World. Both species are carnivores turned vegetarian, although giant pandas have been known to eat fish and wild goats given the opportunity.

Bamboo's low nutritional value means that pandas must eat almost continuously to survive, sleeping for long periods between meals to conserve energy. Bamboo rarely flowers, but when it does all plants over a wide area bloom simultaneously and quickly die. Pandas then suffer from a chronic food shortage, until bamboo seeds germinate and new shoots grow.

GIANT PANDAS WERE FIRST SEEN by Western naturalists in 1869 and have probably always been thinly distributed in the bamboo forests of eastern Tibet, Szechwan and southwestern China. The species has declined rapidly throughout the second half of the 20th century, mainly as a result of habitat destruction.

A wrist bone has become enlarged and elongated in the giant panda, creating an extra pad on the forepaw that acts like a thumb and gives it a high degree of manual dexterity. This 'sixth finger' opposes the other five and allows the animal to grip bamboo stems effectively.

☛ 130–1 ENDANGERED ANIMALS; 147 GRASS.

OLIVE DAY

Archeological investigations suggest that olives (*Olea europea*) have been cultivated in the Middle East since at least 3700 BC. Extensive olive groves have been established in the Mediterranean basin, to supply the fresh fruits and olive oil that are an essential ingredient of the region's cuisine. Many olive trees live for 1,000 years or more.

Olive trees usually crop well in alternate years.

Olive oil, squeezed from the flesh of the fruit, is used in salad dressings, to preserve canned fish and for cooking. Extra virgin oil is the top-quality product obtained from the first pressing of the drupes.

Olives are known botanically as drupes – fleshy fruits enclosing a single, hard seed. Olives are only palatable after they have been soaked in water and then preserved in brine or dressed in spiced oils.

SEVERAL CLOSE RELATIVES of the olive are grown as ornamental plants in gardens, including lilac (*Syringa sp.* – top left), the manna ash (*Fraxinus ornus* – top right) and privet (*Ligustrum vulgare*). The common ash (*Fraxinus excelsior*) is the only member of the olive family (Oleaceae) which is native to Britain. Olive foliage is an ancient sign of goodwill and 'to offer an olive branch' is a well-known idiom denoting a gesture of reconciliation.

☞ *33 SUNFLOWER.*

SHRIKE DAY

Shrikes have an alternative name — butcher-birds. It stems from their gruesome habit of impaling their prey on thorns, storing a larder of corpses that they can eat at a later date. All shrikes have a sturdy, hooked beak and a habit of choosing a high vantage point to survey their surroundings for prey.

Shrikes prefer open habitats, like savannas, steppes and desert fringes. Most species that breed in the north of their range migrate south for the winter.

THE RUFOUS-BACKED SHRIKE, illustrated here, is a southern Asian species which is an aggressive hunter. It kills insects, small animals and fledglings with heavy blows of its beak, then impales them on thorns. The species has a breeding range that extends from the Himalayas to the Philippines.

☞ 350 KESTREL; 118 MIGRATION.

TUBER DAY

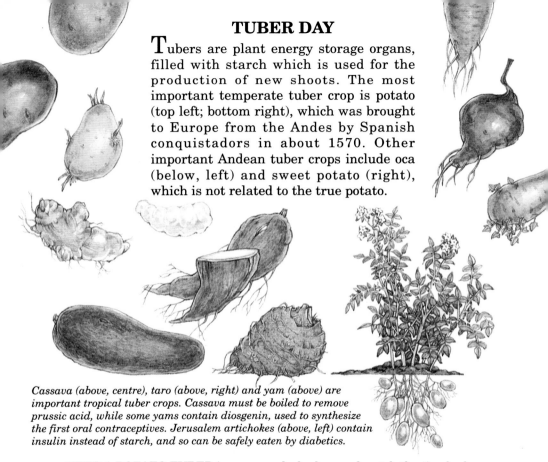

Tubers are plant energy storage organs, filled with starch which is used for the production of new shoots. The most important temperate tuber crop is potato (top left; bottom right), which was brought to Europe from the Andes by Spanish conquistadors in about 1570. Other important Andean tuber crops include oca (below, left) and sweet potato (right), which is not related to the true potato.

Cassava (above, centre), taro (above, right) and yam (above) are important tropical tuber crops. Cassava must be boiled to remove prussic acid, while some yams contain diosgenin, used to synthesize the first oral contraceptives. Jerusalem artichokes (above, left) contain insulin instead of starch, and so can be safely eaten by diabetics.

KEEP A POTATO TUBER in a warm, dark place and watch the tiny buds ('eyes') sprout and grow into shoots. The tuber shrinks as the new growth consumes its starchy energy reserve.

☛ *294 PLANTS SURVIVING WINTER.*

ROBIN DAY

The Australian red-capped robin is a flycatcher, not a true robin.

British gardeners have become familiar with the endearing tameness of the European robin, which will snatch insects from the soil at a gardener's feet, but elsewhere in its range it is a shy and retiring bird. Its brick-red throat and chest feathers matched early postmen's uniforms and earned it a place on Christmas cards in Victorian times; it has become synonymous with Christmas ever since.

The name 'robin' has been used for birds with red breasts all over the English-speaking world, even though their true scientific classification would place them in distinct taxonomic groups. The American robin is really a thrush, in a different subfamily from true robins. The Australian red-capped robin (top left) is unrelated scientifically to either the European or American robin, but shares their shape, size and friendly nature.

EUROPEAN ROBINS are highly territorial birds. Make a crude model robin from wire and feathers, or buy a plastic toy bird and repaint it to resemble a robin. Then place it outdoors and watch. The resident garden robin will attack it furiously. This behavior establishes feeding and breeding areas, ensuring that enough resources are available locally for each breeding pair of robins.

☛ 178 BACKYARD; 168 TERRITORIALITY.

DRAGONFLY DAY

There are 4,500 species of predatory, brightly colored dragonflies and smaller, more fragile damselflies. Despite their fearsome appearance, dragonflies are harmless to humans. Present-day species have wingspans of about 10 cm/4 in.; fossils of those that lived during the Carboniferous reveal that many had wing-spans of almost 1 m/3 ft.

Eggs are often laid on water plant stems and hatch into aquatic nymphs that may take seven years to mature. These have gills in their rectum, providing a form of jet propulsion; when the rectal muscles contract, water is expelled and the animal shoots forward. Nymphs climb from the water to hatch into adults, whose folded wings unfurl as fluid pumps through their network of veins.

During mating the male grips the female round the neck with his tail claspers. She then curves her long abdomen around to touch his and sperm is transferred.

A DRAGONFLY'S ABILITY to catch other insects in flight stems from a combination of large, fast-beating wings, that allow it to hover and fly backward, and exceptional eyesight. If you watch a dragonfly patrolling its territory over a pond on a sunny day, you will see its sudden, darting movements, that correspond to aerial interceptions of prey. Catch some dragonfly nymphs from a pond and keep them in an aquarium. Watch how they catch prey using long, hinged jaws. Remember to return them to the pond to complete their development.

☛ *56 POND, 345 EYE.*

SQUIRREL DAY

All tree-living squirrels share a well-developed sense of balance and good eyesight, giving them an ability to judge distances precisely when they jump between branches. These characteristics are particularly important in the flying squirrels, which have flat membranes of skin between their legs and each side of the body, allowing them to glide between trees, using their tails as rudders.

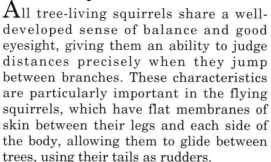

Arboreal squirrels build breeding nests, called dreys, where the young are born in late winter.

Ground squirrels include a number of burrowing species, like prairie dogs of North America, marmots and sousliks that are found across the Northern Hemisphere, and the African ground squirrels. In these species the tail is often reduced and the forelimbs, which are used for digging, are larger and stronger than in tree squirrels.

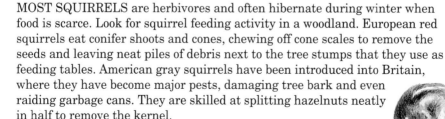

MOST SQUIRRELS are herbivores and often hibernate during winter when food is scarce. Look for squirrel feeding activity in a woodland. European red squirrels eat conifer shoots and cones, chewing off cone scales to remove the seeds and leaving neat piles of debris next to the tree stumps that they use as feeding tables. American gray squirrels have been introduced into Britain, where they have become major pests, damaging tree bark and even raiding garbage cans. They are skilled at splitting hazelnuts neatly in half to remove the kernel.

☛ 103 TAIL; 337 TRACKING.

PUFFIN DAY

The two halves of a puffin's beak open parallel to one another and its palate has backward-pointing spines, allowing it to carry up to 60 small fish back to the nest after every fishing trip.

The multicolored stripes on a puffin's beak only develop during the breeding season, when hundreds of pairs congregate to breed in burrows that they excavate in soft soils covering cliffs and islands. Their feet change color at the same time, from drab yellow to brilliant orange. Like other members of the auk family, they are more at home at sea than on land, and have waterproof plumage, a streamlined body and stubby wings that allow them to swim underwater in pursuit of fish.

The diminutive puffin's major enemy is the greater black-backed gull, which can catch it in flight.

LARGE PUFFINERIES are found around rocky coasts in Britain, Iceland, the Faroe Islands, Norway and along the coast of Alaska. The biggest colonies are on islands, where the birds are safe from ground-based predators like rats and cats. Visit a coastal seabird colony and watch puffins coming in to land. They have almost no tail to steer with, so use their feet as rudders instead.

☛ 43 BEAK; 304 FLAMINGO.

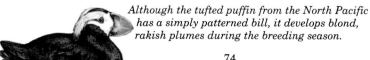

Although the tufted puffin from the North Pacific has a simply patterned bill, it develops blond, rakish plumes during the breeding season.

74

KOALA DAY

The koala eats the leaves of just three of our eucalyptus species. It prefers the leaves of manna gum, Eucalyptus viminalis.

One of the world's favorite animals, the koala lives in eastern Australia, occupying a narrow range from central Queensland to south Victoria. Like its close relative the wombat, the koala has no tail and its pouch points backward. But instead of being adapted for digging, its forefeet have long digits with the thumb and first finger opposed, to allow the koala to grip branches.

In dry weather, koalas switch from manna-gum to swamp-gum leaves which have a higher water content. Chewed carefully into fine diamond-shaped pieces, the leaf material passes down through the stomach and small intestine and is stored in the caecum (appendix) where it is fermented by bacteria for up to eight days.

BACTERIA IN THE KOALA'S GUT convert leaf starch and cellulose into sugar that it can absorb, but the process is slow and the koala's low calorie diet means that it must sleep 18–19 hours each day to conserve energy. Eucalyptus leaves contain many toxins and koalas must carefully select palatable species, at particular stages of growth, to stay alive. Some eucalyptus foliage contains high cyanide levels and this is a frequent cause of death for koalas in zoos. The animal's liver must work overtime to detoxify eucalyptus oils and other compounds, which are a defense against leaf-eating animals.

☛ 141 GUM TREE.

WASP DAY

Wasps may be social, forming annual colonies like bumblebees, or they may be solitary or parasitic. The cells of a bees' nest are provisioned with honey for the developing larvae, but wasps provision their cells with the adults or larvae of other insects or with other arthropods such as spiders. Wasps' nests are made of mud or paper and may be very elaborate.

Mud-dauber wasps provision their nests with stung spiders. The venom paralyzes but doesn't kill, so the larvae's food supply stays fresh.

Paper wasps tear wood from posts and plant stems and chew it to a pulp with which they build their elegant stalked nests.

Wasps are fond of sugar (left) but use it for their own energy needs. The potter wasp (right) folds a paralysed caterpillar on top of its egg.

PARASITIC WASPS are able to dispense with nest building because their prey is their nests. They lay eggs in their host – often a caterpillar or even a spider – and the parasitic grubs feed on the internal organs of their host. Their development is controlled so that the host finally dies when the parasite grubs are ready to pupate. Keep some cabbage white butterfly caterpillars in a cage; you will almost certainly find that some are parasitized by wasps, that will either pupate on the surface of dead caterpillars or emerge after their host pupates.

☞ 325 PARASITES; 82 BUMBLEBEE.

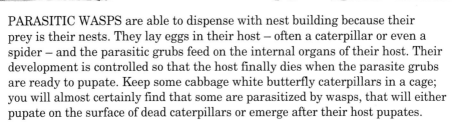

SECRETARY BIRD DAY

Secretary birds build large, untidy nests in the crowns of thorn trees.

A tuft of feathers behind its head, like a bunch of quill pens, gives the secretary bird its name. It is one of the most distinctive birds of the African plains, striding through the grasslands in search of snakes, which it stamps to death with powerful feet that are equipped with short, muscular toes and nail-like claws.

Full-grown secretary birds stand about 1 m / 3 ft. tall and can subdue large snakes. They can walk faster than people usually run and are reputed to congregate at the edge of grassland fires, catching animals that are driven toward them by the flames.

Their eagle-like appearance and predatory habits have led biologists to classify them alongside raptors (eagles and falcons) but they have many unique features and are the only living species of their family.

QUILL PENS MADE FROM BIRDS' FEATHERS were used by secretaries and clerks before fountain pens and word processors were invented. Find a large feather (goose feathers from a farmyard or wildfowl park are best) and cut a nib-shaped point at the end, splitting this lengthways to allow a capillary of ink to flow to the tip. Dip it into ink and try to draw and write with it. Experiment with pointed and flat nibs, to vary the thickness and shape of letters.

☛ *270 EAGLE; 163 SNAKES; 215 MONGOOSE.*

DESERT DAY

Acute water shortage and high daytime temperatures are the major challenges facing desert plants and animals.

North African sandgrouse fly 60 km / 35 mi. to oases and carry water back to their chicks in their breast feathers.

Camels, who store fat in their humps as an energy source, are the best means of transport for human travelers in the desert. They also have an uncanny ability to detect distant rainfall.

The large ears of desert hedgehogs (above) act as heat radiators.

Many desert flowers (below) germinate, flower and set seed after rare rainfall, producing 'desert blooms'.

By midday the sand is unbearably hot and the Namid lizard pauses regularly to raise feet in alternate pairs so that they can cool. Most animals avoid daytime heat entirely.

The blind desert golden mole spends three-quarters of its life burrowing just below the surface, hunting sand swimmers by sound and touch.

Cacti, like the 18-m / 60-ft. tall Carnegia giganteus *of Mexico and Arizona, conserve moisture in water-storage tissues, protected by a thick, waxy surface. Loss of leaves has reduced the surface available for water loss.*

The bizarre Welwitschia mirabilis *survives in the Namib desert by tapping underground water with deep roots and by absorbing condensed dew at night.* Welwitschia *has only two leaves, which grow continually from the base and are shredded at the tips by desert winds.*

78

Animals have evolved many strategies for dealing with water shortages. Scorpions (left) satisfy their moisture needs by using venomous stings to capture other insects, like desert locusts. Gerbils (right), from Asia and Africa, obtain all the moisture they need from seeds. Night sea frogs roll over in coastal parts of the Namib Desert and darkling beetles (below right) stand, head down, on the edge of sand dunes, drinking water that condenses and trickles down their bodies. Australian Holy Cross toads (below left) live in mucous underground cocoons, until rare rainfall coaxes them out to breed in temporary pools.

Movement in loose sand is difficult, but the sidewinder snake solves the problem by throwing loops of its body sideways, leaving a characteristic trail of parallel lines.

Desert foxes, which are nocturnal hunters with enormous ears to dissipate heat and locate faint sounds, have large feet to help them move on soft surfaces.

Tortoises (right) are active mostly at night in stony deserts in the southern United States. Sand swimmers (below right), from the Namib, are legless skinks that treat sand like water and 'swim' through the surface layers by undulating their bodies.

WATCH THE WAY pet gerbils become highly active at night. This is a legacy of their desert past, when nocturnal feeding avoided the perils of daytime heat.

☛ *265 CAMEL; 54–5 UNDERGROUND.*

MANATEE DAY

The mammary glands of a manatee resemble those of a human female, which may account for the widespread belief that they form the basis of the mermaid legend. They are classified as sea cows, or Sirenians, after the Sirens who almost lured Ulysses and his fellow voyagers to their death.

Counts of the annual rings in male manatee tusks show that they live up to 70 years. Females are very attentive mothers, communicating with their calves with squeals, squeeks and chirps.

Three different species of manatee live in Amazonia, West Africa and the West Indies. The fourth species is the dugong of northern Australia and Indo-Pacific coasts.

Sirenians probably share a common ancestor with elephants. They are herbivores, grazing on sea grasses. A manatee's teeth wear rapidly and are continuously replaced from the back of the jaw. Its nostrils are on the top of its head, so it does not need to break the surface with its body to breath. Its vast upper lip is covered with sensory bristles.

WEST INDIAN AND WEST AFRICAN manatees are 4 m/13 ft. long and weigh 1,500 kg/3,300 lbs. They have few natural enemies but large numbers have been slaughtered in the past for their flesh, which tastes like pork. Steller's sea cow, which was twice as large as existing species, was hunted to extinction within 30 years of its discovery, on the Commander Islands off Alaska, in the 18th century. Their slow rate of reproduction and a highly specialized diet of sea grasses makes manatees very vulnerable to hunting and habitat damage.

☛ *26 WALRUS.*

CHICKEN DAY

Domestic chickens, descended from the wild jungle fowl of Asia, are the most numerous birds on Earth. Their varied size and plumage patterns demonstrates how much hidden genetic variation lies within the wild species. Rare genetic variants have been selected and maintained by man for their decorative, meat-producing or egg-laying qualities.

Jungle fowls may have been domesticated originally for cock fighting, which was recorded in China in 1000 BC and was legal in Britain until 1849.

Different breeds have been selected for specific purposes. Bantams are dwarfs and require less space than the decorative long-tailed Yokohama. Marans, bred in Europe after World War II, are noted for their brown eggs. Mediterranean breeds, like the Leghorn and Anconas, were bred by poultry fanciers in America, from Italian stock. The famously productive Rhode Island Red was derived from Leghorns. Wyandottes are named after a Red Indian tribe.

NOTICE HOW FARMYARD CHICKENS retain the wild jungle fowl's behavioral patterns. Hens use their beaks and feet to rummage through the soil for insects and seeds, just as jungle fowl forage in the leaf litter of a tropical forest. Buff Orpington cockerels still issue the same noisy territorial challenges that ring out through Asian jungles at dawn.

☛ *90 TURKEY.*

81

BUMBLEBEE DAY

Bumblebees are members of the same family, Apidae, as honeybees, but their colonies do not persist from year to year. Instead queens hibernate through the winter, establishing a new colony each spring. The first bees to be born into the new colony are workers who service the nest through the summer. Males and new queens are produced in the autumn.

Hibernating queens emerge from crevices and underground burrows after the first few warm days of spring.

They forage for nectar and pollen, and locate a nest site in which they build wax cells.

Workers take over foraging and building from the queen and increase the size of the nest. The next 'generation' of workers is larger.

An egg is laid in each of the few cells which are provisioned with honey.

Small workers emerge from this first batch of eggs.

BUMBLEBEES OFTEN NEST in rodent holes. In spring, before hibernating queens emerge, build a nest that imitates a rodent hole by burying an inverted clay flowerpot so that the drainage hole in its base just projects above the soil surface. Line the base of the cavity with a handful of sawdust or wood shavings and protect the entrance hole from rain with an old tile, propped on stones so the bees can enter.

☛ 76 WASP.

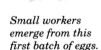

LYREBIRD DAY

The wet eucalyptus forests of Australia are the habitat of the pheasant-sized lyrebirds, whose dull plumage is transformed during their breeding display. Then, the long, lyre-shaped tail feathers are fanned, thrown forward over the head and vibrated while the bird sings and dances.

The lyrebirds are the largest songbirds and are talented mimics. Almost 80 percent of their loud territorial songs may be borrowed from other birds. They can even mimic barking dogs.

Insects form the major part of the diet and are raked from leaf litter with methodical sweeps of the large, clawed feet.

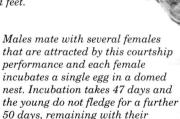

Males mate with several females that are attracted by this courtship performance and each female incubates a single egg in a domed nest. Incubation takes 47 days and the young do not fledge for a further 50 days, remaining with their mother for a further eight months.

Lyrebirds are poor fliers, ascending trees to roost at night by jumping from branch to branch, and gliding to earth at dawn. They are fast, agile runners and are difficult to see in dense undergrowth.

SONG MIMICRY is practiced by many birds. Listen to the calls of urban starlings, who can mimic jet planes and telephones.

☛ *276 BIRD OF PARADISE.*

FOXGLOVE DAY

Valuable drugs are present in many plants and they form a natural medicine cabinet, full of compounds capable of curing illness and disease. Some tropical countries have now begun systematic programs to screen rainforest plants for natural remedies.

*Extracts of European foxglove (*Digitalis purpurea*) have been used for treating heart disorders for centuries. It contains digitalis, a poisonous compound which stimulates the heart if taken in low doses.*

Foxglove is a biennial plant, producing a rosette of overwintering leaves at the end of its first year of growth. In the following year the tall flowering spike elongates.

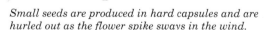

Small seeds are produced in hard capsules and are hurled out as the flower spike sways in the wind.

WATCH THE WAY that bumblebees visit the tubular flowers of the foxglove. The bottom of the tube forms a landing platform and the pattern of spots guides the insect to the hidden nectar. Meanwhile, white pollen is dusted in its hairy back by stamens at the top of the floral tube. You should be able to see the pollen grains on the bee's fur as it backs out of the tubular flower. Occasionally it will pause, before flying off, to comb its hind legs. Open a flower and find the long style and stigma, which collect pollen from the fur of visiting bees.

☛ *332–3 MEDICINAL PLANTS; 162 POISONOUS PLANTS; 344 ALOE.*

PLAINS DAY

A dry climate at the end of the last Ice Age created the grasslands of America's Midwest. These great plains were once inhabited by the largest herds of grazing animals ever recorded.

Habitat loss, through intensive agriculture, has reduced pronghorn antelope numbers from an estimated 40 million to about 400,000. Conservation measures have halted their decline. They are North America's fastest land animal, running at 70 kph/45 mph and leaping 15 m/50 ft. When threatened, they raise conspicuous white hairs on their rump, as an alarm signal to the herd.

Ground squirrels (prairie dogs) underwent a population explosion when settlers killed their natural predators. In 1900 a single colony of 400 million individuals ate enough grass to feed 1.5 million cattle. Systematic poisoning by farmers has since reduced their numbers drastically.

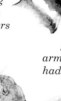

Before white settlers arrived 50 million buffalo provided food and clothing for Sioux, Comanche and Blackfoot Indians. A single kill fed an Indian family for a month. By the end of the 19th century the thundering herds were gone; buffalo hunters, armed with powerful rifles, had slaughtered all but 800 for their skins and tongues.

MOURNFUL HOWLING OF COYOTES (above) is still a familiar sound across the Great Plains at night, despite a century of efforts to destroy them. Sage grouse (top left) and prairie dogs, that both feed on the prairie grasses, are their natural prey.

Prairie fires periodically flare up in the dry grasses in summer. Dry weather and high winds sweep fires forward faster than a horse can gallop, leaving fertile ash that enriches the soil and provides nutrients for deep-rooted plants that survive the blaze.

☛ 54–55 UNDERGROUND; 160 WILD DOG; 147 GRASS.

ARMADILLO DAY

There are about 20 species of armadillo, the smallest weighing a mere 100 g/3.5 oz., and the giant armadillo up to 55 kg/120 lbs. Their skin is remarkably modified to form horny bands and plates of armor connected by normal skin so that they can flex and move. The three-banded armadillo can roll up to form a perfect armored ball.

This fairy armadillo, like the other species, is an accomplished burrower.

Armadillos practice polyembrony – the fertilized egg divides to produce two or more identical embryos. Nine-banded armadillos always have identical quadruplets.

The nine-banded armadillo is the only one found in North America: its hind feet are planted flat on the ground as it walks – a gait known as plantigrade.

Giant armadillos have 80–100 molars that grow constantly and which are the most primitive mammalian teeth known – just pegs of soft dentine with no hard enamel.

UNTIL ABOUT 4 MILLION YEARS AGO North and South America were separate continents and all armadillos were restricted to South America. Southwards migration of advanced northern mammals when the continents became linked, via the Isthmus of Panama, caused extinction of many South American species, including the giant sloth. However, the nine-banded armadillo migrated north and is now a pest of arable fields in the southern states of the USA. The giant armadillo, glyptodon, became extinct in South America in historical times.

☞ *359 ARMOR.*

CORN DAY

Corn (also called maize in Europe and Africa) is the most important cereal after wheat and rice and is used for human and animal food. Sweet corn is harvested before the grains ripen, so that they retain a high sugar content. Popcorn, sold in movie theaters, has small grains whose hard kernels explode when they are heated and the water inside turns to steam. In the United States corn is grown on a large scale for cooking-oil production.

The tassels on the top of the plant are masses of male stamens, releasing pollen. Silky stigmas protrude from the female flowers at the base of lower leaves. Wind carries pollen from tassels to silks, so gardeners who plant sweet corn grow it in blocks rather than rows, to ensure even pollination and well-filled cobs.

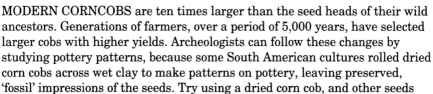

MODERN CORNCOBS are ten times larger than the seed heads of their wild ancestors. Generations of farmers, over a period of 5,000 years, have selected larger cobs with higher yields. Archeologists can follow these changes by studying pottery patterns, because some South American cultures rolled dried corn cobs across wet clay to make patterns on pottery, leaving preserved, 'fossil' impressions of the seeds. Try using a dried corn cob, and other seeds like beans, sunflower seeds and millet, to make your own 'fossils' by leaving their impressions in modeling clay.

☛ *33 SUNFLOWER; 166 CEREALS; 147 GRASS.*

NEST DAY

Birds' nests vary from the shallow, seaweed-decorated gravel scrapes of some shore birds to massive constructions of branches built by eagles. In every case nest building is instinctive behavior, providing a secure site for incubating eggs and raising young.

The European reed warbler builds a cup-shaped nest suspended between reed stems. The American mourning dove builds in cacti, where the plant's sharp spines deter predators.

African and Asian weaver birds build nests suspended from tree branches. The male builds a perch, then extends this into a ring that acts as an entrance for a tear-drop-shaped nest, woven by pushing and pulling fibrous material into loops and knots. Young weavers build practice nests that often fall apart, before perfecting the technique.

Indian tailor birds are warblers that stitch their nests between two leaves, using fibers and cobwebs.

SEARCH A HEDGEROW in winter until you find one of last season's nests. Notice the way that materials like twigs, grass and pieces of wool are woven into the living vegetation of the hedge, to produce a strong, stable platform. Song thrushes line the nest with mud for additional strength, and many species decorate the exterior with moss and lichen, to blend with their surroundings. To appreciate the instinctive skill of a bird, try to build a replica nest using authentic materials.

☞ *250 CUCKOO; 209 BOWER-BIRD.*

BLACK BEAR DAY

The sloth bear has poorly developed teeth and feeds on termites, sucking them up with its mobile lips.

In Asia the Himalayan black bear ranges from Iran to China, with an isolated population on Honshu in Japan. It has a prominent V-shaped white patch on its neck and an endearing habit of rolling downhill in a ball when alarmed.

American black bears (illustrated here) were once common throughout much of the United States. They are now restricted to well-wooded regions, although they sometimes wander into inhabited areas to scavenge. Like most bears, they are omnivores, feeding on tubers, berries, fish and carrion, so the contents of a garbage can can prove irrestistible.

In summer it moves 4,000 m / 13,000 ft. up into the Asian mountains; in winter it hibernates or returns to lower altitudes.

THICK FUR COATS give bears a cuddly appearance which has made them popular subjects for cartoonists and children's writers. Pooh Bear, created by A.A. Milne, is the most famous fictional ursid and if he has a real counterpart it is most likely to be the Malayan or sun bear. This is the smallest species – only about 1.5 m/5 ft. tall – with short, smooth brown fur, a lazy disposition and an extraordinary fondness for honey and syrup. Pooh would approve.

☛ 279 POLAR BEAR.

TURKEY DAY

The traditional Christmas turkey was brought to Europe early in the 16th century by the Spanish who found them a common domestic bird in newly conquered Mexico. A hundred years later turkeys were popular poultry for holidays and feast days. Wild common turkeys still occur in the eastern and southern USA and Mexico.

The Beltsville white, selectively bred in the USA, is now a popular strain among farmers worldwide.

The Norfolk black strain was the standard British turkey for hundreds of years. It is a descendant of the wild-type bronze turkeys reared on Mexican and American farms until early this century.

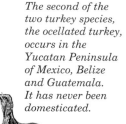

The second of the two turkey species, the ocellated turkey, occurs in the Yucatan Peninsula of Mexico, Belize and Guatemala. It has never been domesticated.

IN THE SEARCH for cheaper meat, food scientists have altered the genetic makeup of the turkey so that it grows rapidly and puts on the maximum amount of weight for the minimum amount of food. It has been selectively bred so that the breast muscle (the part we most like to eat) has become enormous.

In many modern strains the breast is so big that the turkey cannot mate of its own accord. These giant birds have to be helped to reproduce. The female must be injected with sperm taken from a male in order for her eggs to be fertile.

☛ 81 CHICKEN.

BUSH BABY DAY

Bush babies, or galagos, live in African forests. Their appealing looks, enhanced by their immense eyes, make them popular pets and zoo animals. Nocturnal, they feed on insects, supplementing their diet with fruit, flowers, tender leaves and tree gum. Bush babies have acute hearing for locating prey, and can be trapped with calling cicadas tied to a string.

Bush babies build a new spherical leaf nest every two or three weeks.

Needle-clawed bush babies (below) have a claw-like extension in the middle of each nail to hook insects from crevices.

The smallest of the five species, Demidoff's (or the dwarf) bush baby (left), weighs just 60 g/2 oz.

BUSH BABIES, LIKE MOST nocturnal animals, exhibit eye shine: when photographed at night with flash illumination, their eyes glow brightly, like headlights. A crystalline layer at the back of the eye, called the tapetum lucidum, reflects light back through the retina, making night vision more sensitive. You may have noticed that the eyes of cats glow in this way when they are caught in the beam of car headlights. The small round reflectors that mark the center and edges of roads operate on the same principle, reflecting light back directly at its source.

☛ 104–5 NOCTURNAL ANIMALS; 211 LEMURS.

WATER SURFACE DAY

Two groups of animals exploit the water surface as a habitat: those that have developed buoyancy aids and those that can exploit the force of surface tension.

Springtails are scavengers that walk on the water surface.

Hydra (above) exploits surface tension to hang below the pond surface. Whirligig beetles (below) swim in the surface film and have divided eyes that allow them to see above and below the surface simultaneously.

Mucus bubbles keep the sub-tropical bubble raft snail afloat. It eats the tentacles of the planktonic by-the-wind-sailor, a smaller relative of the Portuguese man-of-war.

Portuguese men-of-war drift on the surface, supported by a large, membranous float.

Predatory raft spiders (above) and pond skaters (right) rely on surface tension to allow them to walk on water.

Mosquito larvae hang from the surface, breathing air through siphons.

DEMONSTRATE the strength of the surface film by floating a piece of tissue paper and laying a small needle on top. When the paper becomes waterlogged and sinks, the needle will remain afloat, supported by surface tension.

☞ 176 HYDRA; 56 POND; 254 PLANKTON.

BEAK DAY

A bird's beak is an extension of its jaws, encased in a horny sheath. Its primary function is food gathering, but it is also used for nest building, preening, and as a weapon.

The long beak of a spoonbill is flattened at the end and swept from side to side in the water as the bird wades forward. When prey (usually shrimps) is detected by sensitive nerve endings, the 'spoon' snaps shut and the bird throws back its head, allowing its captive to drop down its throat.

The strong, hooked beak of a parrot tears open tough fruits and crushes seeds and nuts.

Sunbirds, like hummingbirds, are nectar feeders and the long, thin bill of a malachite sunbird is use to suck this sweet liquid from tubular flowers.

The function of a toucan's bloated beak is uncertain. It may be an adaptation to display, rather than feeding.

Fish are often covered with slippery mucilage and cormorants' beaks s are roughened along their edges, to grip their struggling prey.

Flamingos have beaks that are adapted for filtering small animals from shallow pools.

VISIT THE SEASHORE and use binoculars to watch wading birds feeding. Notice that different species, like dunlin, redshank, oystercatchers and curlews, have beaks of different lengths. This allows them to feed selectively on their preferred invertebrate prey, which burrows to different depths in the mud and sand. By evolving varied beak structures, the birds avoid direct competition for identical food resources.

☛ 200 WOODPECKER; 88 NEST; 123 TOUCAN; 205 HUMMINGBIRD; 304 FLAMINGO.

STAR FISH DAY

Together with sea urchins and sea cucumbers, starfish belong to a group of marine animals called echinoderms. The term means 'spiny skin' and the upper surface of star fish is rough to the touch.

Brittle stars have a smaller central body and long, undulating arms. Their tube feet do not end in suckers.

All star fish are radially symetrical and often have five arms, although the sun-stars may have as many as thirteen.

The tube feet are tipped with minute suckers. These grip bivalve mollusk shells, which starfish envelop in their arms. The star fish then pulls relentlessly, until the shell opens and the predator is able to insert its mouth and extendable stomach, eating the mollusk within.

Rows of tube feet are used for moving and feeding. Each foot is coupled to an internal hydraulic system; the muscular tube extends when water is pumped in.

VISIT THE SEASHORE. Find a live star fish in a rock pool, then dig in the sand on the lower shore until you find a live cockle or scallop. Put the shellfish in a bucket with the star fish and watch. The bivalve will flap its shell violently and leap away from the star fish. Water that has contained star fish provokes the same reaction, because the shellfish can detect the chemical secretions of their predator.

☞ 331 SEA CUCUMBER; 153 BIVALVE MOLLUSKS.

LIVING FOSSIL DAY

When an animal or plant is the last living representative of its evolutionary line, it is known as a 'living fossil.' Such organisms are survivors of primitive groups. They are particularly valuable to biologists as they provide structural detail, particularly of their soft parts, that is not preserved in fossils.

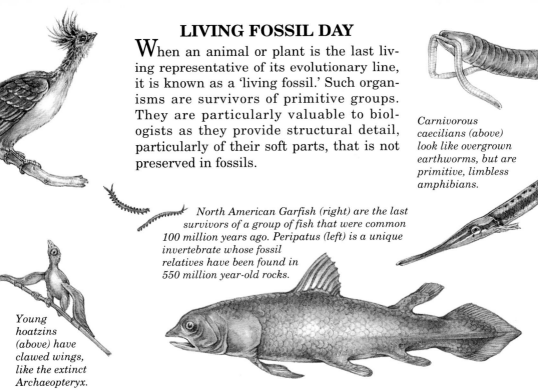

Carnivorous caecilians (above) look like overgrown earthworms, but are primitive, limbless amphibians.

North American Garfish (right) are the last survivors of a group of fish that were common 100 million years ago. Peripatus (left) is a unique invertebrate whose fossil relatives have been found in 550 million year-old rocks.

Young hoatzins (above) have clawed wings, like the extinct Archaeopteryx.

UNTIL 1938 BIOLOGISTS BELIEVED that coelacanths (above) had become extinct 65 million years ago. In that year a living specimen was found in a South African trawler's catch. The discovery became headline news but another specimen was not found until 1952. Over 120 specimens have now been examined and recently coelacanths have been filmed swimming in deep waters off the Comoro Islands, just as they did 380 million years ago.

☛ *170 PRIMITIVE PLANTS; 320 HORSETAIL.*

PEANUT DAY

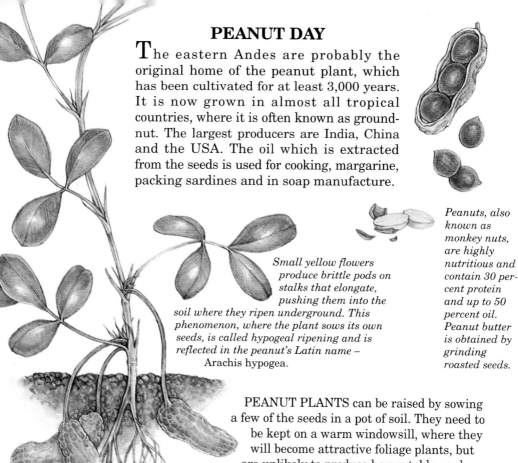

The eastern Andes are probably the original home of the peanut plant, which has been cultivated for at least 3,000 years. It is now grown in almost all tropical countries, where it is often known as groundnut. The largest producers are India, China and the USA. The oil which is extracted from the seeds is used for cooking, margarine, packing sardines and in soap manufacture.

Small yellow flowers produce brittle pods on stalks that elongate, pushing them into the soil where they ripen underground. This phenomenon, where the plant sows its own seeds, is called hypogeal ripening and is reflected in the peanut's Latin name – Arachis hypogea.

Peanuts, also known as monkey nuts, are highly nutritious and contain 30 percent protein and up to 50 percent oil. Peanut butter is obtained by grinding roasted seeds.

PEANUT PLANTS can be raised by sowing a few of the seeds in a pot of soil. They need to be kept on a warm windowsill, where they will become attractive foliage plants, but are unlikely to produce harvestable seeds. Search for nodules on peanut roots. These contain *Rhizobium*, a bacterium which converts atmospheric nitrogen into nitrates for plant growth.

☞ 127 BEAN; 326 PARTNERSHIP.

WOLF DAY

The mournful howl of wolves is becoming a rare sound in North America, as hunters continue to persecute them. These large carnivores inhabit open country and forests, feeding on caribou, deer and even horses. They usually hunt singly or in pairs during the summer but in the winter they congregate in family parties. Howling is a method of calling the pack together.

The common grey wolf has been systematically exterminated over most of its range, in Europe, Asia and North America.

Coyotes, which roam the wilder areas of the North American continent, are smaller than wolves and feed on lesser prey, including rabbits. After centuries of relentless persecution, because they occasionally take young domestic animals, it has been realized that coyotes play a valuable role in controlling rats and other vermin on farms.

THE LAST WOLF IN BRITAIN was killed in Scotland in 1743. A few survive in Scandinavia, Spain and central Europe, but the largest populations are in Asia and the United States. Wolves rarely, if ever, attack humans, unlike domestic alsatians, rottweilers and pit bull terriers, which regularly attack and sometimes kill people.

Look for wolf spiders (right) in gardens, basking in the sunshine on warm stones. They run down invertebrate prey, in the same way that wolves hunt deer.

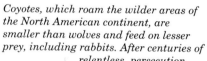

☛ *140 FOX; 160 WILD DOG.*

OSPREY DAY

Ospreys are one of the most widely distributed birds, having colonized everywhere except New Zealand and the polar regions. Large and conspicuous, in flight they are clearly black and white with a short tail and angled wings. In the USA they are called 'fish hawks'.

Ospreys soar in circles 20–40 m / 65–130 ft. above the water surface until they sight a fish, half close their wings and dive, feet first.

The osprey's outer toe is reversible, like an owl's, so a fish can be grasped firmly with two toes in front and two behind.

Ospreys build an enormous nest of large sticks and branches, usually in a tree, and return and add to the nest year after year. Three eggs are laid and the female does most of the incubating.

The osprey returns to its nest or a convenient perch with the fish locked in its claws.

GAMEKEEPERS, CONVINCED OSPREYS took trout and salmon, and egg collectors, who coveted their striking eggs, drove the last ospreys out of Britain at the end of the 19th century. In 1955 ospreys nested in Scotland for the first time in 50 years but egg collectors robbed the nest. In 1958 the Royal Society for Protection of Birds mounted 'Operation Osprey', a round-the-clock guard on the nest. The police and armed forces helped, and the egg collectors were eventually defeated. Now more than 30 pairs of ospreys nest in Scotland.

☞ 270 EAGLE; 360 GANNET.

COFFEE DAY

Coffee originated from Africa but is now grown worldwide as a tropical hill crop. It is a valuable commodity, traded especially in Europe and North America. Brazil is the world's biggest coffee producer, but coffee is important to the economies of many smaller nations in Africa and in Central and South America. Coffee plants require a moist, hot climate and fertile soils.

Coffee flowers have a beautiful scent.

Unripe coffee berries are green.

Roasted chicory roots (right) were widely used in wartime Europe to make a coffee substitute – ersatz coffee – and they are now sometimes added to coffee to provide additional flavoring.

Red coffee berries, known as 'cherries', are ready for picking. Each contains one or two 'beans'.

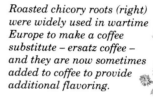

THE COFFEE BUSH, 4 or 5 m/13 or 16 ft. high, is picked, often by hand, and the cherries put through a pulping machine. The slurry of pulp and beans is allowed to ferment then the pulp is washed away and the beans dried in the sun. Dry beans are then put through the hulling machine which removes any remnants of skin and pulp by abrasion. Beans are roasted shortly before use, when they develop their characteristic coffee smell. Roasted beans are ground to powder before coffee is brewed from them.

☛ 44 TEA.

EDIBLE SEAWEED DAY

Coastal communities around the world use seaweeds for food, but the Japanese are the major consumers of these marine algae. Seaweeds are rich in vitamins A and C and also accumulate iodine, so people that eat them never suffer from goiter, an iodine deficiency disease of the thyroid gland.

Brown seaweeds (left) contain alginates, which are used in the food industry, Dulse (right) is eaten in some parts of North America.

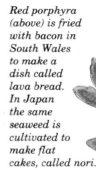

Red porphyra (above) is fried with bacon in South Wales to make a dish called lava bread. In Japan the same seaweed is cultivated to make flat cakes, called nori.

In Ireland, Chondrus crispus (Carragheen moss) is collected to make infusions with cocoa, as a medicine for lung complaints. Sea lettuce (below, left) is sometimes used in salads.

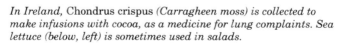

SEAWEED FARMING, for the commercial extraction of natural food additives, is an important industry. If you read the lists of contents in food products like soups and dehydrated foods you will see that you have been eating agar and alginates – seaweed products – for most of your life.

☛ 315 ROCK POOL.

COCKROACH DAY

There are 3,000–4,000 species of cockroach and the group has a long pedigree. Fossils from the Carboniferous period, 320 million years old, are very similar to present-day species. Cockroaches are omnivorous scavengers and almost all are nocturnal. Three or four species are domestic pests, scavenging in kitchens, sewage and waste systems and transferring disease organisms between them.

In the wild cockroaches live in cracks beneath bark, in rock crevices and between leaves on the forest floor. Their flattened shape is an adaptation to living in narrow spaces.

Cockroach eggs look like small beans. Newly hatched nymphs (above) are almost white but quickly turn brown.

The American cockroach, Periplaneta americana *(right), is the largest pest species, up to 8 cm / 3 in. long.*

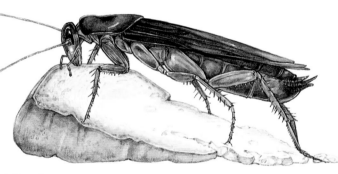

COCKROACHES ARE EXOPTERYGOTE ('outside-winged') insects – the wings develop progressively outside the body with each molt (left). Endopterygote ('inside-winged') insects have a larval stage which metamorphoses via a pupal stage to a fully winged adult. Immature exopterygotes are termed nymphs, not larvae, and there is no pupal stage. Cockroach nymphs molt between 5 and 12 times (depending on species) over a period of several months, before they become adult.

☛ *273 LOCUST.*

STRANGE-NOSED FISH DAY

Large numbers of species can live together in a single habitat when each has unique adaptations which allow it to exploit a particular food source more efficiently than competitors. The noses of fish are often highly specialized for hunting certain types of prey.

The extended, drooping nose of the elephant-snout fish allows it to pick up worms from the bottom of African lakes, where it hunts at night by detecting prey with electric discharges.

Atlantic needlefish have a long beak armed with razor-sharp teeth, used for gripping prey.

The nose of a hammerhead shark also contains an electrical prey-location system and its widely spaced eyes have an extended field of vision.

Paddlefish live in the Mississippi and Yangtze rivers and grow to a length of about 3 m / 10 ft. This includes a 1-m / 3-ft. snout, whose function is a mystery. One possibility is that it contains an electrical sensor for detecting plankton swarms. Other theories suggest that it is used for digging in mud, beating aquatic organisms from plants or as a stabilizer to balance the downward pressure of its gaping mouth. The closely related sword-nosed sturgeon has a similar snout, used for disturbing mollusks and other prey.

Sailfish, and the related swordfish and marlins, have long snouts that may be used as weapons. Swordfish swim at 100 kph / 60 mph, and can puncture the bottom of boats and the flesh of whales.

☛ 93 BEAK; 254 PLANKTON; 1 SHARK; 148 STRANGE NOSES; 119 KILLER WHALE.

TAIL DAY

A tail is much more than an evolutionary afterthought. Depending on the animal, it can be used for climbing, threatening, balancing, displaying and expressing emotions.

Both pangolins (above left) and New World monkeys like the woolly spider monkey (left) have prehensile tails that are used to grip branches. The pangolin's tail is also a very effective weapon and can inflict serious wounds with its covering of sharp scales.

The fine tail plumes of quetzals, red-tailed tropic birds, hummingbirds and magpie jays are sexual ornaments, designed to attract admiring females.

The elephant's tail is like a short leather whip and is used for flicking flies from its hindquarters.

When a skunk raises its tail, it is a sign that it is about to spray enemies with stinking fluid from its anal glands.

Kangaroos' tails act like the third leg of a tripod, helping them to balance when they sit up and acting as a counterbalance when they hop. The tails of ring-tailed lemurs are also vital balancing organs.

WATCH THE MOVEMENTS of the tail of a domestic cat. As with other mammals, like foxes, lions and tigers, it is used to maintain balance during the twists and turns of the chase. But its angle also changes with its owner's moods, depending on whether these are aggressive or submissive. Even whales use tails for communication, 'lobtailing', or splashing the surface.

☛ 22 HARVEST MOUSE; 151 PEACOCK; 189 SQUIRREL MONKEY.

NOCTURNAL ANIMALS
DAY

Large animals that hunt at night are usually equipped with an acute sense of smell and exceptional eyesight, allowing them to find their prey in darkness.

The slow loris stalks its prey with slow, deliberate movements, then grabs it suddenly.

The linsang is one of many cat-like animals, including genets and civets, that hunt in darkness, preying on chickens, young domestic animals, small mammals and birds. Many of these cats are seldom seen by humans and little is known about their natural history.

In the Australian outback the echidna, a monotreme or egg-laying mammal, digs at night for termites, insects and worms.

Aerial hunters of the night include bats, which have a sophisticated echolocating system for navigating and catching moths in total darkness. Ecologists use electronic bat detectors to pick up these signals and monitor bat populations. Each species has its own distinctive ultrasonic call. Many other mammals navigate at night by detecting scents that they use to mark out the boundaries of their territories.

South American owl monkeys are the only nocturnal monkeys. Large, forward facing eyes give exceptional night vison.

Australian honey possums feed exclusively on nectar, which they collect at night using their long, frilled tongues.

Much remains to be discovered about the biology of species like the slender loris, whose nocturnal life style makes them difficult to study.

Tarsiers, which range throughout the Philippines, Sumatra and Borneo, have large ears and huge eyes, whose dark pupils contract to pinpoints in daylight. They feed on insects and small birds, moving through the trees in a series of flying leaps.

Darkness presents communication problems for nocturnal animals. Tawny owls' hooting is an audible courtship signal. Glowworms (bottom) court one another by emitting flashes of light from a luminescent tail organ.

The habits of nocturnal European badgers have been intensively studied using infrared cameras.

TAKE A FLASHLIGHT into a garden after dark and search for the small animals that attract nocturnal hunters. You should find dozens of slugs crawling over the vegetation, worms coming to the soil surface and moths attracted to night-scented flowers. These are all at the bottom of a food chain that feeds frogs and mice and ultimately the larger predators, like hedgehogs, badgers and owls.

☛ 345 EYE; 271 BAT; 253 OWL; 363 BADGER; 286 BIOLUMINESCENCE.

MAGNOLIA DAY

Fossils reveal that today's magnolia flowers have many similarities with the blooms of the earliest flowering plants. Other primitive flowers, like degenaria from Fiji (bottom right), suggest that many of the plants that existed in the age of dinosaurs may have resembled the magnolia, with large numbers of stamens and ovaries.

There are 125 magnolia species distributed throughout the Himalayas, Japan, Malaysia and North America.

Magnolia seeds are produced in a cone of tough carpels.

The first animal pollinators of flowers were probably beetles that visited flowers to eat pollen and ovules and accidentally pollinated the ovules that survived their predations. More advanced flowers have evolved nectar as a reward for visiting insects, which are dusted with pollen as they drink the energy-rich liquid.

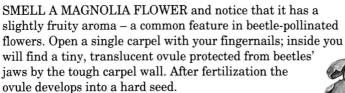

SMELL A MAGNOLIA FLOWER and notice that it has a slightly fruity aroma – a common feature in beetle-pollinated flowers. Open a single carpel with your fingernails; inside you will find a tiny, translucent ovule protected from beetles' jaws by the tough carpel wall. After fertilization the ovule develops into a hard seed.

☛ *196 PARTS OF A FLOWER; 318 PINE.*

CICADA DAY

Cicadas belong to an insect suborder called the Homoptera, all of which feed by sucking sap from plants. Adults lay eggs in twigs but the larvae crawl down the trunk and use their enlarged front legs to burrow underground, where they tap the sap in roots. Nymphs hatch and crawl up tree trunks into the shady foliage, where they undergo several molts before they reach full adulthood.

Bladder cicadas have large, distended abdomens.

The transparent, membranous wings of cicadas are only completely formed after the last nymphal molt.

Magicicada septendecim holds the record for slow subterranean development, spending seventeen years underground. Mass emergence of cicada nymphs often occurs, with thousands leaving the soil and climbing tree trunks, where adults live for two or three weeks, singing their courtship song before they breed and die.

CICADA MATING CALLS are produced by a pair of rigid abdominal membranes which are vibrated by a muscle so that they click. Air sacs below make the sound resonate. You can achieve the same effect by holding a large sheet of cardboard by its edges and wobbling it, producing a deep sound like rolling thunder. Try wobbling smaller pieces of thin rigid plastic to produce higher notes. You can make the sounds resonate by holding the plastic or cardboard horizontally above a large cooking pot.

☛ 273 LOCUST.

SEA HORSE DAY

Sea horses belong to a group of fish called pipe fish, with elongated bodies, mouths that are extended into long snouts and a single dorsal fin which ripples constantly, propelling the fish with effortless grace. In sea-horses the head is turned 90 degrees and a prehensile tail allows the animal to grip seaweeds or mates.

The sea horse's long snout is used like a vacuum cleaner, sucking in small food particles from some distance.

Sea horses are distributed throughout the warm seas of the world and the Mediterranean species is occasionally carried on warm ocean currents to the south coast of Britain. The most spectacular sea horses occur in tropical oceans; the leafy sea-dragon (below) of south Australian waters trails long appendages that camouflage it among seaweed.

THE BREEDING BEHAVIOR of sea horses is as unusual as their appearance. The female fish lays her eggs in an armored chamber (marsupium), in the male's belly. He fertilizes the eggs and then broods them for about four weeks, while they are nourished by secretions from the spongy wall of his brood pouch. Then, over a period of 24 hours, he undergoes a series of shuddering contractions as the perfectly formed young seahorses are expelled in large numbers. They fend for themselves from the moment they are born.

☛ 152 MOUTHBROODING; 305 MARSUPIAL.

PANGOLIN DAY

Pangolins are armored with overlapping scales. These are soft when the pangolin is born, but soon harden. A pangolin can roll into a ball when frightened, protecting its head and soft underparts. All pangolins can climb trees – the three African forest species are tree-dwelling and use their prehensile tail as an extra limb or hook. It may also be used as a weapon.

The pangolin's name comes from the Malay 'tenggiling' – the animal that rolls up.

Its powerful claws are used to break open anthills and termite-mounds.

The 1-m/3-ft.-long nocturnal pangolin has no teeth but uses its sticky tongue to catch termites and ants.

A PANGOLIN'S SCALES are very like fingernails or toenails and are made from the same material – keratin. This has a characteristic sweet and sickly smell when burned. Ask for help to burn some nail-clippings. A pangolin scale would smell the same if singed. Now test some wool, bristles from a brush, a feather, and some strands of hair. Wool, hair and feathers are keratin and should smell like nail-clippings. Real bristles are stiff hairs, often from pigs, and also consist of keratin, but many brushes have plastic or plant-fiber bristles.

☛ *103 TAIL.*

SLOTH DAY

The sloth is the slowest land mammal with a top speed of only 2 kph/ 1.25 mph.

Sloths are bizarre Amazonian mammals that spend most of their lives hanging upside-down. They are well adapted for this lifestyle, able to rotate their heads through 270 degrees, and their hair lies in the opposite direction to that of other mammals so that water can run off.

Because a sloth doesn't groom itself, its coat grows green algae. At a distance it may just resemble a dark bunch of leaves.

A three-toed sloth spends 18 hours of each day asleep and the remaining time browsing slowly on leaves and shoots.

Sloths hang and move in trees using their hook-like claws. On the ground they cannot walk but sprawl and drag themselves along.

THE SLOTH'S HEART beats at only 15 pulses per minute, but the hyperactive shrew has a pulse rate approaching 1,000. Your heart beats to pump blood round your body. Each beat makes arteries and veins swell slightly with the pulse of blood. Feel the pulse on the inside fold of your wrist at the very base of your thumb using the first two fingers of your other hand. Count the pulses for a minute to find your heart rate. Now run on the spot or run up and down stairs, and take your pulse again. It should have speeded up. Your heart beats faster to keep up with the demand for extra oxygen and fuel.

☛ *326 PARTNERSHIP.*

110

PRICKLY PEAR DAY

Introduced into Australia as a hedging plant, prickly pear usurped thousands of miles of grazing land in the early years of this century.

A native of Central America, the prickly pear, *Opuntia*, is a cactus but it is not a typical, slow-growing well-behaved species. Outside its normal environment it can be a serious pest, growing rapidly to produce impenetrable spiny thickets up to 3 m/10 ft. high, choking off other vegetation and injuring livestock.

Scientists dispatched to Central America found that Opuntia *there was kept in check because it was attacked regularly by the caterpillars of a small moth.*

Caterpillars of Cactoblastis cactorum *were taken to Australia and bred to provide large numbers for release into the wild.*

Within ten years Opuntia *was no longer a pest in Australia.* Cactoblastis *is a highly successful control agent because its larvae will feed only on prickly pear.*

PRICKLY PEAR FRUITS, called tunas or Barbary figs, are eaten in Central American and Mediterranean countries, either fresh or cooked. They are often sold in larger European supermarkets. Buy some, peel them and eat the pulp (taking care not to get any spines in your hands or mouth), then spit out the seeds and plant them in seed compost. Keep these warm and moist and they should germinate, producing a fast-growing cactus.

☛ *149 CACTUS.*

CABBAGE

Red cabbages get their color from special pigments called anthocyanins.

The cabbage, *Brassica oleracea*, is remarkable for the vast array of varieties that have been produced under cultivation from a single ancestral form. The wild cabbage (below, left) is a native of rocky coastal areas in Europe. In cultivated cabbages the leaves develop as a tight ball on the main stem. In Brussels sprouts the axillary buds develop as tight balls of leaves, miniature cabbages, ranged along the stem.

Broccoli (above) produces a cluster of multiple flower heads instead of a single head, and it is the bunched immature flower buds that we eat. Purplish-tinted varieties turn green when boiled.

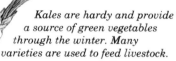

Kales are hardy and provide a source of green vegetables through the winter. Many varieties are used to feed livestock.

EXTRACT BLUE ANTHOCYANIN PIGMENT from red cabbage by boiling some leaves in a little water and straining the juice. The pigment changes color, depending on whether the water it is dissolved in is acid or alkaline. Add alkaline washing soda to one sample to make it turn green. When you add vinegar to another sample it should turn pink – a sensitive test for acidity.

☛ *197 DYE.*

GIANT CLAM DAY

In the world of fiction, giant clams are dangerous animals, clamping tight around the feet of unwary divers. In reality they are threatened bivalve mollusks that are rapidly disappearing, due to relentless collection for food and as curios. Clam meat is a dietary delicacy in the Indo-Pacific region and the adductor muscles, that pull the clam shells together, sell for high prices.

All seven species contain single-celled algae called zooxanthellae, which photosynthesize and produce carbohydrates that feed the clam, so the animals depend on light energy in shallow, sunlit waters.

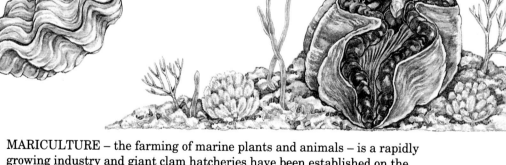

MARICULTURE – the farming of marine plants and animals – is a rapidly growing industry and giant clam hatcheries have been established on the Solomon Islands in the Pacific. Young clams need only clean, warm water and sunlight. They are cultured in tanks of sea water until they reach a length of about 2 cm/0.75 in., then in ocean nurseries in plastic cages until they reach 20 cm/8 in., and are then large enough to transfer onto reefs. They grow about 10 cm/4 in. per year for the first 7 years, but giant specimens live for 50 years or more. Clam farming should help to prevent the destruction of natural populations.

☛ *153 BIVALVE MOLLUSK.*

FERN DAY

Ferns are ancient plants – they colonized the earth 200 million years before the flowering plants and formed much of the forests in which the dinosaurs would have lived. Ferns can be just 2.5 cm/1 in. long, but tree ferns (left) with their tough fibrous trunks can reach 25 m/80 ft.

Many ferns are epiphytes, living on the trunks or branches of trees.

Fern fronds are the equivalent of a flowering plant's leaves. They emerge from the ground tightly coiled, then unroll. Fern spores develop in sori – brown patches on the underside of the frond (above, right).

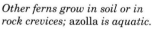

Other ferns grow in soil or in rock crevices; azolla *is aquatic.*

PLACE A FERN FROND, with its ripe sori facing downward, on white paper. By morning a dusting of brown spores will cover the paper and these can be sown on the surface of damp peat, in a pot that is covered with a plastic bag and kept in a shady, damp place. Tiny heart-shaped prothalli (as seen in the middle of the page, above) will grow. Male sperm cells on these will swim to female cells and fertilize them; from this embryo a tiny new fern will grow, as the prothallus withers away.

☞ 170 PRIMITIVE PLANTS; 320 HORSETAIL; 62 MOSS.

GNU DAY

Otherwise known as the wildebeest, the gnu is really an ungainly antelope. There are two species: the white-tailed and (illustrated here) the brindled gnu. Confusingly they are also known as the black and blue wildebeest, respectively. Gnus are native to the savanna plains of Africa where they are one of the most numerous grazing animals.

Before the start of the East African wet season the wildebeest trek south and west in vast herds toward the areas where the rain will fall first.

Herds raise clouds of dust large enough to be visible from cruising jet airliners and they are able to smell rainfall up to 100 km / 60 mi. upwind.

ALERTED BY SMELL to the breaking of the dry season, leaders turn the herd upwind toward the impending rainfall. As new grass begins to grow in response to the rain, the wildebeest arrive to crop the young shoots. The arrival of the wildebeest and many other plains grazing animals means fresh prey for lions and cheetahs. There is abundant food for all, and the wildebeest give birth here in the East African wet season with plentiful food for mothers and calves. As the wet season ends, the herds re-form and begin their annual migration back north and westward to the summer feeding ground.

☛ *118 MIGRATION; 59 DEER.*

STRAWBERRY DAY

Strawberries are insect-pollinated and visited by bees.

The first strawberries were grown in Europe in the 1600s from plants introduced from the east coast of America, and this old-fashioned species is still used for jam making. In the 1700s a west coast strawberry species was introduced. Descendants of the hybrids between this and the east coast species are today's familiar strawberry plants.

Cultivated strawberries have to be protected with nets against birds, squirrels and mice.

Strawberries are 'false fruits' – the seeds are on the outside of the fleshy and swollen receptacle, originally the base of the flower. Each seed or 'pip' is a fruit in its own right.

Wild alpine strawberries are never eaten by birds, unlike their cultivated cousins.

Many strawberry varieties multiply vegetatively from buds that sprout from creeping surface stems, called runners.

IDENTIFYING AND CLASSIFYING ORGANISMS involves the comparison of many characteristics; relying on superfical resemblances can be misleading. The strawberry tree (left) has strawberry-like fruits but belongs to the heather family (Ericaceae). True strawberries are members of the rose family (Rosaceae) – notice the close similarity between wild rose and strawberry flowers.

☛ 38 WILD ROSE.

SHELL DAY

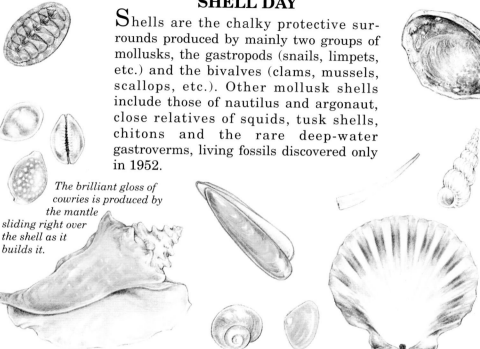

Shells are the chalky protective surrounds produced by mainly two groups of mollusks, the gastropods (snails, limpets, etc.) and the bivalves (clams, mussels, scallops, etc.). Other mollusk shells include those of nautilus and argonaut, close relatives of squids, tusk shells, chitons and the rare deep-water gastroverms, living fossils discovered only in 1952.

The brilliant gloss of cowries is produced by the mantle sliding right over the shell as it builds it.

Cone shells are hunters, harpooning worms, other mollusks and even small fish with a dart that delivers a lethal nerve poison. At least ten people have been killed by cone shells.

Scallops are bivalves ('two-shells') and have well-developed eyes around the edge of the mantle, the fleshy outgrowth of the body that lines the two halves of the shell. They can swim.

USE A FIELD GUIDE to identify flat periwinkles and collect this species from seaweed beds. You should find yellow, brown, olive green, red, orange and banded specimens. They are all one species but, as with many organisms, their color varies depending on their diet.

☛ *153 BIVALVE MOLLUSK; 34 NUDIBRANCH; 355 SNAIL.*

MIGRATION DAY

Animals migrate to avoid adverse seasonal weather and to reach breeding and feeding grounds. These journeys often involve immense distances and precise navigation. Birds will frequently migrate several thousand miles and then return to their original nest site, year after year.

Eels migrate from European rivers to the Sargasso Sea, where they breed. Elvers retrace their parents' transatlantic journey using instinctive navigation.

Humpback whales and most other whale species breed in tropical seas but adult males migrate annually to higher latitudes, to exploit the plankton-rich feeding grounds of the Antarctic.

Arctic terns nest in sub-arctic regions during the northern summer then migrate south, to the Antarctic ocean, to avoid the northern winter and to exploit the feeding opportunities of the southern summer.

Monarch butterflies migrate from North America to the southern United States and Mexico to avoid the northern winter.

African wildebeest spend the dry season in woodlands but the beginning of the rainy season is the signal for an annual mass migration to southern grasslands, where rainfall turns the dry savanna into luxuriant grazing lands. Long columns of thousands of wildebeest, sometimes swathed in clouds of dust, sometimes fording rivers, provide one of the epic spectacles of life on the African plains.

MANY INSECTIVOROUS European birds, like warblers, swifts and cuckoos, migrate south in winter when no food is available, and return in spring.

Visit coastal areas in spring and autumn, when large numbers of exhausted migrants make landfall or congregate to return to the wintering grounds.

☛ 154–5 HIBERNATION; 362 EELS; 128 ARCTIC TERN.

KILLER WHALE DAY

Killer whales will use their heads as battering-rams to break through ice-floes 1 m / 3 ft. thick to get at seals.

Killer whales are widespread across the world's oceans, but commonest in the Arctic and Antarctic. Males can be 10 m / 35 ft. long and weigh 6 tons; females are half the size of males. They hunt in packs or 'pods' of 2 to 40 individuals for small and, especially, injured whales and for seals, dolphins and penguins.

Members of the dolphin and porpoise family, killer whales are intelligent and playful. In seaquariums they have been trained to give spectacular displays. 'Orky' has lived at Marineland in Los Angeles since 1964 and is the biggest killer whale in captivity.

Seals are not even safe on a beach – killer whales swim rapidly towards the shore, drive themselves up the beach and seize a seal before flopping back into the water.

HERBERT PONTING, photographer on Scott's Antarctic expedition of 1911, carried his heavy camera and tripod onto ice floes to photograph killer whales. The whales began tilting the floes to try and tip Ponting into the water and he had to run for his life. Yet no diver or seaquarium trainer has ever been attacked by a killer whale.

☛ *102 STRANGE NOSED FISH; 1 SHARK; 23 DOLPHIN.*

HEARING DAY

Sound production and detection is an essential part of the lives of vertebrate animals, who use it for communication, hunting and prey detection. Songs are an important element of courtship in animals as diverse as grasshoppers, frogs, birds and whales.

Bats use ultrasonic squeaks to locate moths at night. Some moths detect these sounds and escape by dropping to the ground.

Long-eared owls' ear tufts are for display only. Owls have asymmetric ears, allowing them to locate rustling prey in darkness.

Large ears are more efficient sound collectors but may also serve a second purpose in some animals; in elephants, fennec foxes and jack rabbits they are well supplied with blood vessels and act as heat radiators.

Scores of frog species live in tropical forests, producing a cacophony of nocturnal calls. Each species has its own frequency.

Dolphins also communicate and hunt using high-pitched ultrasound.

DEMONSTRATE THE BENEFIT of large ears, using a small portable tape recorder, a microphone and a large plastic funnel. Attach the microphone in the funnel base, aim it at a sound source and record. Then remove the microphone from the funnel and record the sound. Play both recordings back at the same volume setting and you will see how the plastic 'ear' enhances the sound-collecting capacity of the microphone. Make a collection of recorded bird songs, experimenting with different mechanical 'ears' for your microphone.

☛ 345 EYE; 317 SCENT AND TASTE; 78–9 DESERT.

SPEED DAY

Relative speeds often control the delicate balance between predators and prey in food chains.

Tortoises, moving at a sedate 1 kph / 0.6 mph, have traded speed for an armored carapace that protects their limbs and head. Snakes are also slow movers, preferring to ambush prey, although black mambas can reach 15 kph / 10 mph in short bursts on level ground.

Long legs are an important adaptation for fast running. The furious pace of a mouse will only propel it at a few kilometers per hour, while the apparently effortless gallop of camels and giraffes carries them along at 40–50 kph / 25–30 mph.

Running foxes and hares have similar speeds of about 60 kph / 37 mph, but the hare's greater agility and ability to turn rapidly often allows it to escape death. Ostriches are the fastest flightless birds, with a speed of about 65 kph / 40 mph, while swifts are among the fastest flying birds, reaching 170 kph / 105 mph during courtship flights.

THE OUTRIGHT ANIMAL speed record holder is the peregrine falcon, which is reputed to reach speeds of 350 kph/215 mph when diving during territorial displays. The fastest animal on four legs is the cheetah, which is capable of reaching 100 kph/60 mph over short distances when pursuing impala, which are slower but have greater stamina. Use a stopwatch to measure how long in seconds it takes snails, woodlice (sow bugs) and other small invertebrates to cover a 10 cm/4 in. course, and use a calculator to work out the speed in kilometers or miles per hour.

☛ 359 ARMOR.

JAPANESE MACAQUE DAY

Japanese macaques are the northern-most primates apart from man. They live at heights above 1,600 m/5,000 ft. on the mountains of Honshu, Japan's largest island. The Barbary apes, another macaque species, living on the Rock of Gibraltar, are the only wild monkeys in Europe.

Adult Japanese macaques cuddle close to their young to keep them warm during snowstorms.

In the Shiga highlands of the Joshinetsu-Kogen National Park, Japanese macaques survive during the bitter Japanese winter by bathing. Hot rock deep within the volcanic mountains of Honshu heats water that wells up as hot springs and collects in steaming pools. The monkeys sit up to their chests in warm water as the snow falls. Thick fur keeps out the worst of the winter cold.

PUT A BOWL OF HOT WATER (just hot enough to be bearable) to the left of the kitchen sink, and a bowl of cold water to the right. Fill the sink with lukewarm water. Put a hand in each bowl; after one minute plunge both into the sink. The water in the sink is a uniform temperature, but your left hand tells your brain that it's cool and your right hand tells it that it's hot. It takes a few moments for the brain to interpret the conflicting signals that the nerves in your hands are sending.

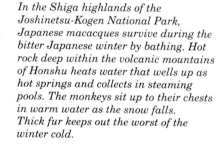

☛ *43 SNOW; 283 DEEP SEA.*

TOUCAN DAY

Toucans look as if they have their heads stuck in the end of a gaudily-painted cow-horn. Their ridiculous bills make even hornbills look conservative. The Tupi Indians long ago named the large species 'toco', corrupted by Europeans to 'toucan', and the smaller of the 37 species 'arassari', the name used for them today. Unlike woodpeckers, toucans cannot excavate nest sites.

The red-necked toucan is very similar to Cuvier's toucan (right) except for its red-edged bib.

The larger toucans inhabit the lowland rainforests of Central and South America while the smaller species tend to live in the hill and mountain forest of the Andes, moving up and down the slopes as particular trees come into fruit.

Toucans eat mainly fruit, tearing it with the serrated edges of their bills and tossing the pieces to the back of their throats.

ORNITHOLOGISTS HAVE LONG PUZZLED over why toucans should have developed such unwieldy bills. It isn't necessary to have a bill almost as big as one's body to eat fruit. It may be that the bill and its pattern play some part in courtship and social ritual, as in hornbills, but the evidence for this is flimsy. It certainly contributes to the disruptive pattern of most toucans, a pattern that seems to recur time and again among rainforest animals – bold patches of dark and light color that break up their outlines.

☛ *93 BEAK.*

BEAVER DAY

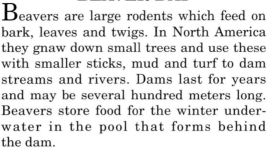

Beavers are large rodents which feed on bark, leaves and twigs. In North America they gnaw down small trees and use these with smaller sticks, mud and turf to dam streams and rivers. Dams last for years and may be several hundred meters long. Beavers store food for the winter underwater in the pool that forms behind the dam.

Beavers have been parachuted into mountain areas in North America to build dams to prevent soil erosion.

The beavers' lodge is a dome of logs with underwater entrances and dry chambers above water level.

The underwater entrances give beavers access to their food supply when the pool is frozen over.

Eurasian beavers are a different geographical race from the North American ones and rarely build dams or lodges.

Beaver dams slow the flow of rivers and prevent flooding.

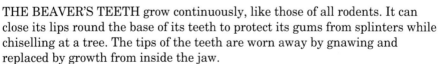

THE BEAVER'S TEETH grow continuously, like those of all rodents. It can close its lips round the base of its teeth to protect its gums from splinters while chiselling at a tree. The tips of the teeth are worn away by gnawing and replaced by growth from inside the jaw.

Beavers use their front teeth, called incisors, for cutting wood. Our incisors grow quickly then stop, and are replaced just once, at the age of seven, with a set that must last for the rest of our lives. Eat a carrot in front of a mirror, to see how your incisors work.

☛ *329 RIVERBANK.*

BANANA DAY

Banana trees, up to 10 m/33 ft. tall, are not trees at all but giant herbaceous plants, their 'trunks' formed from the tightly wrapped leaf bases. Originally from Southeast Asia, the edible varieties are sterile hybrids probably developed by prehistoric people. Now bananas are grown throughout the tropics, especially in Central America and the Caribbean, by planting pieces of the root.

Once all the fruits have developed, the stalk may carry 200 bananas and weigh up to 40 kg / 90 lbs.

The drooping flowering stalk has male flowers among the purple bracts at the tip and female flowers behind them.

Female flowers develop into seedless bananas but, as the plant is sterile, the male flowers have no role.

The bananas we see in Europe and North America are chosen from the hundreds of varieties, because they can survive several weeks in transit from the tree to us, the consumers.

GREEN BANANAS are ripened when they arrive in Europe by ethylene gas, which triggers ripening in many fruits. Put a green and an overripe banana in a closed plastic bag in a warm cupboard. Keep one green banana aside, for comparision. After two days the green banana in the bag should have ripened, under the influence of ethylene emitted from the overripe fruit. The untreated banana should still be green.

☛ *6 PINEAPPLE.*

TAMARIN AND MARMOSET DAY

These tiny monkeys, the biggest with a body length of about 33 cm/13 in., comprise 20 species restricted to the rapidly shrinking forests of central and eastern South America. Mostly insectivorous, marmosets are especially partial to sweet tree-sap which they tap by gnawing through bark. Sap holes are scent-marked and vigorously defended.

Geoffroy's marmoset is a race of the common marmoset; it lives in the forest canopy and eats mainly insects.

Monkeys from the Americas have sideways-facing nostrils while Asian and African monkeys have downward-facing nostrils.

White-faced saddle-back tamarin.

Golden lion tamarin – restricted to the coastal forest of Brazil.

Fluffed fur of 20-cm / 8-in. long cotton-top tamarins (below) exaggerates their size.

MARMOSETS AND TAMARINS are very sensitive to habitat disturbance, which has brought several species to the verge of extinction. Only 2 percent of Brazil's coastal forest – the habitat of the golden lion tamarin – remains and only about 500 animals survive in the wild. Captive breeding and release, coupled with education and encouragement of landowners to retain woodland, is the only hope of survival for this species. The illegal pet trade threatens many marmoset species, which often die in captivity.

☛ *130–1 ENDANGERED ANIMALS.*

BEAN DAY

Beans and peas are the seeds of plants belonging to the family Leguminosae – the legumes. A legume pod – the fruit – contains numerous beans. They are an important part of our diet for they are very nutritious and can be grown in a variety of climates in a variety of soils. Some people in India live almost entirely on beans of various species.

Beans can be grown in poor soil because they are able to manufacture their own fertilizer. Their roots have nodules containing symbiotic bacteria which 'fix' nitrogen from the air. The resulting nitrate is used by the bean plant to make protein.

TEST BEANS for the presence of starch, protein and fat. Liquidize fresh beans in a blender and dilute some of the liquid in a test tube with water. Add a few drops of iodine and shake; if the liquid turns black, starch is present. Add 1 ml of caustic soda (DANGER! – see end of book) plus 1 ml of copper sulphate solution to another sample and shake. If the contents turn violet, protein is present. Soak dried, crushed beans in dry-cleaning fluid overnight, then allow the drained-off liquid to evaporate in a shallow dish; if fat is present, a greasy residue will remain.

☛ *96 PEANUT.*

ARCTIC TERN DAY

Arctic terns make one of the epic migratory journeys of the animal world, traveling to their breeding sites north of the Arctic Circle in spring and returning to Antarctic feeding grounds in winter. The feat is all the more remarkable because they mate for life and pairs return to the same nest sites every year, after a 30,000-km/20,000-mi. round trip.

Sailors called terns 'sea butterflies' because of their bouncing, fluttering flight. Terns are plunge divers, hovering above the water and dropping onto fish with deadly accuracy.

Arctic terns defend nest sites by attacking intruders. Their sharp beaks draw blood from scalps of people who venture too close to their eggs.

MOST TERNS BUILD a rudimentary nest, relying on the natural camouflage of their eggs among stones on shingle banks to protect them from predators. The chicks' mottled plumage serves the same purpose. Test the effect of camouflage by painting small hens' eggs to resemble various backgrounds like shingle and sand. Use book illustrations of sea-birds' eggs as a painting guide and test the effect by asking your friends to find your test samples hidden against an appropriate background. Use unpainted eggs as a control.

☛ 118 MIGRATION; 289 CAMOUFLAGE.

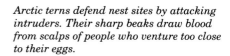

MOOSE DAY

Moose are polygamous and bulls roar out mating calls in autumn, smashing through undergrowth in eager anticipation when they hear females respond. North American Indians mimicked female moose calls, luring courting males into an ambush.

Moose live in the forests of Alaska, Canada and the northern USA. Their antlers are heavier and broader than any other deer species. The European elk, which inhabits forests and marshes across northern Europe, is smaller than its American relative but its habits are very similar. Female moose and elk lack antlers.

Summer is spent wading in lakes and rivers, feeding on water lilies and escaping the swarms of flies and mosquitoes that are a constant torment in subarctic regions. Heavy winter snow buries vegetation but the height and weight of a moose allows it to bend saplings to reach tender shoots. They avoid deep snow, where they would become trapped and easy prey for pumas and wolves.

NATURALISTS OFTEN PLAY tape-recorded calls of hidden birds and animals, to induce them to respond and reveal their whereabouts. Listen to recorded tapes of bird songs and animal noises and use them to learn to identify unseen animals.

☛ *59 DEER.*

Calves are unable to run with their mothers until they are ten days old and do not become fully independent until the end of their second year.

ENDANGERED ANIMALS DAY

Animals become endangered when populations breed too slowly to replace individuals that have died. Destruction of habitats and hunting for valuable products like fur, meat and horns has reduced population sizes.

The nocturnal indri, the largest living lemur, is now extremely rare, due to logging in Madagascar's mountainous rainforests. Zoos may be its only hope of survival.

Rhinoceroses are illegally killed for their horns, which are used in folk medicine and for dagger handles and ornaments in Asia and the Middle East.

Habitat destruction has led to the near-extinction of golden lion tamarins.

Asiatic black bears, ranging from Iran to Japan, are reputed to be less afraid of humans than other bears. This, together with habitat destruction, has been their downfall.

Poachers kill mountain gorillas for their heads and hands, which are sold as souvenirs. Less than 500 gorillas survive in the mountains of Rwanda, Uganda and Zaire.

An estimated 300,000 blue whales lived in the oceans in the 1920s, before hunting for meat and oil almost exterminated them. Despite a whaling ban in 1966, less than 15,000 survive. Similar disastrous overexploitation has decimated populations of other large whale species.

Tigers and jaguars were formerly shot in enormous numbers for sport, but are now mainly killed illegally by poachers, who sell skins on the black market. The wearing of animal skins, once a necessity for primitive man, continues as a fashion amongst the rich and famous.

Like many large mammals, the giant panda requires large tracts of undisturbed, specialized habitat. It may well vanish, along with its bamboo forest home, unless breeding success in zoos can be increased. As the logo of the World Wide Fund for Nature (WWF), it has come to symbolize the plight of endangered animals everywhere.

The pigmy hippopotamus inhabits dense tropical rainforests of Liberia and the Ivory Coast and is one-tenth the size of its semi-aquatic cousin. Many details of its biology are unknown and may remain so if it continues to disappear at the present rate.

Gelada baboons are no longer common on the grasslands of the Ethiopian plateau, due to agricultural development.

Orangutans are still locally common in Borneo and Southern Sumatra, where forest destruction threatens its survival. Leadbeater's possum (below), an arboreal Australian marsupial, is endangered for similar reasons.

HELP TO CONSERVE WILDLIFE by joining and working for conservation organizations.

☛ 321 DODOS AND EXTINCTION; 310 RHINOCEROS; 67 PANDA; 119 KILLER WHALE.

CATERPILLAR DAY

Caterpillars are the larvae of moths or butterflies. While some species feed as adults, many do not and their caterpillars must store all the food that the pupal and adult stages will need. Caterpillars are vulnerable to attack by predators such as birds, and parasitoids, such as chalcid wasps. They have evolved a variety of defenses to assist in their survival.

Privet hawk moth larvae (below) rear up to startle predators – stripes form disruptive camouflage.

Caterpillars of sycamore (top left), pale trussock (top right) and garden tiger moth (right) have long hairs that make them difficult for a bird to swallow.

Puss moth larvae have a non-typical shape and a dorsal stripe to break up their appearance – tail 'horns' can extrude pink filaments to confuse an attacker.

MANY THOUSANDS OF SPECIES are leaf miners. These caterpillars are minute enough to tunnel between the upper and lower surfaces of a leaf, mining away a transparent blotch or winding tunnel (a serpentine mine) that is easily seen when the leaf is against the light. If you search the leaves of oak trees in summer or early autumn you will find blotch mines and serpentine mines. Follow the course of a serpentine mine and see how the tunnel has widened as the larva has grown. You may be able to see the semi-transparent larva feeding at the end of the tunnel.

☛ 306–7 MOTHS AND BUTTERFLIES.

FIG DAY

Figs grow in Mediterranean and warm temperate climates and are one of the sweetest fruits, with a 50 percent sugar content. Fig trees are small, up to 10 m/ 30 ft. tall, and the leaves may be three- or five-lobed. Figs are dried like dates, canned or eaten fresh. Because of their thin skins they cannot be transported easily, so figs are best eaten fresh from the tree.

The flowers of the fig are borne inside the fruit.

Depending upon variety, figs can be green, brown or purple.

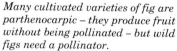

Many cultivated varieties of fig are parthenocarpic – they produce fruit without being pollinated – but wild figs need a pollinator.

TINY FIG WASPS pollinate wild figs. They arrive carrying pollen and crawl in through the small hole at the end of the fruit. Inside, they pollinate all the female flowers and begin to lay eggs, but their long ovipositors can only reach the ovaries of female flowers with short styles, which form galls, inside which the next generation of fig wasps develop. Intact long-styled flowers develop seeds. Male wasps hatch and mate with females, which collect pollen and exit through a tunnel in the fruit wall cut by males, then seek out new figs to breed in.

☛ *143 DATE; 76 WASP; 237 EXOTIC FRUIT.*

BUTTERFLY FISH DAY

Many marine carnivores use the eye of their prey as an aiming point, but in the butterfly fish this is disguised with a dark stripe. A false eye spot near the tail makes it hard for a predator to tell one end from the other, especially if its prey swims backward slowly. A moment's hesitation and confusion represents the difference between life and death on a coral reef.

The butterfly fish's long snout is used like forceps, to pick food from crevices.

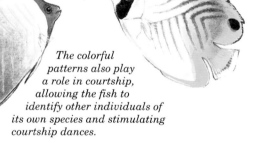

The colorful patterns also play a role in courtship, allowing the fish to identify other individuals of its own species and stimulating courtship dances.

YOUNG EMPEROR BUTTERFLY FISH (below, left) have a completely different color pattern than adults, which may signal to full-grown fish that the young are not rivals for territories or mates.

Some butterfly fish in northern Australia and New Guinea are immune to stings of sea anemones and will feed on them, unless the anemones are protected by a clown fish, which is reputed to drive the butterfly fish away.

 37 FISH PARTNERSHIP; 289 CAMOUFLAGE; 330 CRYPSIS; 208 ZEBRA.

KANGAROO DAY

W hen Europeans colonized Australia there were 48 different species of kangaroo. Now six are extinct, four endangered and thirteen are described as 'vulnerable'. The brush-tailed bettong now occupies less than 1 percent of its former range. Smallest are musky rat kangaroos. Weighing only 500 g/18 oz., they are the most primitive of living kangaroos and the only species to retain big toes.

Male red (left) and eastern gray (right) kangaroos can be distinguished by their noses.

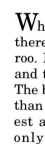

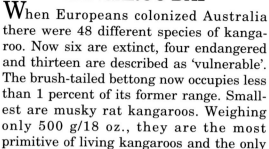

A young red kangaroo weighs less than 25 g/1 oz. at birth. It remains suckling in the mother's pouch for about eight months.

The largest kangaroo is the red – males weigh up to 90 kg/ 200 lbs. A common species, it is culled for meat and hides. Although excellent meat, most is just used for pet food.

FEMALE RED KANGAROOS operate a production line for young. The tiny joey, little more than an embryo, has to climb more than 30 cm/12 in. into the mother's pouch when it is born and attach itself to a teat at the base of her pouch. Meanwhile, a second, larger teat nearer the pouch opening is used to feed a year-old joey who has recently left the pouch for good. The female mates within a few days of the birth, and the fertilized egg is kept 'on hold' until the female is feeding only one joey. At this point the egg develops rapidly and another joey is born.

☛ 108 SEA HORSE; 152 MOUTHBROODING; 305 MARSUPIAL.

JAPANESE CRANE DAY

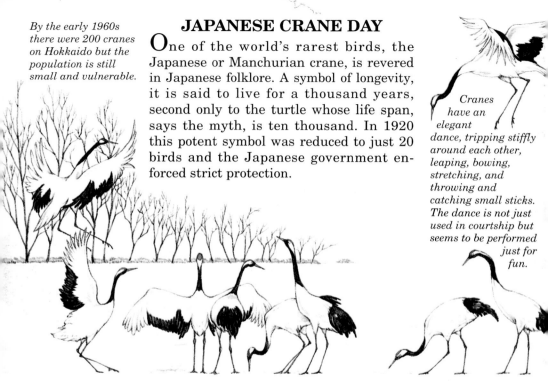

By the early 1960s there were 200 cranes on Hokkaido but the population is still small and vulnerable.

One of the world's rarest birds, the Japanese or Manchurian crane, is revered in Japanese folklore. A symbol of longevity, it is said to live for a thousand years, second only to the turtle whose life span, says the myth, is ten thousand. In 1920 this potent symbol was reduced to just 20 birds and the Japanese government enforced strict protection.

Cranes have an elegant dance, tripping stiffly around each other, leaping, bowing, stretching, and throwing and catching small sticks. The dance is not just used in courtship but seems to be performed just for fun.

THE SLOWNESS of the recovery of the Japanese crane from near-extinction has been due to several setbacks as well as its slow breeding. It nests once a year and lays two, rarely three eggs. Migrating cranes were frequently shot for food by starving troops at the close of World War II. After the war, occupying forces poached cranes on a number of reserves in northern Japan. Then, in the Korean War, battles were fought across the cranes' wintering grounds. Left in peace, Japanese cranes are thought to have a lifespan of 30–50 years.

☛ *263 CROWNED CRANE; 246 HERON; 221 STORK.*

136

KOMODO DRAGON DAY

Although they cannot spit fire like mythical dragons, Komodo dragons hiss aggressive challenges. Their tongues dart out contiuously, acting as sense organs.

Old explorers' maps often carry the inscription, 'Here be dragons.' Such warnings were not taken seriously until scientists first discovered these giant lizards on the Indonesian islands of Komodo, Rintja, Padar and Flores in 1912. Komodo dragons are the world's largest lizards, reaching a length of over 3 m/10 ft., and are descendants of a reptilian group that evolved during the Jurassic period, about 180 million years ago.

The dragon's favorite prey are young goats and pigs. In the early 19th century, when Komodo was a convict colony, the dragons were reported to have eaten humans.

ONLY A FEW HUNDRED Komodo dragons exist, but such large predators have probably never been numerous on their small island habitats. They are voracious carnivores, at the top of a food chain, and such animals are always relatively rare. They depend on the pyramid of life, preying on large herbivores, which in turn depend on plant food. Their future depends on the preservation of their food chain, by protecting their whole habitat. They are good swimmers and commute between islands in search of prey, so it is possible that they can colonize other islands.

☛ *199 LIZARD; 163 SNAKES.*

LICHEN DAY

Lichens are compound organisms, a fungus and an alga living together. The fungus provides the support and the anchorage and absorbs moisture from the air. The alga makes food for both by photosynthesis. Growing on rocks or trees, lichens are rarely conspicuous but they are quietly successful and can grow at over 7,000 m/23,000 ft. in the Himalayas and within 4 degrees of the South Pole.

Trailing fronds of Usnea trap moisture from misty air.

Red swellings on this trumpet-lichen are fungal spore patches.

Slow-growing rock-dwelling lichens colonize gravestones. They are very sensitive to air pollution and city graveyards contain only one or two species.

Xanthoria lichens make bright yellow patches on rocks near the sea. Lichens were traditionally used to dye Harris tweed.

MOST LICHENS reproduce by releasing dusty particles – soredia – which contain the fungus and the alga and are carried in the wind to a suitable habitat. Fungal spores are a riskier reproduction method, because they must land next to a suitable alga to develop the lichen partnership. The alga can lead an independent existence, but the fungus cannot.

In extreme habitats some lichens take 50 years to cover 1 cm^2/one-sixth of a square inch, and large, dinner-plate-sized lichens in mountains may be thousands of years old.

☛ 326 PARTNERSHIP; 11 FUNGI.

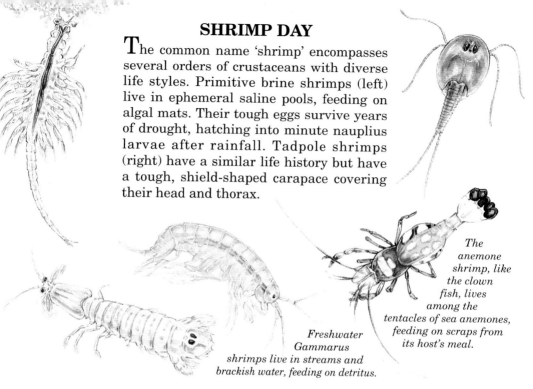

SHRIMP DAY

The common name 'shrimp' encompasses several orders of crustaceans with diverse life styles. Primitive brine shrimps (left) live in ephemeral saline pools, feeding on algal mats. Their tough eggs survive years of drought, hatching into minute nauplius larvae after rainfall. Tadpole shrimps (right) have a similar life history but have a tough, shield-shaped carapace covering their head and thorax.

The anemone shrimp, like the clown fish, lives among the tentacles of sea anemones, feeding on scraps from its host's meal.

Freshwater *Gammarus* shrimps live in streams and brackish water, feeding on detritus.

MANTIS SHRIMPS (above, left) reach a length of 30 cm/12 in., and their forelimbs are massively enlarged. These are used to smash carapaces of crabs and mollusks with a single, devastating blow. Large crabs are first disarmed by preliminary blows to their pincers. Shrimps can usually be found in rockpools on sandy beaches. When alarmed they shoot backward, with a powerful flick of the tail, so the best way to capture a shrimp is to place the net behind it and scare it from the front.

☛ 37 FISH PARTNERSHIP; 308 CRAB; 269 LOBSTER; 315 ROCK POOL.

FOX DAY

Foxes are small canids with pointed skulls and bushy tails. Most are solitary hunters, feeding mainly on rats and mice.

American red foxes show a variety of mutant color forms, with seasonal variations. Silver fox, with a black coat flecked with white-tipped hairs, is highly valued in the luxury fur trade.

The North American gray fox is the only species that regularly climbs trees to hunt. It favors the warmer regions of the continent.

The common or red fox has an enormous range, occurring throughout Europe, much of Asia, Japan, North Africa and North America. In Europe and America it has taken to living on the waste products of urban society and has become so adept at raiding garbage cans that it is now a familiar sight in many cities.

The smallest fox is the fennec, of African and Arabian deserts. Hairy feet allow it to run on loose sand. Large ears act as heat radiators and sound detectors.

FOXES EXCAVATE LARGE breeding tunnels, called earths, on south-facing slopes. These are conspicuous, with a fan of soil spread around the entrance and an acrid smell, produced by scent-marking with urine. Food remains – bones and feathers – often litter the entrance. Find a set, conceal yourself at a distance when twilight falls, and watch through binoculars as the animals emerge.

☞ 97 WOLF; 160 WILD DOG; 78-9 DESERTS.

South American 'foxes' are really specialized wild dogs. The pampas fox or maned wolf is a long-legged species living on the grassy plains.

140

GUM TREE DAY

The 450 species of gum tree, which are all species of eucalyptus, dominate large parts of the Australian and Tasmanian landscape. They include *Eucalyptus regnans*, the world's tallest flowering plant, which reaches a height of over 100 m/300 ft.

Gums are fast-growing timber trees and have been planted in many countries, but are also prolific seeders and tend to be invasive. Unwanted trees on grazing lands in Australia are killed by removing a ring of bark.

Eucalyptus is the staple diet of koala bears, which have a digestive system that is modified to cope with the tough leaves.

Gum trees' juvenile foliage has a different shape and color from the mature leaves. Ornamental species, like the Tasmanian blue gum, are often regularly clipped to encourage the growth of the more decorative young foliage.

AROMATIC EUCALYPTUS oil provides an excellent cure for blocked noses and is one of many herbal remedies that are available in drugstores.

☛ *75 KOALA.*

The Coolibah tree, made famous in the Australian national song 'Waltzing Matilda', is Eucalyptus microtheca, *which produces one of the strongest and hardest timbers.*

DUNG DAY

Dung is formed from food residues that animals are unable to digest, and from the moment that it hits the ground it becomes the center of a miniature ecosystem. Its rich content of decomposing nitrogenous nutrients and fibrous material makes it an excellent substrate for fungal growth and a warm, moist habitat for insect larvae.

Pilobolus is a tiny fungus, a mere 2 cm/ 0.8 in. tall, that thrives on cow-pats.

Dung beetles, in the family Scarabaeidae, play a vital role in the health of soils and pastures. Some excavate burrows in cow dung and lay their eggs within, tending their larvae until they leave the burrow. Others roll the dung into balls and bury it, to provision a larval chamber. In this way they break down cowpats, that would otherwise foul pastures and prevent cattle grazing. In Australia, the problem of persistent cowpats from imported cattle, which were not processed by native scarabs, was only solved by the introduction of dung beetles from Mexico and Africa.

INVESTIGATE THE LIFE HISTORY of a fresh cowpat. The first insects to arrive are dung flies (bottom right); males court females on the surface, where the latter lay their eggs. The larvae eat dung, then pupate. Old, crusty cowpats are covered with dung fly exit holes, where pupae have hatched. Cowpats also have a characteristic flora of coprophilous (dung-loving) fungi. Caps of *Coprinus* species (top right) liquify and their inky spores are carried on dung fly feet. *Pilobolus* (top left) fires its spores up to 2 m/6.5 ft.

☛ 337 TRACKING; 256–7 BEETLES; 11 FUNGI.

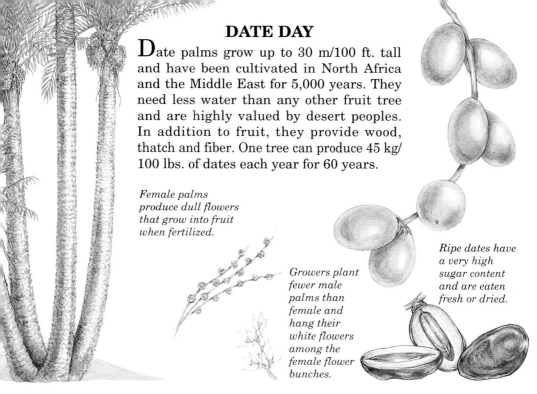

DATE DAY

Date palms grow up to 30 m/100 ft. tall and have been cultivated in North Africa and the Middle East for 5,000 years. They need less water than any other fruit tree and are highly valued by desert peoples. In addition to fruit, they provide wood, thatch and fiber. One tree can produce 45 kg/ 100 lbs. of dates each year for 60 years.

Female palms produce dull flowers that grow into fruit when fertilized.

Growers plant fewer male palms than female and hang their white flowers among the female flower bunches.

Ripe dates have a very high sugar content and are eaten fresh or dried.

DRIED DATES, once a Christmas treat in Europe, are now available all year round. Produce from the traditional exporters, Morocco and Tunisia, has been joined by dates from California. Make the Arabic sweet date halva, using two cups of pitted and finely chopped dates. If you can't get fresh dates, use dry boxed ones but rinse off some of the excess sugar. Add half a cup each of chopped walnuts and almonds. Mix the dates and nuts and roll them into firm little cylinders on a chopping board sprinkled with confectioner's sugar. Slice the cylinders with a sharp knife and serve.

☛ *237 EXOTIC FRUITS.*

SHEEP DAY

Sheep were first domesticated about 10,000 years ago, from a mouflon-like ancestor (left), possibly *Ovis vignei* of Central Asia. Selective breeding to enhance the density, length, thickness and strength of the wool has resulted in more than 800 distinct varieties of sheep today.

Although meat and leather are important products, wool is the most valuable commodity that we get from sheep. Woollen cloth fragments have been found in archaeological remains of most ancient civilizations, and it was probably the first fiber to be spun and woven.

Thick wool is an excellent insulator, which allows sheep to survive in the cold temperate climate of Britain's hill farms. Woollen clothing has also allowed man to colonize and survive in harsh environments.

COLLECT WOOL SCRAPS from barbed wire or hedges and spin it into yarn. Sharpen one end of a 20-cm/8-in. pointed stick, cut a narrow notch at the other, then push the stick through a potato. Tease and twist a 30–40 cm/12–16 in. length of wool: tie the end to the pointed tip and lock the other in the notch at the other end. Spin the stick and tease the wool, until you have a length of yarn. Repeat the procedure, until you have a ball of wool.

☛ *19 WILD SHEEP; 313 GOAT.*

CAVE DAY

Natural caverns are formed by seepage of underground water, which dissolves soft rock strata. The end result is a network of tunnels that form a secure and specialized habitat for a range of uniquely adapted animals.

Such concentrations of mammals create massive deposits of droppings on the cave floor, which slowly decompose through microbial action. Green plants cannot survive in the darkness, so this excrement forms the base of a food chain that supports several highly specialized detritus feeders, like blind isopods. These woodlouse-like creatures scavenge in the darkness, where they have no need for vision.

Dry caves are perfect bat roosts and in some countries they house enormous numbers of these flying mammals. The Gomanton Caves of Borneo contain several million bats of eight different species. Bracken Cave in San Antonio, Texas, sometimes hosts up to 20 million Mexican free-tailed bats.

Many cave animals are sightless and 38 species of fish, from 13 different families, are known to have become adapted to underground life in the tropics.

STALAGMITES (which point upward) and stalactites (which hang down) are formed over thousands of years by the constant dripping of lime-laden water. Each droplet deposits a few molecules of lime, forming massive accretions that often become tourist attractions. The lime scale that accumulates in tea-kettles in hard water areas is deposited in exactly the same way.

☛ *282 CAVE ANIMALS.*

HIPPOPOTAMUS DAY

Common hippopotamuses are widespread throughout sub-Saharan Africa in suitable habitats. They spend most of the day half submerged in slow-flowing rivers, forming herds of up to 60 individuals among which females are dominant. The West African Pygmy hippopotamus is much smaller (225 kg/500 lbs.) and lives in swamp forest.

Hippos emerge from the river at night to graze on grass and low plants.

Large hippos weigh up to 4.5 tons and, with the white rhino, are second only in bulk to elephants.

The enormous yawn is a sign of aggression. Hippos look peaceable but they kill more people in Africa each year than do lions. The tusks are the lower incisor teeth and they can inflict appalling wounds.

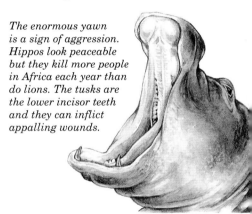

Hippos are said to sweat blood, but the oily pink secretion is a waterproofing skin lubricant.

HIPPOS BATHE BY DAY and feed in the cool of the night out of necessity. Few mammals survive if their body temperature rises above 40–42°C/104–108°F. The daytime temperature in the hippos' habitat often rises above the critical point beyond which, with all their bulk, they cannot lose heat. Elephants have enormous ears that act as heat exchangers, but the hippo has no such adaptation and must rely on a cool river to keep its body temperature down.

☛ *130–31 ENDANGERED ANIMALS.*

GRASS DAY

Grasses represent one of the largest and most important plant families, containing over 8,000 species. These include bamboos and all the major cereals, including wheat, rice and maize. Grass flowers are wind pollinated, and their florets open to reveal feathery stigmas that filter pollen from the air. The stamens have long, slender filaments, so that their anthers shed pollen into the air stream.

Reed beds form in freshwater and brackish marshes and are an important habitat for several birds, including reed warblers.

Couch grass is an invasive weed which spreads with brittle underground stems, or rhizomes.

Tufted hair grass forms large clumps of leaves that feel rough to the touch and have grooves running along their surface.

Rye grass is a fast-growing, grazing-resistant species which is widely sown in pastures.

GRASSES ARE UNIQUELY adapted to grazing by animals. Trim the ends from young rye-grass leaves and notice how they continue to grow from their base; cell division takes place at the leaf base, not in the tips and edges as in most plants.

☛ *166 CEREALS; 87 CORN; 161 RICE.*

STRANGE NOSES DAY

The human nose serves as an entry and exit channel for air and as a sense organ, but in many animals the nose has important additional functions.

The elongated nose of the giant anteater is perfect for penetrating crevices in ants' nests and houses a long, worm-shaped, sticky tongue.

Its sense of smell is at least 40 times more sensitive than that of humans.

Hammer-headed fruit bats are the largest bats in Africa and their long muzzles give their noisy chattering a resonant quality.

The saiga's doleful expression is due to a drooping, mucus-lined nose that filters and warms the air before it enters the lungs.

Proboscis monkeys are confined to the mangrove forests of the river-banks of Borneo. Their 18-cm/7-in. noses are most highly developed in males. In young monkeys the proboscis points upward, but it droops as they age. Its function may be to create resonance in the calls that males use when communicating with the troop.

The prehensile muscular trunk of an elephant is the perfect organ for breaking down succulent branches.

ANIMALS LIKE THE GIANT ELEPHANT SHREW (below) rely on scent for detecting prey and for this their elongated snouts house extra receptors. In some species, snout shape helps to create distinctive sounds by modifying the vibrating column of air that the voice box generates. Try pinching your nose and singing, and note the effect on your voice.

☞ *317 SCENT AND TASTE.*

148

CACTUS DAY

The word 'cactus' is commonly used to describe any succulent or spiny drought-tolerant plant. Strictly, it only applies to members of the family Cactaceae, which are almost all confined to the New World. Old World succulents are in different families and have evolved the same adaptations under similar environmental stresses – a case of convergent evolution.

African living stones have two swollen, water-storage leaves with a surface pattern that mimics a pebble, hiding them from grazing animals. Flowers sprout from the cleft between them.

Echinocereus pentalophus *(right) has typical, brightly colored cactus flowers, with many petals and stamens. The Angolan* cissus *(left) is a member of the grape family (Vitaceae), which has evolved succulent, cactus-like adaptions to conserve water.*

Tall stems carry the flat pads of Galapagos prickly pear beyond the reach of the islands' giant tortoises.

MANY CACTI, like the ferociously spiny *Ferocatus* (below, left), are more or less spherical – minimizing their surface area relative to their volume and so reducing water loss. A thick layer of wax on the surface also prevents surface evaporation and cacti can survive protracted droughts. Leave a cactus unwatered for several weeks before measuring its diameter with dividers. Then water it and measure the plant's diameter again; it will have expanded, reflecting the amount of water reabsorbed.

☛ 21 TORTOISE; 289 CAMOUFLAGE; 330 CRYPSIS; 173 PLANT DEFENSES.

CARP DAY

Carp are native to Central Europe and Asia and have been introduced into many countries. The Romans probably brought them to Britain and they were stocked as a food fish in monastery ponds in Medieval times. Ornamental carp have been bred for at least 4,000 years in China, where they were fed on silkworm feces.

Wild carp are exceptionally long-lived fish, surviving for over 40 years and eventually weighing up to 18 kg/40 lbs. They have been bred for food and sport, but many decorative varieties have also been artificially selected.

Mirror carp have fewer, exceptionally large scales that are mainly concentrated along the lateral line. Some varieties have also been bred without scales, giving their skin a leathery appearance.

The attractively colored golden carp has been bred for ornamental pools. Decorative carp are particularly popular in Japan, where intensively bred koi carp fetch high prices.

BREEDING NATIVE CHINESE GOLDFISH, with a wide range of fin shapes and colors, became an art form during the T'ang dynasty (AD 650). The fish have been popular pets in Britain since they were first introduced in 1691. Carp have three small bones of their inner ear which are connected to their swim bladder. This gives them acute hearing and they can be trained to respond to sound. If you ring a bell whenever you feed a pet goldfish, it will eventually come to the surface to feed when the bell is sounded, even when no food is supplied.

☛ 45 TROUT; 48 FISH KISSING & COURTSHIP.

PEACOCK DAY

Males of almost all species compete with other males to attract mates, breed and so pass on their genes to the next generation. This process, known as sexual selection, means that a male must convince a female that he is fitter, stronger, and more successful than any of his rivals. Birds use song, fine feathers and complex behavior patterns during courtship to convey this message to potential mates.

Peacocks normally carry their train of tail feathers behind them, but raise them in a fan during courtship, revealing a dazzling pattern of false eyes. The feathers are vibrated at the same time, creating a loud rustling.

THE PEACOCK'S COURTSHIP can be watched in many zoos and ornamental bird collections. Compare its behavior with the less spectacular but equally effective plumage displays of the closely related pheasants and cockerels.

☛ 364 PHEASANT;
276 BIRD OF PARADISE;
81 CHICKEN.

The combined spectacle of color and sound is guaranteed to attract a female's attention, but eventual breeding success goes to the male that produces the best display.

151

MOUTHBROODING DAY

Fish eggs and the juveniles that hatch from them are a highly nutritious food source for a wide range of animals. Their low survival rate means that some fish must lay millions of eggs to ensure that a few reach adulthood and perpetuate the species. This high wastage has led to the evolution of behavior patterns and adaptations where the adult fish protects the offspring.

The South America arawana carries its eggs in its mouth.

The female of the Paratilapia multicolour carries parental care one stage further and protects the young fry in a special brood pouch in her mouth.

Shoals of tiny fish swim around the head of a mouthbrooding mother, disappearing into her mouth in an instant when danger threatens.

A MOUTH FULL OF EGGS makes eating difficult so many mouthbrooders, like the jawfish, hide their eggs for a brief period while they feed, before returning them to their mouths. Mouthbrooding is carried out by males in several fish species.

The most efficient form of parental protection occurs in fishes like the rainbow surfperch of the west coast of the United States, which is ovoviviparous. Its eggs hatch within its body and the fish gives birth to fully developed young.

☛ *108 SEA HORSE.*

BIVALVE MOLLUSK DAY

The two halves of a bivalve shell are joined by a tough ligament and close when powerful adductor muscles contract. All are filter feeders, drawing in a current of water over the gills and trapping and carrying food particles to the mouth in a stream of mucus.

Teredos (shipworms) burrow into submerged wooden timbers. The toothed shell valves gouge tunnels when they are twisted back and forth by the muscles of the foot. The animal may eventually grow to 30 cm / 12 in. long, excavating a tunnel sealed with limey plates (called pallets) on the end of its foot.

Lustrous pearls are formed when oysters secrete concentric layers of aragonite, a form of calcium carbonate, around sand particles that lodge in the soft mantle tissues.

In the past, shipworm infestations have sunk wooden ships and weakened wooden dykes in Holland; today, concrete and steel constructions and anti-fouling paints have limited the damage that teredos can do.

Bivalves include several economically important edible species, such as mussels, which anchor themselves to exposed, rocky shores with tough byssus threads.

BUY A FEW MUSSELS at a fish market. Open them up and look for the fleshy mantle, which secretes the shell, and the delicate gills, which extract oxygen from the water.

☞ 117 SHELL; 343 SLUG; 355 SNAIL; 34 NUDIBRANCH; 30 OCTOPUS; 228 CUTTLEFISH AND SQUID.

Sand gapers use a muscular foot to bury themselves in sand, drawing water over the gills with long, extending inhalent and exhalent siphons. These protrude through an opening in the edge of the shell; hence the name 'gaper'.

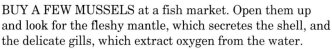

HIBERNATION DAY

Food shortages and freezing conditions force many animals to hibernate through the winter. During this deep sleep the heart pulse rate slows dramatically and the animal's metabolic rate drops to a minimum.

Squirrels hibernate in secure nests constructed from twigs in the branches of a tree, wrapping their bushy tails around themselves for extra insulation against the winter cold.

Reptiles and other cold-blooded animals must bask in sunshine to maintain their body temperature.

Only fertilized queens of many social insects, like wasps, survive the winter by hibernating in crevices and outhouses. All the workers are killed by the first frosts, but the queens emerge in spring to found a new colony.

The most important autumn task for hibernating animals is to eat continually, accumulating enough fat energy reserves to last until spring. Golden hamsters store caches of food before sleeping, so that a convenient top-up supply is available when they awaken. Red squirrels may break hibernation and forage if the winter conditions are mild, digging up nuts that have been buried in autumn.

The woodchuck, a North American ground squirrel, sleeps for eight months of the year, emerging in February.

The state of summer suspended animation is called estivation and is practiced by snails during periods of summer drought. They seal their shells with a mucus epiphragm, which glues them to bark and rocks and prevents water loss.

154

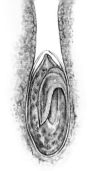

When water supplies disappear African lungfish burrow into mud and secrete a mucus cocoon, surviving for up to four years by slowly breaking down muscle tissue.

Shelter and security are the key criteria for choosing a hibernation site. Bats and bears sleep in dry caves. Bats hibernate communally, packed together for mutual warmth.

Three-toed terrapins burrow into the mud around ponds during the winter.

Communal hibernation is common in insects. Ladybugs can often be found clustered in large numbers in the dry security of conifer foliage.

Only the slow, rhythmic rise and fall of the rib cage and a gentle snoring show that hibernating bears are sleeping, and not dead.

WINTER IS A GOOD TIME to search for hibernating butterflies in old buildings, roof spaces and outhouses, where they may emerge on occasional sunny days. Provide these early risers with a piece of cotton wool soaked in dilute sugar solution, so that they can replenish their energy supplies before settling down again to sleep through until spring.

☞ 294 PLANTS SURVIVING WINTER.

Monarch butterflies of North America migrate several thousand kilometers to the southern United States and Mexico, hibernating in vast communal groups in trees and migrating north again in spring.

155

DARWIN'S FINCHES DAY

Many thousands of years ago, a flock of finches was blown by a storm nearly 1,000 km/600 mi. from South America to the isolated Galapagos Islands. There were almost no other birds there to compete – insect-eating, fruit-feeding and wood-pecking niches were wide open. From the one ancestral species, different finch populations evolved slowly and now different species do different ecological jobs in the Galapagos Islands.

The cactus ground finch has a down-curved bill and split tongue. It feeds on prickly pear nectar and fruits.

The large ground finch has a deep and powerful bill similar to that of a bullfinch for crushing fruit and seeds.

The woodpecker finch has a stout, straight bill which it uses like a woodpecker. But it doesn't have the woodpecker's long tongue to extract insects from its diggings, so it uses a twig or cactus thorn to pick out grubs.

THE GALAPAGOS FINCHES were studied by Charles Darwin during the voyage of the *Beagle* in 1835. There are now 14 different species. This marvelous example of adaptive radiation became another piece of evidence to support his theory of evolution – species were not 'fixed' and the overall characteristics of populations would change as the more successful variants within them prospered in a new environment in which the variation was advantageous.

☛ *21 TORTOISE.*

SEEDLING DAY

A seed contains a minute, embryonic plant surrounded by a food store. Both are protected by a tough seed coat, or testa, allowing some seeds to remain dormant in the soil for decades or even centuries.

Most of a castor bean seed is composed of food reserves.

Germination is triggered by uptake of water through the micropyle, a minute pore in the seed coat. The cells inside then expand, generating pressure on the rigid testa, which ruptures. Proteins, carbohydrates and fats in the unfurling seed leaves sustain the early growth of the root and shoot.

Coconuts are surrounded by a thick fibrous husk. They float in seawater and germinate when they are cast up on beaches. The young embryo germinates from one of the small circular scars at the end of the nut. The white, oil-rich endosperm secretes coconut milk and sustains the embryo during its early growth.

Castor beans store oil as an embryonic food source. In rice the storage product is largely carbohydrate, while beans store high concentrations of protein.

SOAK
PEA SEEDS
overnight, strip off the testa and dissect out the tiny embryo. This is a perfect plant in miniature, poised for growth.

☛ *180–1 SEED DISPERSAL; 127 BEAN; 161 RICE.*

Brazil nuts have a high oil content, a concentrated energy source that allows the seedling to grow rapidly toward the light.

HORSE CHESTNUT DAY

All thirteen species of horse chestnut have palmate leaves, arranged like the fingers on a hand. The winter buds are covered with a thick layer of protective resin, which prevents frost damage.

Collecting 'conkers' – the nuts from horse chestnut trees – is a traditional autumn ritual for children in Britain, but it is one with a relatively short history. The species was introduced from its native Albania and northern Greece in the 16th century and its magnificent display of flowers quickly made it a popular parkland tree.

Horse chestnut flowers are pollinated by bumblebees. Each flower has yellow spots at the base of its petals and after pollination these change from yellow to red. Bees' eyes are insensitive to red and the color change may act as a signal that the flowers are no longer worth visiting for nectar.

THE REFERENCE TO HORSES in the common name of this tree stems from its use by Turks to treat ailments of horses. Recent research shows that the 'conkers' also contain medicinal compounds that can also be used to treat humans. There are seven species of horse chestnut in North America, where they are called 'buckeyes,' because the brown nuts with their pale blotch resemble the eye of a deer. Wood from Ohio buckeye was once used for carving artificial limbs.

☛ *332 – 3 MEDICINAL PLANTS.*

YEW DAY

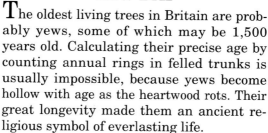

The oldest living trees in Britain are probably yews, some of which may be 1,500 years old. Calculating their precise age by counting annual rings in felled trunks is usually impossible, because yews become hollow with age as the heartwood rots. Their great longevity made them an ancient religious symbol of everlasting life.

Archers' longbows were traditionally made from the tough, elastic timber of yew, which bends without splitting. The strongest wood comes from trees grown in the Mediterranean climate and much of the wood for English longbows was probably imported from Europe, an early example of international trade in strategic military equipment.

Yew leaves and seeds are poisonous to humans and farm animals, but the seeds are dispersed by birds. The bright red, fleshy coating is called an aril and has evolved to attract birds, whose vision is particularly sensitive to the red end of the spectrum.

LOOK FOR LARGE YEW trees in old churchyards. There are separate male and female trees: males have small yellow strobili that shed pollen in March; females bear red fruits.

☛ 318 PINE; 314 REDWOOD.

Biochemists have recently discovered that yews on the Pacific coast of the United States contain a compound called taxol, which is an effective treatment for certain forms of cancer. Their discovery is a clear illustration of the value of plants as a source of medicines.

159

WILD DOG DAY

Wild members of the family Canidae are important carnivores of open grasslands and usually have long legs for running down prey.

The raccoon dog of Japan, China and Korea is the only canid that does not bark and is also the only member of the family to live in dense forest undergrowth.

Dingos are the wild dogs of Australia and were probably introduced by aboriginal settlers. There are few large carnivores in the Australian fauna and the dingo is the largest and most important. They are nocturnal hunters and often kill farm livestock.

Cape hunting dogs live in packs of six to twelve, allowing them to bring down larger animals, like zebra. Packs often travel great distances over the savannas south of the Sahara.

South American bush dogs are amongst the least known members of the family. They live in the tropical forests of Brazil and the Guianas and are about the size of a small badger. They run in packs and feeds on capybaras.

AN ENORMOUS VARIETY of domestic dogs, ranging from poodles to rottweilers, have been bred from the original wild-dog ancestor, demonstrating the hidden range of genetic variation that is present in wild animal species. In the wild, mutant individuals with abnormal faces, fur, leg lengths, body shapes and behavior are unable to compete with normal animals and are ruthlessly eradicated by natural selection. In the world of show-dog breeding, they are carefully nurtured.

☛ 97 WOLF; 140 FOX; 12 HYENA.

RICE DAY

Rice provides the staple food intake for over half of the world's population and is the world's most important crop for direct human consumption. It has been cultivated in China since at least 2800 BC and dominates agriculture in most Asian countries. The crop is also grown in southern Europe and in the southern United States.

Upland rices are grown in fields in the same way as wheat, watered by normal rainfall or irrigation. Deepwater rices are grown in deltas of rivers like the Brahmaputra, Ganges and Mekong. Their stems elongate as the flood waters rise and the crop is harvested from boats.

'Green revolution' rices are dwarf, high-yielding plants that can benefit from heavy fertilizer applications without growing tall and being flattened by typhoons.

PADDY RICE IS GROWN in flooded fields, where the water level is gradually lowered as the crop matures. The harvested grains are milled to remove their brown outer layers, producing the familiar white rice. This cooks much faster than brown rice but is nutritionally inferior, since milling removes much of the protein. You can germinate brown rice grains by soaking them overnight in water, then sowing them on a wet paper towel. Transfer germinated grains to seed compost and keep them warm and wet; eventually, you may be able to harvest a rice crop on your windowsill.

☛ *147 GRASS; 87 CORN.*

POISONOUS PLANTS DAY

Plants have evolved a wide variety of chemical toxins to protect them from grazing animals. These include deadly poisons like curare (used by South American Indians to tip arrows), strychnine (once popular as a rat poison and as a murder weapon in detective novels), ricin (a lethal protein from castor beans) and coniine (the poison from hemlock, used to kill Socrates).

Snowdrops contains alkaloids.

Henbane was used to murder the King of Denmark in Shakespeare's 'Hamlet'.

Baneberries are deadly but were once used to treat St. Vitus' dance.

Buttercups (right) and pasque flowers (left) contain poisons that also have medicinal value.

DRIED, GROUND ROOTS of irises (top left) were once used to produce the violet-scented orris root, which was used to powder wigs in Georgian times. Roots of several species contain medicinal alkaloids which are highly toxic when taken in uncontrolled doses.

Learn to recognize poisonous plants, for your own safety. Deadly nightshade (*Atropa belladonna*) berries look like black cherries (above, right), but two fruits are sufficient to kill a child. The plant is named after Atropos, the mythical Fate whose job was to sever the thread of life.

☛ 332–3 MEDICINAL PLANTS; 230–1 HERBS; 248 POISONOUS FUNGI; 174 KILLER SNAKES.

SNAKES DAY

Snakes, which are limbless reptiles in the order Squamata, probably evolved from burrowing lizards but most modern snakes live above the ground or in trees. All are predators and most either kill prey with deadly toxins injected through biting fangs, or by suffocating their victims in the coils of their body. Only 20 percent of the 2,700 snake species are venomous.

Snakes regularly slough off old skin as they grow. The shed skin that is left behind is a perfect, inside-out, transparent replica of its owner.

Rattlesnakes' hollow fangs can be erected to point forward and inject venom when the snake lunges at its victim. Their tails are composed of dry horny segments which are shaken as an aggressive threat.

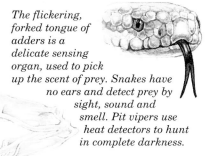

The flickering, forked tongue of adders is a delicate sensing organ, used to pick up the scent of prey. Snakes have no ears and detect prey by sight, sound and smell. Pit vipers use heat detectors to hunt in complete darkness.

SOME SNAKES LAY EGGS in soil and vegetation and leave them to hatch; other species are viviparous, with eggs that hatch inside the snake's body, so that it then gives birth to live young.

☞ 174 KILLER SNAKES.

Pythons capture their prey in biting jaws, which have backward pointing teeth for a secure grip (above). Then they throw coils around their meal, crushing it to death and swallowing it whole. Flexible ligaments in their jaws allow them to ingest prey that is much larger than their own diameter.

163

GIANT HOGWEED DAY

Giant hogweed comes from southwestern Asia and was introduced into British gardens in the 19th century. It quickly escaped from cultivation and has spread rapidly along riverbanks. Its sap sensitizes skin to ultraviolet light, causing painful blisters on the hands and arms of people who handle it. Children who use the hollow stems as blowpipes develop blisters around their mouths and need hospital treatment.

Giant hogweed is a biennial, forming a rosette of massive leaves in its first season and then producing flowering stems that may reach 5.5 m / 18 ft. These are crowned by a giant umbel of flowers, which develop into seeds that have aromatic oil glands embedded in them.

There are many examples of alien plant introductions which have become pests. Japanese knotweed was also introduced into Britain as an ornamental, but its creeping stems make it almost impossible to eradicate; it now infests thousands of acres of waste ground, particularly alongside rivers, canals and roads.

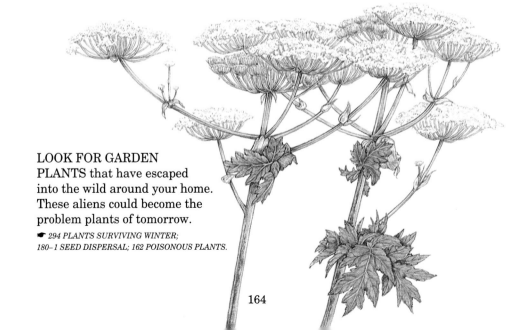

LOOK FOR GARDEN PLANTS that have escaped into the wild around your home. These aliens could become the problem plants of tomorrow.

☛ *294 PLANTS SURVIVING WINTER; 180–1 SEED DISPERSAL; 162 POISONOUS PLANTS.*

MARINE WORM DAY

Most of the marine worms that live in the mud and sand along the low tide mark are bristle worms, that belong to the class Polychaeta. Their stiff bristles – or chaeta – are often attached to paddle-like arms, that allow them to swim. The ragworm (left) is one of the commonest active species and is a predator, with powerful jaws. It can often be found under stones. Other species, like *Eupolymnia nebulosa* (right), live in burrows and trap passing animals and detritus in long tentacles.

When disturbed, the 12 cm / 4.5 in. long Spirobranchus gigantica *instantly withdraws its spiral of tentacles.*

Many polychaetes build protective tubes of sand (right). Retractable tentacles protrude like feather dusters, absorbing oxygen and filtering food from the water current. At least half of the tube lies below the sand surface.

LUGWORMS (left) live in U-shaped burrows, filtering food from seawater and leaving a distinctive coiled worm cast at low tide. Dig for polychaete worms in the intertidal zone. Most live in the top 40 cm/16 in. of sediment and can be captured by sieving silt and sand. Transfer them to a white dish of seawater, when some burrowing and tube-living species will extend tentacles that resemble writhing snakes or exotic fans.

☛ 214 EARTHWORM; 283 DEEP SEA.

CEREALS DAY
Bread and wheat

Settled civilization only began when people learned to cultivate crops. European agriculture arose about 10,000 years ago, in the countries bordering the eastern Mediterranean. The first farmers selected wheat varieties (right) which had lost the ability to shed their seeds, and this allowed them to harvest the crop and store the seeds dry in a granary, for winter food supplies.

Oats (above) are used for animal feed and for breakfast cereal.

Rye (far left) is used for bread making. Barley (left) is mainly grown for animal feed.

BREAD WHEAT (above, right) flour contains elastic proteins which trap carbon dioxide bubbles from fermenting yeast. These cause the bread to rise, producing the spongy bread that is popular in Europe and North America. Durum wheats (top right), which are grown in the eastern Mediterranean for pasta and spaghetti production, lack this property. Knead some dough, using a mixture of flour, water and yeast, and watch the dough rise. Then bake it and cut the bread open, to reveal the imprisoned gas bubbles.

☛ *161 RICE; 87 CORN; 147 GRASS.*

HAIR DAY

Color may be used for camouflage by hunters or the hunted. The leopard's spots provide camouflage in savanna grassland as it waits – an ambush predator.

Hair is a feature peculiar to mammals, although the protein keratin, from which hair is formed, also forms feathers, nails, claws and the outermost layer of skin in other groups of vertebrates. Hair provides mammals with an insulating layer to retain body heat and provides a medium in which color patterns can be developed for recognition or camouflage.

Pale winter coats in Arctic animals such as this fox are formed from hair with little or none of the black pigment (melanin) present in the darker summer coat.

Cats raise their fur by contracting muscle fibers under the skin, pulling the individual hairs upright. This is used to make the animal look larger in threatening displays.

IF YOU PULL A HAIR OUT from your head you will see that it is swollen at the end. The swelling is newly formed keratin in which the molecules have not locked (cross-linked) together. Unlock keratin molecules by soaking hairs in an alkali such as washing soda (sodium carbonate) (care!). The hair swells and becomes soft. If you twist the hair and transfer it to acid conditions (vinegar) the molecules will lock together holding the hair in its new shape. This is the basis of a permanent wave.

☞ *359 ARMOR; 279 POLAR BEAR.*

TERRITORIALITY DAY

Animals of many species take an area for themselves either individually (e.g. tiger) or as a group (e.g. meerkats). This area is their territory and its use may be for mating or for resources such as food or nesting material. Territoriality is the name given to the behavior used to establish, mark and defend that territory.

Male speckled wood butterflies defend a sunlit patch of leaves in woodland, wait for females to settle there to warm themselves, then mate with them.

Male ruffs establish a mating area – a lek – within which individual males fight for an individual territory. Females then enter the lek area and pick their mates – males with a central territory are preferred.

Lumbering male walruses defend territories on Arctic beaches to provide space for their harems of up to 50 females.

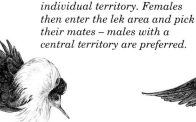

TIGERS IN SOUTHERN NEPAL have large territories, the boundaries of which they mark to warn off intruders by spraying urine and anal gland secretions, and by leaving feces and scratch-marks on trees. Female territories are about 20 sq. km/8 sq. mi.; those of males two or three times this size.

Park wardens track tigers and plot their territories using radio direction-finders. Each tiger wears a collar with a radio transmitter that gives off a unique signal. Collars and batteries are replaced from time to time by trapping the tigers and tranquilizing them using a hypodermic dart-syringe.

☛ 71 ROBIN.

BIRCH DAY

The tiny, wind-blown seeds of silver birch disperse the tree so efficiently that many foresters consider it to be a weed, but its bark was once a valuable commodity. Birch bark peels from the trunk in large sheets and has been used for making roofing tiles in Lapland and Norway, as writing paper and clothing, and for covering baskets and portable canoes in North America.

Birch trees are a valuable resource for wildlife and over 300 species of insect feed on them. The seeds from the pendent catkins are eaten by finches in early winter.

The foliage turns a spectacular bright yellow in autumn and brightens the edges of conifer plantations. Large 'witches' brooms' of coalesced twigs are often visible after the leaves have fallen; these are caused by a fungus called Taphrina, *which invades twigs and causes buds to proliferate. The contorted wood grain inside these fungal galls was once prized in Russia for making thin wooden bowls of great beauty.*

BIRCH TREES are generally short-lived and they are often eventually killed by razor strop fungus, *Piptoporus betulinus*, whose flat white brackets erupt from dying branches. If you collect an old bracket fungus and keep it in a plastic box covered with muslin you will find that several different insect species will hatch from it. Even after death the tree acts as a habitat for a variety of wildlife. Birches make a graceful addition to a wildlife garden, casting light shade and attracting insects like the emerald moth and the birch shieldbug.

☛ 227 OAK; 178 BACKYARD.

PRIMITIVE PLANTS DAY

In addition to the flowering plants and conifers familiar to all of us, there are three other obscure and primitive groups of plants – the cycads, the ginkgos and the gnetophytes. These are "living fossil" groups which evolved long before the flowering plants evolved and colonized the Earth. Each is now represented by just one or a few surviving species.

Ginkgo biloba *(top right), the last remaining ginkgo, is native to China but widely grown as an ornamental tree. Because of the appalling smell of the flesh around the seeds, it is usual to grow only male ginkgos.*

Cycads look like dwarf palm-trees. They occur in Africa, eastern Asia and the Americas, and are common on the east coast of Australia. Two hundred million years ago they were the dominant land plants.

Welwitschia mirabilis *(below), the strangest of the 35 living gnetophytes, grows in the Namib Desert. It has just two leaves, which grow continuously and fray away at the tips – about 5 m / 15 ft. of leaf remains intact. Some plants may be 2,000 years old.*

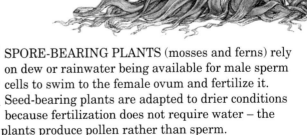

SPORE-BEARING PLANTS (mosses and ferns) rely on dew or rainwater being available for male sperm cells to swim to the female ovum and fertilize it. Seed-bearing plants are adapted to drier conditions because fertilization does not require water – the plants produce pollen rather than sperm.

☛ *114 FERN; 62 MOSS.*

FLYING FISH DAY

Gliding fish would be a more accurate name for the members of the Exocoetidae, a family of fish with enlarged fins that are used as wings. Their pectoral fins, just behind the head, are elongated and flattened; when the fish swim rapidly, at speeds of up to 32 kph/20 mph, they break through the water surface and glide for nearly 400 m/ 1,300 ft. During these gliding flights they are sometimes lifted by rising air currents, landing on the decks of small boats.

The California flying fish is one of several species that have taken to the air to escape predators. Only its pectoral fins are enlarged, but in the four-winged flying fish the extended pelvic fins provide additional "wing area".

The freshwater butterfly fish is an air-breather of African rivers, swimming close to the surface and sometimes skittering along the surface and taking to the air. It was first discovered by a butterfly collector, who caught one in a net while it was in flight.

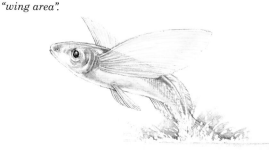

DURING FLIGHT most flying fish flap their tails but not their 'wings', so they do not fly in the true sense, like birds and bats. The exception is the South American characin or hatchet fish, with a deep chest housing muscles that vibrate the pectoral fins, allowing the fish to taxi on the surface and make short, buzzing flights.

☛ 52 RAY.

CATTLE DAY

Cattle are bred for many purposes. Highland cattle are a hardy beef breed, while Herefords were originally developed for ploughing and Jersey and Holstein-Fresians are dairy breeds.

Domestic cattle have provided milk, meat and leather and acted as beasts of burden since prehistoric times. European and North American domestic cattle (*Bos taurus*) are descended from the wild aurochs (*B. primigenius*). This forest-dwelling bovid was painted by Stone-Age man on cave walls and was still common throughout Europe during Roman times, but by 1627 it had been hunted to extinction.

Zebu cattle, with prominent humps, are revered by Hindus, who are not allowed to harm or sell them but do use them for riding or as draught animals.

Watussi cattle are farmed in Uganda and their exceptionally long horns make them instantly recognizable. European cattle do not survive well in Africa, where they are prone to diseases like sleeping sickness; zebu breeds, like the Watussi, replace them.

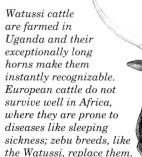

THE HUMPED CATTLE, or zebu, of India and Africa are a distinct subspecies of auroch, *Bos primigenius namadicus*, and their resistance to disease makes them suitable for humid and arid climates. In Australia and the United States they are known as Brahman cattle and are farmed for beef.

Visit an agricultural show to see all the breeds of domestic cattle side by side. They range from diminutive Dexter cattle, bred for small farms, to Normandy cattle which can each produce over 27,000 liters/7,000 gallons of milk per year.

☛ *144 SHEEP; 3 PIG; 313 GOAT.*

PLANT DEFENSES DAY

Plants lie at the base of almost every food chain and are eaten by countless herbivorous animals; stinging hairs, prickles and thorns are a first line of defense against browsing animals.

The brittle hairs of stinging nettle pierce the skin of potential grazers and release irritating acid.

Hollow thorns of some acacia trees (below, right) act as nests for ant colonies. The relationship is symbiotic; the ants have a secure home and the tree benefits because they remove caterpillars and deter browsers.

Thorns have evolved from the stems of leaves (petioles) that have lost their leaf blade. In hawthorn they are long and woody, deterring animals from browsing on the lower branches of the tree.

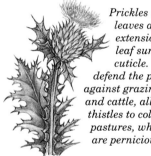

Prickles on thistle leaves are tough extensions of the leaf surface cuticle. These defend the plant against grazing sheep and cattle, allowing thistles to colonize pastures, where they are pernicious weeds.

The stems of desert cacti (below) have taken over the role of photosynthesis from the leaves, reducing the surface area of the plant and minimizing water loss. In many species the leaves have become spines – a necessary defense in desert environments, where food is scarce for herbivorous animals.

PLANTS CAN SOMETIMES RESPOND to attacks by strengthening their defenses. Plant two nettles in separate flowerpots (use gloves!) and keep well watered and fed with fertilizer. Then cut one plant back to ground level, to simulate grazing, and count the number of stinging hairs on a length of a regenerated shoot and on an identical length of stem from the unmolested plant. Repeat the experiment several times and you should find that the regularly cut plant develops a denser covering of stinging hairs in response to repeated 'grazing'.

☛ *162 POISONOUS PLANTS; 69 SHRIKE; 88 NEST.*

KILLER SNAKES DAY

Snake fangs are modified teeth, connected to a gland that produces venom instead of saliva. Back-fanged snakes, which have grooved fangs that inject relatively little venom, are not particularly dangerous, although people have been killed by the African boomslang. The elapsids, or front-fanged snakes, are deadly and have deeply grooved teeth that inject a large dose of poison.

The long-nosed tree snake is typical of many arboreal species, gliding through branches, well concealed by its camouflage colors.

The South American anaconda is the largest of all snakes, reaching 11 m / 36 ft. in length. Anacondas are not venomous; instead, they envelope large mammals in their coils, frequently drowning them before swallowing them whole.

American coral snakes are generally brightly colored, warning potential predators that they are highly venomous.

African egg-eating snakes specialize in swallowing eggs whole and often raid hen-houses. Long projections on their backbone crush the egg as it passes into the gullet.

THE LARGEST AND MOST AGGRESSIVE poisonous snake is the king cobra, or hamadryad, of India, Malaysia and China. It reaches a length of 5 m/16 ft. and is exceptionally aggressive, rearing up and expanding its hood to threaten any large animal that approaches. Its natural prey is other snakes. Snake charmers pull out the fangs or sow up the mouths of their cobras, so that there is no chance of them being bitten.

☛ *163 SNAKE; 199 LIZARDS; 356–7 RAINFOREST CANOPY.*

ROADRUNNER DAY

Roadrunners are aberrant cuckoos that are capable of weak flight but which prefer to run. They have long, muscular legs and sprinting individuals have been clocked at well over 30 kph / 20 mph.

Roadrunners make over a dozen different call sounds, but the 'beep! beep!' of their cartoon counterpart is not part of their vocal repertoire. In other respects their antics are almost as remarkable as those of the fictional bird that spends its life outwitting Wile E. Coyote. They feed on large grasshoppers and desert reptiles amongst the buffalo grass and chaparrel scrub of the southwestern United States, and are adept at killing rattlesnakes.

Roadrunners kill their prey with furious blows of their sharp, heavy beaks. They continue to pound snakes and lizards long after they are dead, breaking their bones and making them easier to swallow and digest.

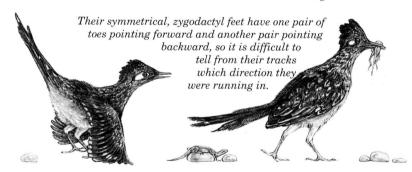

Their symmetrical, zygodactyl feet have one pair of toes pointing forward and another pair pointing backward, so it is difficult to tell from their tracks which direction they were running in.

ROADRUNNERS ARE ALSO KNOWN as 'chaparral cocks', and their semi-desert habitat has few trees. They usually nest in the tops of tall cacti, constructing large, untidy nests that are protected by the cactus spines.

Animals have provided a constant source of inspiration for cartoonists. Birds, mice, ducks, bears and rabbits have provided some of the most enduring movie attractions. Why not create your own cartoon character, based on your favorite animal in this book?

☛ 250 CUCKOO; 88 NEST.

HYDRA DAY

The phylum Cnidaria includes planktonic comb jellies, jellyfish, and sessile sea anemones and hydroids. Hydra is a fresh-water hydroid but most of its class are marine animals, often forming branched colonies on brown seaweeds.

Cnidarians are endowed with a deadly feeding mechanism. Their tentacles carry microscopic weapons called nematocysts, containing a toxic thread which is discharged at an acceleration of 40,000 times gravity when a prey item brushes against a trigger hair, called a cnidocil. As the prey struggles it brushes against further cnidocils, until its body is penetrated by hundreds of barbed, toxic threads. When it is paralyzed, it is drawn into the Cnidarian's body cavity and digested.

Hydra usually remains attached to weeds and stones but can hang from the surface film. It also moves by somersaulting.

SEARCH FOR FRESHWATER HYDRA on waterweeds in ponds and for marine hydroid colonies on seaweeds, near the low-water mark on seashores. Freshwater hydra are easy to keep in aquaria, where you will be able to watch their lethal feeding mechanism at work on water fleas.

☛ 219 JELLYFISH; 254 PLANKTON; 339 SEA ANEMONE.

Hydroids usually reproduce by budding off new individuals from the body wall, but when conditions are harsh they reproduce sexually, with males releasing sperm that fertilize eggs in the female.

176

BLOODSUCKER DAY

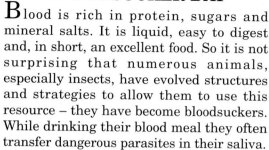

Blood is rich in protein, sugars and mineral salts. It is liquid, easy to digest and, in short, an excellent food. So it is not surprising that numerous animals, especially insects, have evolved structures and strategies to allow them to use this resource – they have become bloodsuckers. While drinking their blood meal they often transfer dangerous parasites in their saliva.

Tsetse flies bite cattle and man in tropical Africa, transmitting sleeping sickness. The female tsetse uses her blood meals to develop a single egg at a time to the stage of a fully mature larva which is laid and immediately pupates.

Leeches inject anticoagulant into their victim to prevent the blood clotting as they cut a circular hole. The anti-coagulant is long-lasting which is why leech bites bleed so much.

Vampire bats specialize in drinking blood from the ankles of horses and donkeys as they sleep. The bat sneaks up on its prey by crawling along the ground and bites a hole with its teeth.

BLOODSUCKERS face two problems. Blood clots when exposed to rough treatment and air, and getting through the skin of the host is painful to the victim. The bloodsucker must avoid getting its mouth parts clogged with congealed blood or have the wound seal before it has finished feeding. It must also bite painlessly so the victim doesn't notice and slap or scratch. Many bloodsuckers therefore inject saliva which contains anticoagulants and mild anaesthetics. These produce inflammation and irritation after the bloodsucker is gone – the itch of a mosquito bite.

☛ 325 PARASITE; 49 LICE; 194 MOSQUITO.

BACKYARD DAY

Soil or concrete, large or small, your backyard will contain a surprising number of plants and animals. Some will live there because part of it mimics a natural habitat – stone or brick walls and paving are cliff and rock substitutes. Look for lichens on walls and fences and for moss growing in cracks, and look for the animals that feed on them.

Some of the animals in your backyard live on your waste. Woodlice (sow bugs), beetles and millipedes will be living in your compost-heap.

The animals that prey on others are often nocturnal. Use a flashlight to search for spiders, harvestmen and centipedes. Night-time is the most active period for slugs and snails.

Garbage cans and bags attract wasps, flies and ants by day. At night rodents, foxes, cats, raccoons and possums attack garbage cans around the world. Many animals have become adapted to urban life, thriving on waste food scraps discarded by householders.

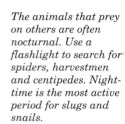

MAKE A SMALL GARDEN or paved city yard into a wildlife haven, by planting herbs and shrubs that offer food and shelter for insects and by providing winter food and spring nest sites for birds. A bird-table and nest box will attract birds into city centers and a small pond will provide a habitat for amphibians and insects. Buddleia and sedum are nectar-rich plants for butterflies, moths and bees which can be grown in large pots in a paved yard. Herbs like mint and thyme grow well in medium sized pots and attract bees.

☛ 56 POND.

ABYSSAL FISH DAY
(sea monsters)

These bizarre fish come from the abyssal zone of the ocean, more than 2,000 m/ 6,500 ft. below the surface, where cold, darkness and pressure are intense. Many have luminous spots to attract mates or prey. Food is scarce here and may consist of other abyssal fish or dead animals drifting down from above.

The anglerfish's luminous lure attracts prey within range of needle-sharp teeth.

Male anglerfish attach themselves to the first female they meet and live as a parasite for the rest of their lives, their only function being to fertilize the female's eggs.

At 4,000 m/ 13,000 ft. deep the pressure is 1,000 kg per square centimeter/ 14,000 lbs. per square inch – 550 times the pressure of a car tire. The fishes' internal pressure is the same, so they burst if they are brought to the surface quickly.

☛ *283 DEEP SEA.*

Virtually just gut and teeth, gulpers can take prey larger than themselves.

179

SEED DISPERSAL DAY

A seed is a plant-survival capsule, equipped with a dispersal mechanism and a food store. Seeds are formed in the ovary of a plant and in some species this develops into an edible fruit.

Apples are known as false fruits, or pomes, because the seeds and ovary are enclosed in the swollen receptacle.

Drupes are fruits like cherries, with sweet flesh covering a single stony seed. A blackberry is a collection of drupes.

In strawberries the hard seeds are distributed over the surface of a swollen flower base, or receptacle, which is edible.

Peas and beans have a succulent fruit wall which develops enormous tensions in its walls as it dries out. Seeds are hurled away from the parent plant when the pod splits violently. Plant breeders eliminate this dispersal mechanism from crops, so that the seeds can be harvested before they are shed.

Lotus flowers develop into large flat-topped fruits that bend over, so that the seeds drop into the mud. There are many stories of extreme seed longevity attached to the lotus, but the record for the oldest viable seed belongs to an arctic lupin, whose seeds germinated after 10,000 years in frozen mud in the Yukon.

True berries are succulent fruits that contain a large number of seeds, like the tomato.

180

Hooked fruits of burdock become entangled in the fur or feathers of mammals and birds and can be carried long distances before they are released.

The long plumes of old man's beard act as parachutes for wind dispersal.

The membranous wing of a sycamore seed makes it spin like a helicopter rotor as it falls, slowing its descent so that the wind carries it further. Conifer seeds have similar wings and spin to the ground when cones open on dry days.

Many fruits, like rose hips, are fleshy and brightly colored, to entice animals to eat them. Hard, woody seeds within fruits are tough enough to pass unharmed through the gut of a bird, which may fly long distances before the seeds are ejected in droppings. The sudden appearence of blackberry seedlings on the tops of high walls demonstrates how effective this dispersal mechanism can be.

Some fleshy fruits, like those of Sterculia tragacantha *(above)*, have an edible covering of the seed, called an aril, which has evolved to attract birds.

Hundreds of tiny seeds are shaken from pores around the top of a poppy capsule when it sways in the wind.

COLLECT MUD from the soles of your shoes or a car tire in autumn. Spread this on the soil surface in a flower pot and identify the seedlings that germinate, grow and flower. Humans, who are highly mobile, are very efficient seed dispersers.

☛ *157 SEEDLING.*

HARE DAY

The European brown hare has long, black-tipped ears, whereas a rabbit's ears are shorter and uniformly colored. Hares don't burrow – they are solitary and live in a depression (a form) in open ground which is also where the female gives birth. The young leverets are fully furred when born, unlike baby rabbits which are born blind and naked in the safety of a burrow.

Brown hares have a crazy courtship display – males run, jump, jink and box (below). Occasionally one may knock out another or even the female who was the object of their display.

Large ears act as radiators to lose excess heat as well as give the hare acute powers of hearing.

Arctic hares (left) have small ears to lessen heat loss and are white all year round. The Snowshoe hare turns white in winter and grows bristles on the sides of its feet to support it when it walks on snow.

MARCH AND APRIL – when they indulge in their mating antics – are the best months for hare watching. You will need binoculars, warm clothes, a vantage point that overlooks a landscape of rough pastures and hedgerows, and plenty of patience. Hares are most active at dawn and dusk, when they move out from the cover of hedgerows to feed on short grass and young cereal crops. During the middle of the day they often rest, motionless, in their forms.

☛ *57 RABBIT.*

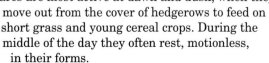

ONIONDAY

Onions are biennial plants, storing sugars in their swollen leaf bases (the onion bulb) through the first year, then growing some more before flowering and producing seeds in their second year. The stem of the onion is the small solid lump at the base of the bulb to which the roots are attached. Onions and their relatives contain allyl sulphide – the pungent component that makes your eyes water.

Garlic bulbs (top, right) separate into cloves, each of which can grow into a separate plant the following year.

Leek bulbs are long and slender, grown by 'blanching'. Leek seedlings are replanted deeply to prevent the leaves separating too near the base.

PLACE AN ONION on top of an old jam jar of water, so that the water just touches the bulb base. Leave it on a warm windowsill. Leaves will sprout and roots will grow into the water, which will need refilling regularly. Look closely at the roots and you will see fine root hairs that absorb water and nutrients. If you have a microscope, look at a root tip in water. You should see the individual cells of the root hairs.

☛ 70 TUBER.

RAT DAY

Rats and mice are rodents, with continuously growing incisor teeth that they use for gnawing. Between the incisors and the grinding cheek teeth there is a long gap, the diastema, into which the lips can be sucked to close the mouth while the rat gnaws through inedible materials in search of food.

The black rat (below) is a worldwide pest and carrier of disease, including bubonic plague, transmitted from rat to man by rat fleas.

Blind mole-rats (above) from Greece create tunnels over 30 m / 100 ft. long. Their fur can lie forward or back, so they can move easily in either direction in their burrows.

Bubonic plague killed 25 million people in Europe between the 14th and 17th centuries; 10 million died in India between 1890 and 1920.

Rodents destroy more than 40 million tons of human food each year. But fewer than 10 of the 500 species of rat are pests; most species do not impinge on man.

INQUISITIVE, INTELLIGENT and very, very cautious, rats are difficult to trap and even more difficult to poison. They are wary of unfamiliar food, often sampling it then waiting some time, as if testing for ill effects, before returning to take more. Pest controllers engage in an ongoing battle of wits with rats to protect our food and our health. New rat poisons are often only short-lived miracles. Rats breed rapidly, and quickly evolve resistance to new rodenticides.

☛ 210 ANIMALS IN THE HOUSE; 312 HOUSE MOUSE.

GOOSE DAY

Geese are members of the family Anatidae, which also includes the swans and ducks. Geese are thought of as being intermediate between the two but, unlike ducks and swans, they are largely terrestrial and feed on grasses. They are particularly fond of tender new growth, and several species have become pests of young wheat and barley.

Geese migrate to take advantage of the rapid growth of their food in spring and early summer. Barnacle geese spend the summer and breed in Greenland and Spitzbergen, migrating to Britain and Germany for the winter.

Webbed feet, adapted for swimming, testify to the goose's close relationship with ducks and swans.

Snow geese feed and breed in the Alaskan and Canadian tundra then migrate south for the winter – a 3,000-km/2,000-mi. journey to the southern states of the USA.

THE HAWAIIAN GOOSE, or nene, endemic to the islands of Hawaii, has been reduced to probably no more than 200 individuals in its original habitat. Its decline has been due to hunting and to the depredations of introduced wild dogs, pigs and mongooses (which take eggs and fledglings). But this bird is adaptable, and stock from the Honolulu Zoo has bred freely on reserves overseas so that there are now more Hawaiian geese in Britain, for example, than in Hawaii.

☛ 336 DUCK; 299 SWAN.

CARNIVOROUS PLANTS
DAY

Plants that grow in poor soil, or in peat that is leached by heavy rain, struggle to get enough minerals (especially nitrates) to grow properly. Carnivorous plants solve the problem by trapping insects, digesting them, and absorbing the juices along with the vital minerals.

Butterwort traps insects on sticky leaf-hairs.

Sweet and sticky droplets on the purple hairs of the sundew can trap very large insects: this dragonfly is too big for the leaf to fold over and sandwich it.

Backward-pointing hairs direct insects into the pitcher plant's drowning pool.

THERE ARE THREE TRIGGER-HAIRS on each side of the Venus flytrap leaf. Touched once, there is no response – raindrops cannot cause a false alarm. But if more than one hair is touched at the same time, or if a hair is touched twice, the two halves of the leaf fold together in about three seconds, imprisoning a fly behind the spines. The halves press closer, the fly is digested, and its juice absorbed into the leaf. The trap opens again, ready for another victim, within three or four days.

☛ *322 PEAT BOG.*

186

BURROWING OWL DAY

Burrowing owls are found in prairie and pampas grassland all the way from the western states of the USA south to Tierra del Fuego. They live in burrows that they excavate themselves or use old burrows made by prairie dogs or other mammals. In Argentina they may share the tunnels of the viscacha – a 10-kg/22-lbs. rodent that seems to tolerate its strange lodger. Marauding snakes are a constant underground hazard.

Unlike most owls this species is active during the day. Its comical appearance is enhanced by its habit of bobbing up and down on its long legs to get a better view over the grass close to its burrow.

Most of the owl's hunting is done in the cool period in the early evening. It flies low, looking for insects with its enormous yellow eyes, and is able to hover almost silently, like a kestrel.

FOR DAY-TO-DAY LIVING the owl is happy to use other animals' abandoned holes. But for breeding it prefers to build its own burrow. This may be up to 3 m/10 ft. long and may make part use of an old viscacha burrow. Sometimes an abandoned viscacha warren – a viscachera – will be taken over and modified by several families of owls.

At the end of the tunnel the owls hollow out a nest chamber and line it with grass and there the female lays 6–12 white and almost spherical eggs. Parents take turns incubating the eggs and, later, feeding the young.

☛ 54–55 UNDERGROUND.

FLEA DAY

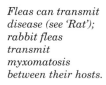

Fleas are highly specialized wingless insects that have evolved from a flying, fly-like ancestor. There are nearly 2,000 species, all blood-sucking parasites of bird or mammal hosts. Adult fleas are shiny and flattened, allowing them to slip between the host's fur or feathers. Flea larvae are inconspicuous, living in nests or burrow linings and feeding on skin dust and detritus.

Most fleas are 1–2 mm / 0.05–0.1 in. long, but fleas from the mountain beaver can be 8 mm / 0.3 in., the diameter of a pencil, in length.

The famous jump of the flea – up to 200 times its own length – is made possible by resilin, a special elastic protein that stores considerable energy. On release, the resilin straightens the flea's back legs, catapulting it into the air.

Fleas can transmit disease (see 'Rat'); rabbit fleas transmit myxomatosis between their hosts.

Cat fleas rest and digest in carpets between meals. If the cat is absent for more than two or three weeks, the starving fleas will try and feed on any passing mammal. After a long holiday when the cat has been boarded out, the owner may become covered with fleas on returning to the house.

SOME FLEES FEED on adult and nestling birds and their larvae and pupae can be collected from abandoned birds' nests. Put the nest in a plastic bag and keep it warm. Hatched fleas will patter against the plastic when you disturb the bag. Pick one up on a paintbrush dipped in denatured alcohol and examine its flattened, armored body and powerful back legs with a magnifying glass or microscope.

☛ *325 PARASITE; 49 LICE.*

SQUIRREL MONKEY DAY

Squirrel monkeys are members of the family Cebidae, which with the Callitrichidae (marmosets and tamarins) comprise the New World monkeys, the platyrrhines ('flat-noses'). These monkeys of the Americas are an entirely different group from those of the Old World (Asia and Africa) – the catarrhines – and there are numerous features that distinguish the two.

The two species of squirrel monkey live in the tree canopy of the Amazon basin rainforests. Their food consists of insects, fruits, seeds and flowers.

NEW WORLD MONKEYS have three premolars (grinding cheek teeth) on each side of the upper and lower jaw while Old World monkeys only have two. The thumb is not opposable: in other words it is at the end of the hand, not at the side, and to grasp an object a New World monkey must fold all five digits over toward the palm. Old World monkeys can move their thumb in a different plane from their other digits, allowing more sophisticated hand movements.

☛ *126 TAMARIN.*

189

AFRICAN PLANTS DAY

Africa is a vast continent, with plant habitats that range from mountaintops to baking deserts, and its flora is equally diverse. Epiphytes, like this member of the Scrophulaceae (left) growing on a thorn tree, are plants that live on the surface of other plants without harming them. Tropical rainforests have a rich flora of epiphytes, which exploit the branches of trees to gain access to light.

Africa's savannas are dotted with drought-tolerant acacia trees, whose flowers resemble powder puffs (right). These thorn trees are browsed by elephants and giraffes. When they are wounded, some species exude sticky gum arabic, which is collected and used commercially in the manufacture of chewy candies.

Desert rose (above) grows in arid parts of East Africa and is fearsomely poisonous. Its sap is used to tip poison arrows, and in tribal trials by ordeal. Its thick stems store water during droughts.

INSECTS ARE the main flower-pollinating agents in temperate regions, but tropical flora attract vertebrate pollinators. The nectar in the tubular flowers of Cape heaths (above), that dominate the flora around Cape Town's Table Mountain, attract sunbirds. Deep red sausage tree flowers dangle on long peduncles, allowing easy access to pollinating bats; the blooms then develop into gourd-shaped fruits (right). This trait, where flowers have extended peduncles, is known as flagelliflory.

☞ 296 AUSTRALIAN PLANTS; 241 GIRAFFE; 356–7 RAINFOREST CANOPY.

SKUNK DAY

Skunks have the unenviable reputation of producing the foulest smell in the animal kingdom. There are ten North and South American species. They belong to the weasel family (Mustelidae), all of which have a gland under the tail producing a scent for territory marking. In skunks this gland has become highly developed for defense.

Skunks raise their tails as a warning to intruders.

The Spotted skunk does a handstand to make itself look bigger.

If display doesn't work, a skunk sprays the intruder. The jet carries 3 m / 10 ft., and the fluid is highly irritating to skin and eyes as well as smelling revolting.

TERRITORIAL BEHAVIOR is one way by which animals can ensure themselves adequate supplies of food and space – by marking off and protecting an area for their exclusive use. Scent is often used as a marker.

Watch how dogs behave when taken for a walk down a street. They urinate deliberately on landmarks such as lampposts to claim them as their own. They will spend a considerable amount of time investigating the individual urine scents left by other dogs and will often try to override them by adding theirs.

☛ 168 TERRITORIALITY.

PIGMENTATION DAY

Color has many purposes in living organisms. It can act as a form of communication, when pigment changes occur during the breeding season, or can provide camouflage. Purple pigments in plants act as filters to protect leaves from damaging ultraviolet radiation. Green chlorophyll in leaves and red hemoglobin in blood have distinctive colors that are related to the way in which their chemical structure absorbs and reflects light.

Color has no communication or camouflage value in the darkness of caverns, so cave salamanders (above) have little body pigment.

In shallow coastal waters cuttlefish show a bewildering array of color patterns. These are under nervous control and the animal can communicate with several other animals simultaneously, by altering patterns on different parts of its body.

PIGMENTS, LIKE MELANIN IN HAIR and in the cuttlefish's pigment cells (chromophores), are produced by a series of chemical steps. If any of these go wrong, then pigments fail to form and the result is an albino, like the white gorilla above. Sometimes melanin synthesis can be activated by hormone or temperature changes, so the anole (right) can change color from yellow, through green, to brown and black.

☛ 197 DYE; 306–7 BUTTERFLY; 228 CUTTLEFISH AND SQUID; 43 SNOW; 145 CAVE.

CARIBOU OR REINDEER
DAY

Reindeer, or caribou, are large deer native to the cold conifer forests and Arctic tundra of Greenland and North America. In Europe the caribou is semidomesticated and known as the reindeer. It is herded in Scandinavia and Siberia, and by Eskimos in northern Canada, for milk, meat and hides. It is also used as a pack animal and to draw sledges.

Caribou fawns are born in spring on the high tundra where new plant growth in early summer provides ample food.

Wolves have adapted to the caribou's migrations and follow them south, picking off the young and the weak.

Caribou migrate southward from the tundra to the forests in winter to find food and to escape predation by wolves.

The reindeer stag's antlers are used in display in the breeding season; males fight using mainly their feet.

THE CARIBOU'S 1,000-KM/600-MI. JOURNEY, made twice a year, utilizes trails used for centuries. As the migrating caribou run the gauntlet of predators, mainly men and wolves, scavengers such as lynx, foxes and crows gather along the route to share the spoils. Logging and burning of northern forests has depleted the caribou's habitat, and the building of oil pipelines has disrupted migration trails. The number of caribou has dropped sharply.

☛ 129 MOOSE.

MOSQUITO DAY

Mosquitoes are a specialized group of Diptera (flies) whose larvae develop in stagnant fresh water. They are small insects and must contend with the surface tension to get their eggs into the water and to emerge through the barrier formed by the water film. The bloodsucking habits of female mosquitoes have made the group notorious.

A female mosquito lays eggs through the water film.

The pupa hangs from the water film, breathing through siphons.

Adults emerge through the pupal thorax into the air above the water film.

Older larvae are streamlined and swim by wriggling.

Larvae feed on microscopic algae and particles of detritus.

Male mosquitoes feed on nectar but females suck blood to provide protein to develop their eggs.

BITING FLIES transmit numerous diseases between animals and between people. Among these are filariasis (a minute parasitic worm which causes terrible disfigurement), arboviruses, sleeping sickness, yellow fever, onchocerciasis (river blindness), leishmaniasis and encephalitis. Mosquitoes transmit malaria, responsible for more than a million deaths a year. Examine mosquitoes with a magnifying glass; males have much larger, bushier antennae than the bloodsucking females, but both have a long, tubular proboscis.

☛ *177 BLOODSUCKER.*

LEMMING DAY

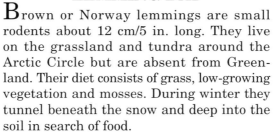

Brown or Norway lemmings are small rodents about 12 cm/5 in. long. They live on the grassland and tundra around the Arctic Circle but are absent from Greenland. Their diet consists of grass, low-growing vegetation and mosses. During winter they tunnel beneath the snow and deep into the soil in search of food.

Lemmings breed prolifically – they can produce 8 litters of 5 or more young per year and can breed when only 5 weeks old.

At this population level food resources run out rapidly. Overcrowding, disease and hunger trigger mass emigrations in search of space and food. Meanwhile, predators such as owls and foxes find an abundance of food and their populations rise.

Within three years this sparse population can increase to 30 lemmings per 1 ha/2.5 acres.

Lemming populations increase rapidly from a low of just one lemming every 4 ha/10 acres if food is plentiful.

MASS EMIGRATIONS OF LEMMINGS from the tundra areas can be spectacular, especially in mountainous areas where the moving animals are funnelled into valleys. Lemmings can swim short distances but they can drown easily in choppy water. This is the source of the myth that lemmings commit mass suicide by diving into fjords. They don't – a few lemmings are just unlucky. Lemming population explosions, followed by mass starvation, occur regularly, on a 3–4 year cycle.

☛ 184 RAT.

PARTS OF A FLOWER DAY

Flowers have evolved to ensure that the male pollen, produced in the stamens, reaches the stigma where it can germinate and grow down to fertilize the female egg cells in the ovary. The usual agents of pollen transfer are wind, water, insects, birds and bats. Floral parts have become highly modified to attract animal pollinators and ensure that their vital task is performed efficiently.

The dangling blooms of fuchsia deposit pollen on the heads of hummingbirds, which hover below to collect nectar.

Meadow cranesbill, like many insect-pollinated flowers, has guide lines on the petal which orientate bee visitors toward the nectar source. Bees can see ultraviolet light and many flowers have ultra-violet reflective patterns that are visible to insects but not to humans.

Passion flowers are pollinated by birds and the delicate ovaries, containing ovules that might be damaged by a bird's probing beak, are situated on a short stalk, well away from the nectaries.

COMPARE THE BLOOMS of white dead nettle (left) with those of honeysuckle (above, right). The dead nettle flower is visited by bees. Stamens hidden in the hood of the bloom ripen first, shedding pollen onto a bee's back, which then carries it to another flower and rubs it onto a receptive stigma when it enters the bloom in search of nectar. The long floral tube of honeysuckle excludes all pollinators except hawkmoths, which hover in front of the blooms and drink nectar through their long tongues.

323 FLY-POLLINATED FLOWER; 190 AFRICAN PLANTS; 251 BUTTERCUP.

DYE PLANTS DAY

Modern synthetic dyes are usually made from coal tar by-products, but plants were the main source of coloring before these became available. Plants contain many different dye molecules, including purple anthocyanins and yellow caroteins, but these colors often fade quickly when they are used to dye cloth.

Weld, or dyer's rocket, provides a greenish-yellow dye for coloring wool. It was once cultivated in Yorkshire and other centers of the wool industry.

Powdered turmeric root produces a deep yellow food coloring that is often used as a cheap substitute for saffron in rice dishes.

Safflower florets yield a range of yellow- and tan-colored dyes, which are used in India.

The Picts, an ancient British tribe, used the blue dye from woad to stain their bodies. It was cultivated until the 17th century as a source of cloth dyes, until replaced by blue dyes from tropical indigo plants and then by synthetic dyes.

Boiled madder roots produce a rich, tomato red pigmentation.

DISSOLVE A TEASPOONFUL OF TURMERIC in 3 cups of water and use the yellow solution to tint drawing paper. Boiled red onion skins can be used to dye wool a rich brown, after it has first been washed in detergent and soaked in an alum mordant.

☞ 112 CABBAGE.

SPICE DAY

The use of many spices predates the written word – coriander seeds have been found in Stone Age graves. Today they are an essential element of fine cuisine, but their original purposes may have been to disguise the smell and flavor of decaying food and as an ingredient in folk medicine. Their enormous value in the Middle Ages stimulated many great European voyages of discovery, to open up trade routes.

Cloves from Sulawesi are unopened flower buds. Their oil relieves toothache.

Slightly bitter caper flower buds flavor Mediterranean fish dishes.

Pimento berries from Jamaica have a blend of flavors – hence their alternative name, allspice.

Mustard from the Mediterranean is used to spice a wide range of dishes.

Star anise is an eight-seeded fruit used whole or ground in southern Chinese cookery – essential in making char sue pork.

Indian cardamoms are unripe seed capsules that give mild curries a flowery aroma.

Coriander seeds from Asia flavor curries and stews.

MAKE A SWEET-SMELLING pomander for a closet by studding an orange with cloves and hanging it from a loop of ribbon. Victorian writers claimed that the scent freshened clothes and kept moths away.

☛ 317 SCENT AND TASTE; 183 ONION; 230–1 HERBS.

Saffron (above, left), which is dried stigma tissue from Turkish crocuses, is one of the most expensive of all spices and is used to color and flavor rice.

Garlic (above, right), a member of the onion family, is one of the key ingredients in many French and Mediterranean dishes, imparting a rich flavor.

LIZARD DAY

Lizards are found throughout the world – a successful group with 350 species. Like all reptiles they are unable to produce heat internally and are 'cold-blooded'. They must maintain their preferred body temperature by adapting their behavior – basking in the sun or sheltering in a cool place when the air temperature is too high.

Whiptail lizards (opposite) are parthenogenetic. There are no males; females develop from unfertilized eggs.

Amphisbaenians (top, right) are a separate group halfway between snakes and lizards. Near-blind and limbless, they live in soil, feeding on insects and small vertebrates.

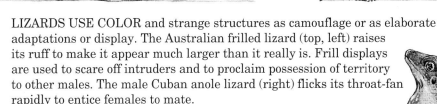

LIZARDS USE COLOR and strange structures as camouflage or as elaborate adaptations or display. The Australian frilled lizard (top, left) raises its ruff to make it appear much larger than it really is. Frill displays are used to scare off intruders and to proclaim possession of territory to other males. The male Cuban anole lizard (right) flicks its throat-fan rapidly to entice females to mate.

☛ 324 ESCAPE AND DEFENSE.

WOODPECKER DAY

Superbly adapted to life among trees, the 179 woodpecker species have invaded most forested areas of the world except Australia and Madagascar. Zygodactyl feet and long, curved nails help them grip bark; the stiff tail is used as a prop while the bird hammers into tree-trunks with its stout chisel-like bill to find insect larvae, sap, or to build a nest hole.

The lesser spotted woodpecker is 15 cm / 6 in. long; the almost identical greater spotted woodpecker is 25 cm / 10 in.

Red-headed woodpeckers' bills hit a tree with an impact velocity of 2,000 kph / 1,250 mph generating a force of about 1,000 G.

The American acorn woodpecker chisels holes in bark and stores acorns in them for the winter.

Woodpeckers' tongues are long, slender and muscular with backward-pointing barbs at the tip. When the woodpecker has opened up a larval tunnel it spears and draws out the grub with its tongue.

LISTEN for the distinctive drumming of woodpeckers in spring, when they are calling mates and investigating nest sites by hammering their bills in a fast drumroll on tree trunks. Sometimes, especially in the USA, they may do this to a metal chimney or tin roof of log cabins, producing a sound that has been mistaken for gunfire. When you are bird watching, notice how woodpeckers work their way up a tree, moving spirally and listening for insect larvae as they go.

☞ *93 BEAKS.*

ANT DAY

Ants are the most abundant group of carnivorous and scavenging animals. They are particularly important in the tropics, with more than 12,000 species. A single hectare (2.5 acres) of rainforest may support more than 8 million ants living in or on the soil or in the trees. Many ants make permanent nests but African driver ants are nomadic (right), carrying eggs, larvae and queen in their marauding columns as they hunt for prey.

Australian tree ants' leaf nests are sown together with silk.

Desert honeypot ants store sugar and water through dry summers in their grossly distended abdomens.

Wings are temporary, developed only by special reproductive ants which swarm, mate and found a new colony.

Ants may share their nests with other animals; the white woodlouse helps keep the nest clean.

ANTS, LIKE TERMITES, bees and wasps, are social insects. Individual castes within the colony are adapted for particular tasks. The sole function of the queen is to lay eggs, while workers tend the queen, rear the larvae and forage for food. Short-lived males mate with queens then die, while soldiers with large jaws defend the nest. Find an ants' nest by searching under stones on sunny, south-facing hillsides. Notice how workers carry larvae to safety when the nest is disturbed.

☛ *82 BUMBLEBEE; 41 ANTEATER.*

LONG NECKS DAY

Long necks have been evolved by many animals. They are used to gain an advantage in feeding – to take food that other animals cannot reach. The food exploited may be fresh leaves in a high tree; a long neck may enable a long-legged animal to take food from the ground, or allow a floating animal to dip its head deep below the water surface to feed. A long neck gives animals an elevated viewpoint, so that they can spot distant predators.

Giraffes' necks allow them to browse savanna trees that are beyond the reach of competing antelope.

The flamingo's height is offset by the long neck (above) that allows it to filter food from shallow lake water. The swan (left) searches in deeper water for succulent pond weed and algae.

CAMELS AND OSTRICHES use their necks to feed on new growth of grass and herbs at ground level. No long-necked animal can now reach the very tops of forest trees, and the leaves there are left to leaf monkeys and insects. But dinosaurs exploited this resource: 120 million years ago herds of 100-ton brachiosaurus grazed leaves from treetops 10–15 m/30–45 ft. above the ground.

☛ 242 OSTRICH; 241 GIRAFFE; 299 SWAN; 265 CAMEL; 304 FLAMINGO.

GORILLA DAY

There are three distinct races of gorilla. Very little is known of the first two. The Western lowland gorilla has populations in Cameroon and possibly Gabon and the Congo; the Eastern lowland race is in Zaire. It is separated from populations of the Western lowland gorilla by the low-lying swamps of the Congo basin.

The third gorilla race, the mountain gorilla, occupies a small area of high forest, 2,500–3,700 m/ 7,500–11,000 ft. above sea level, around the Virunga volcanoes and Mt. Karisimbi, straddling the borders of Rwanda, Zaire and Uganda. It is this small and endangered population that has been studied intensively, and has been the focus of enormous international conservation efforts.

A dominant silverback male leads a troop of up to 30 individuals. He scares off intruders by hooting and roaring, ripping up and throwing vegetation, beating his chest, then crashing about in the vegetation and thumping the ground with his fists.

A male gorilla can weigh 200 kg/450 lbs. and stand 1.8 m/6 ft. tall. Females are smaller, weighing about 80 kg/180 lbs. Gorillas have black skin and black hair but mature males have a silver-gray saddle on their backs. Males have a bony ridge on top of their heads which acts as an anchorage for the powerful

☛ *225 CHIMPANZEE; 285 ORANGUTAN; 130 ENDANGERED ANIMALS.*

Despite their reputation, gorillas are slow and peaceful animals with a strictly vegetarian diet.

The hind wings are reduced to a pair of drumstick-shaped projections – halteres – which act as balancing organs.

FLY DAY

There are 85,000 species of fly that live in a vast range of habitats. Blowflies – the familiar blue- and greenbottles – breed in garbage dumps. Some flies breed in corpses, and forensic entomologists can advise the police of the time of death of murder victims from the knowledge of the habits and life cycles of the species concerned.

Eggs are often laid on dead animals.

Maggots hatch and feed in putrefying flesh, secreting enzymes to liquefy it before sucking it up.

Adult blowflies break out of the puparium, crawl to the soil surface and inflate their wings. Their scientific name – Diptera – refers to the fact that all true flies have only two wings whereas other flying insects have four.

Full-grown in a few days, maggots burrow into soil and pupate.

BLOWFLIES CAN BE REARED in a plastic box half-filled with sawdust. Place a small piece of liver on top of the sawdust and leave the open box in a sheltered, shady place out of doors in the summer. As the meat decays, flies will be attracted to the smell and will lay groups of tiny, white eggs. Once the maggots hatch and feed, the smell will diminish, but do not do this experiment indoors, or touch its contents. Once the maggots are fully grown and the meat has disappeared, put the lid on the box and wait for the adults to hatch.

☛ 323 FLY-POLLINATED FLOWERS.

HUMMINGBIRD DAY

Masters of aerial maneuver, hummingbirds can fly forwards, backwards, sideways and straight up and down. Only one of the 320 species has a wing-beat slow enough for the wings to be visible – the wings of the others beat at speeds of up to 80–100 strokes per second.

The Cuban bee hummingbird is the world's smallest bird. The size of a large bumblebee, it weighs less than 2 g/0.07 oz.

The secret of the hummingbird's flying skill is in its ability to twist its wings to provide lift on both upstroke and downstroke.

Hummingbirds probe flowers for nectar using their long beaks and tubular or brush-shaped tongues.

HUMMINGBIRDS GAIN the large amounts of energy they need for flight from the sugar in nectar. Protein comes from small insects. Flowers don't just give nectar away; it is provided so that the nectar-drinkers will pick up one flower's pollen and carry it to fertilize another. Hummingbirds get pollen brushed onto and off their beaks and heads as they visit flowers.
Like many of the plants visited by hummingbirds, zucchinis need help in fertilization. Try growing one, and use a paintbrush to transfer pollen from the male anthers to the stigma of a female flower.

☛ 196 PARTS OF A FLOWER.

SPIDERS DAY

Spiders extrude several types of silk from spinnerets on their abdomen. The threads of a web are kept taut by microscopic liquid droplets that are secreted as the silk is produced. Their surface tension 'reels in' slack silk, so when a fly collides with the web this spool of silk extends and prevents the web from breaking under the impact. Once the fly is eaten, the surface tension in the droplets 'winds in' the slack silk again.

The nerve toxin of a black widow spider from the southern USA can kill a child.

Female crab spiders are much larger than their mates.

Arachnophobia – fear of spiders – is common, even in countries where there are no poisonous species. Many large tropical spiders are harmless and surprisingly gentle creatures.

Ant spiders live in ants' nests and have an extended body, to mimic their insect hosts. Only their extra pair of legs gives them away.

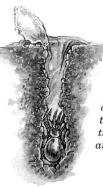

Trapdoor spiders live in a silken tunnel, capped with a trapdoor, and race out to grab any prey that blunders into trip wire threads around the entrance.

Bird-eating spiders of tropical forests rarely bite and can be handled, albeit carefully. They feed on large insects and birds, rather than insects. They reach a diameter of 25 cm / 10 in. and live for up to 20 years. Large tropical spiders are sometimes imported into Europe accidentally in bunches of bananas.

Many spiders detect the presence of struggling insects in their webs by sensing vibrations transmitted through the silk. The blind spider that lives in rain forests relies solely on its sensitivity to touch and vibration to detect its surroundings.

Spiders' silk is extremely strong in relation to its diameter. The webs of Nephila species have been used as fishing nets.

Lycosid or wolf spiders have a fraught courtship. The male must convince the larger female that he is not a potential meal. This involves hours of posturing and signaling with palps on his head, before he can pass sperm to her in his pedipalps. If he tried to make more intimate contact, the female would probably eat him. She carries her fertilized eggs around in a silk-covered ball, and when the spiderlings hatch they ride on her body until they are large enough to fend for themselves.

Species in the genus Microthena have protective spines on the abdomen, acting as a deterrent to hungry birds.

The fishing spider lives in marshes and is powerful enough to catch small minnows that swim close to the surface.

GARDEN SPIDERS eat their old webs and make new ones every night. Watch the whole process by keeping one in a large aquarium. Web construction always begins in the same way, with the constration of a framework, before a spiral of silk is wound outward from the center. Feed the spider by putting flies in the web and watch the way that it wraps its prey in a shroud of silk.

☛ 178 BACKYARD.

ZEBRA DAY

A 'family group' of zebras consists of a stallion, five or six mares and their foals. Such groups join together to form larger herds, the size of which depends on the richness of the grazing.

The zebras of the savannahs of southern and eastern Africa are closely related to the horse, so much so that Lord Rothschild, the zoologist, employed four zebras to pull his carriage. There are now three species of zebra – Burchell's, Grevy's and the mountain zebra. They differ in details of stripe pattern and in the number of chromosomes each has. The fourth species, the quagga, became extinct in 1883.

Oxpecker birds sit on the zebra's back and feed on ticks and biting flies.

Herds mingle with other grazing animals – wildebeest, eland, ostrich – an arrangement that provides mutual protection. The ostrich's acute eyesight and elevated viewpoint complement the zebra's keen sense of smell, to give warning of predators.

THE ZEBRA'S disruptive coloration works in a special way, confusing predators by its combination of vertical and horizontal components. The effect is greatest when a lion attacks a herd and several individuals scatter simultaneously – the result is a blur of vertically and horizontally striped irregular shapes. The lion's momentary confusion may allow its selected prey to escape. Find a book with illustrations of World War II merchant ships. Notice that some vessels in convoys were painted with zebra stripes, making it difficult for submarine commanders to pick them out as targets.

☛ 289 CAMOUFLAGE.

BOWER-BIRD DAY

The males of many kinds of animal compete for the chance to mate with a female. Competition is often physical or involves providing food. So a female can select a mate to fertilize her eggs from whom her offspring will inherit characteristics of physical or hunting prowess that will enhance their chances of survival.

Early explorers thought the 3-m / 10-ft. high gazebos with fenced moss gardens and scattered fresh flowers were playhouses built by native children. They are the work of the 20-cm/8-in. long male crestless gardener bower-bird of western New Guinea.

The 'avenue' is two walls of sticks on a soft mat of twigs. The bird makes a paint from bark scrapings, soil, charcoal and saliva and paints the walls using a brush of leaves held in its beak. The floor of the avenue is decorated with colored stones, shells, leaves and flowers. His work done, the male waits to see if his artwork will attract a mate.

A female satin bower-bird inspects an avenue; the male waits hopefully.

SOME SORT OF EVOLUTIONARY ACCIDENT has made the elaborate display of the bower-birds involve using natural materials that they have to collect themselves whereas their closest relatives, the birds of paradise, display using remarkably modified feathers. Male bower-birds use large amounts of time and energy in building their bowers, so much so that they are some of the worst mates in the bird world. After mating, the female is left to build her own nest and rear the young alone.

☛ 276 BIRD OF PARADISE.

Wood-boring beetle.

ANIMALS IN THE HOUSE
DAY

Many organisms find our houses and their contents their ideal homes. There are food scraps, dust, wood, natural fibers and even other animals and plants to eat. To a wood-boring beetle, there is little difference between fine furniture and a dead tree; both offer food and shelter. Molds break down wallpaper as easily as they digest dead leaves.

House spiders are fishermen of the air, spinning their webs to catch insects.

Woodlice live in damp, dark corners.

Carpet- and clothes-moth larvae eat wool.

Minute bed mites feed on flakes of dead skin, dried saliva and other secretions. The average bed contains millions of them.

Mice eat almost anything and rarely need to drink. They rip up paper and fabrics for nest material.

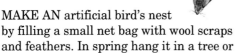

MAKE AN artificial bird's nest by filling a small net bag with wool scraps and feathers. In spring hang it in a tree or wedge it in a wall, out of direct sunlight. Retrieve the bag in autumn and put the contents in a jar closed with fine netting. Look for moth larvae among the feathers. Eventually clothes moths, whose natural habitat is birds' nests, should emerge. Three common genera are *Tineola* (golden forewings), *Tinea* (brownish, with black dots) and *Monopsis* (silver dot on the forewing).

☛ 178 BACKYARD.

LEMUR DAY

Lemurs are found only on the island of Madagascar in the Indian Ocean where no fewer than six of the 20 species are in danger of extinction. Their habitats are being destroyed through clearance of forest and the further destruction of vegetation by fire, cattle and goats.

Dwarf lemurs, the smallest, are only 13 cm / 5 in. long and weigh 60 g / 2 oz.

Indris have no tail; agile in trees, they move on the ground by hopping on their hind legs.

The largest, ring-tailed lemurs, are the size of a cat. They move around on the ground in troops of up to 20 with their tails held up like flags. The young ride on their mothers' backs.

The aye-aye's incisor teeth grow continuously, like a rodent's; it gnaws wood and hooks out beetle larvae with its long fingers and nails.

LEMURS, ALONG WITH LORISES, tarsiers, monkeys and apes, are primates, like you. Check that you are a primate. You should be able to grip branches with your thumb opposed to other digits, which should all have fleshy, sensitive pads underneath. Your claws should be flattened into nails and you should be able to turn your palm uppermost to put food in your mouth. Your eyes should be on the front of your head, giving stereoscopic vision – to see why this is important to primates, try eating with one eye closed.

☛ 203 GORILLA; 225 CHIMPANZEE; 67 PANDA.

RACCOON DAY

Well-known across North America, the raccoon has a distinctive striped tail and black burglar's mask – appropriate for an animal renowned for raiding dustbins for food. Its German name, 'wasch-baren' (wash-bear) describes its habit of 'washing' food items in its dexterous and almost monkey-like forepaws.

Raccoons doze in a tree perch during the day and descend to feed at night.

Raccoons' thick winter coats help conserve energy. Mating occurs in February and the young are born in early spring.

Raccoons hibernate in the colder parts of their range. Away from human settlement, raccoons feed in streams and pools on shellfish, small turtles, frogs and fish. But they will eat almost anything they come across, including fruit and vegetables.

MAN'S FOOD-SCRAPS and garbage dumps now provide a way of life for many animals and birds. Possums in Australia and New Zealand, and foxes, rats, crows, rats and mice in Europe all frequent rubbish tips. The rodents in turn attract owls and kestrels. Check whether your garbage can is ever raided. Look for clues, like footprints, tooth-marks and droppings, that might help to identify the visitor that rattled your garbage can lid in the night.

☞ 178 BACKYARD; 67 PANDA.

BUDGERIGAR DAY

A popular cage bird, the budgerigar (*Melopsittacus undulatus*) is a small parrot. Wild budgerigars are found across the drier parts of the Australian continent. They may form flocks of up to 10,000 individuals that migrate several hundred kilometers in search of food and water during dry periods.

Budgerigars court and mate shortly after rain which brings a flush of new plant growth to near-desert regions, providing food for the young.

Budgerigar flocks feed at dawn and dusk, mainly on grass seeds which are particularly abundant several weeks after a rainstorm has passed across an arid area. Budgerigar flocks can form whirling clouds at a food source or a water hole. This behavior confuses predators such as hawks and is comparable with that used by impala.

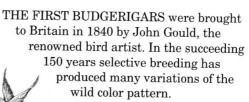

THE FIRST BUDGERIGARS were brought to Britain in 1840 by John Gould, the renowned bird artist. In the succeeding 150 years selective breeding has produced many variations of the wild color pattern.

☛ 247 IMPALA.

EARTHWORM DAY

Earthworms play a vital role in recycling and in keeping soil in good condition. As they burrow they ingest soil, grind it (and the decaying organic matter in it) and digest some of its content. Some waste soil is dumped on the surface as curly 'worm casts'. Worms also feed on dead leaves which they pull into their burrows, thereby speeding up the breakdown of the leaves and their incorporation into the soil.

Earthworms continually mix soil, bringing nutrients to the surface, adding and grinding in dead plant material, and aerating the soil and improving its drainage by their burrowing.

Each segment of a worm, seen here in cross section, contains internal organs.

Earthworms are both male and female. Mating worms (right) exchange sperm. A sticky ring formed by the swollen 'saddle' is slid off the body, collecting eggs and sperm as it goes, and forms a cocoon in the soil.

BUILD A WORMERY as described in the back of this book and stock it with worms. Watch the way they move, anchoring parts of their bodies with fine spines (chaetae) and then elongating or shortening by using radial or longitudinal muscles in their body wall.

☛ *284 MOLE; 54–5 UNDERGROUND.*

MONGOOSE DAY

There are 48 different species of mongoose living in Africa, Madagascar and Asia. They live on insects, small mammals and reptiles and birds' eggs.

The small Indian mongoose was introduced by humans into many of the islands of the West Indies and Pacific with the intention of controlling rats in cane plantations. It bred rapidly and became a pest, killing native animals and chickens. On some islands it has driven ground-nesting birds to extinction.

Agile, intelligent and sharp-toothed, mongooses are one of the few animals that will attack and kill venomous snakes.

Unusual banded tails are found in some mammals from Madagascar including the ring-tailed mongoose (below) and the ring-tailed lemur.

"RIKKI-TIKKI'S EYES GREW RED AGAIN, and he danced up to Karait with the peculiar rocking, swaying motion ...."

You can read the story of Rikki-Tikki-Tavi, the snake-killing Indian mongoose, in Rudyard Kipling's *The Jungle Book*, first published in 1904. The Walt Disney film of the same name, telling the story of Mowgli, is taken from *The Second Jungle Book*, but Kipling's books contains six other tales. After nearly a century Kipling's books, which accurately portray animal behavior, remain immensely popular.

☛ *174 KILLER SNAKES.*

HORNBILL DAY

Hornbills inhabit Africa and Asia, and nest in holes in trees. The male helps seal the female into the hole using mud and droppings, leaving only a narrow slit through which he feeds her and, later, the nestlings. After sometimes as long as three months the parents break open the hole, which has protected the family from monkeys and tree snakes, and release the fledglings.

The bony knob on the rhinoceros hornbill's beak is called a casque – it may be used as a weapon by competing males.

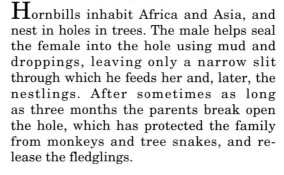

Hornbills eat fruit, insects, small animals, and other birds' eggs and nestlings.

The great hornbill is more than 1 m / 3 ft. long. Its yellow coloration is staining from the gland used to preen its feathers.

THE HORNBILL'S WING BEATS are very noisy and the 'whoosh-whoosh' it makes is familiar to explorers in rainforests. The bird's Malay name, based on its loud call, means 'chop down your mother-in-law bird'. The 'WUP-WUP-WUP' of the call sounds like an ax being applied to the stilts of a Malay house, chopping faster and faster, 'KE-WOP, KE-WOP, KE-WOP', then 'HA, HA, HA, HA' as the son-in-law runs away laughing as the house topples.

☛ *123 TOUCAN.*

MARINE TURTLE DAY

There are six species of marine turtle living in the world's tropical and sub-tropical seas. Unlike tortoises, they cannot completely retract their head and limbs into their shells. They feed on fish and jellyfish or, like the green turtle, on seaweed. Female green turtles nest every 2 – 4 years, coming ashore to lay up to 8 batches of up to 10 eggs each in a hole dug in a sandy beach.

Turtles have no teeth but instead have a sharp, horny beak.

Leathery turtles 'cry' as they lay their eggs – a gland near the eye excretes excess salt. Overcollection of turtle eggs for food has drastically reduced their breeding success.

MARINE TURTLES are endangered in most parts of their range. Many are trapped and die in fishing nets. Leathery turtles mistake plastic bags or other floating trash for jellyfish – their staple food – and die after eating them. Many turtle-nesting beaches have had tourist hotels built almost on top of them.

☞ *21 TORTOISE; 199 LIZARD.*
58 GECKO; 163 SNAKES.

217

TAPIR DAY

The tapir's skull is similar to that of the horse or rhinoceros, to which it is closely related. Protruding incisor teeth graze vegetation, which is then ground between the large flat cheek teeth.

There are four species of tapir – three in South America and one in Southeast Asia. The South American tapirs (right) are brown, but the Asiatic or Malaysian tapir has a striking black and white pattern (below). A distinctive feature is the tapir's trunk – a sensitive, flexible extension of the nose and upper lip used to sniff, probe and grasp vegetation and bring it towards the mouth.

Brazilian tapirs live near water, swim well and often wallow in rivers. Asiatic tapirs prefer to stay within the forest.

The young of both Old and New World tapirs have stripy coats like young wild pigs – good camouflage in light-dappled forest.

THE STRANGE DISTRIBUTION OF TAPIRS is a relict distribution. We know from fossils that up to about 5 million years ago tapirs were distributed across the Asian continent, including Europe. During a warm period less than 2 million years ago they migrated to North America across dry land in the area of the present-day Bering Strait and moved south to tropical America. Populations in North America and Europe died out, leaving just the species we see today.

☛ 148 STRANGE NOSES; 27 DONKEY; 208 ZEBRA; 310 RHINOCEROS.

JELLYFISH DAY

Jellyfish are coelenterates, a group of simple animals that includes sea anemones, corals and hydras. Coelenterates have two basic body plans – the polyp, little more than a blind-ended length of gut with a mouth surrounded by tentacles, and the medusa, a free-swimming bell. Most polyps, like the hydra and coral polyps, are permanently attached to a surface, but some are free-swimming.

The Portuguese man-of-war (left) is a colony of specialized polyps. One forms a gas-filled 30-cm / 12-in. floating bladder that supports the rest.

Other polyps perform one of three functions – feeding, reproducing or killing. Killer polyps form trailing strands, up to 12 m /40 ft. long, armed with special stinging cells called nematocysts.

JELLYFISH LIKE THE SEA WASP (top right) and polyorchis (bottom right) are medusae – a single individual rather than a colony. The tentacles, much of the bell surface and sometimes the stomach lining are armed with venomous nematocysts.

Serious stings, including those from the sea wasp and Portuguese man-of-war, sometimes prove fatal.

 ☛ *176 HYDRA.*

219

COCOA DAY

The source of chocolate, cocoa was originally a Central American tree but is now grown widely throughout the tropics. Rarely more than 7.5 m/25 ft. tall, the trees are often grown in the shade of taller species such as avocado. The flowers are strange – they bud out from the trunk and main branches. From the fertilized flowers, large 20-cm/8-in. green pods develop. These turn red or yellow when they ripen.

Pods are cut down, split open, and the beans scooped out into a pile along with some of the slimy pith.

Covered with banana leaves, the bean pile is allowed to ferment for ten days.

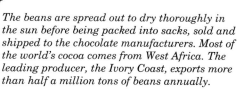

The beans are spread out to dry thoroughly in the sun before being packed into sacks, sold and shipped to the chocolate manufacturers. Most of the world's cocoa comes from West Africa. The leading producer, the Ivory Coast, exports more than half a million tons of beans annually.

IN A CHOCOLATE FACTORY the beans are roasted and crushed. Shell fragments are removed in an air blast. The 'nibs' of cocoa contain more than 50 percent of cocoa butter – grinding between rollers turns them into an oily liquor. Some of the liquor is pressed – the butter is squeezed out to leave cocoa cake (ground up to make cocoa powder). Milk, sugar and the extra cocoa butter are added to the rest of the liquor and the mixture is poured into a 'conching' machine. The warm mixture is ground to a smooth paste with granite rollers, then poured into polished molds.

☛ 309 SUGAR CROP.

STORK DAY

Storks are represented in all the warmer parts of the world by one or more of 17 species. The European white stork has been believed to be a bringer of good fortune since the Middle Ages, especially in Germany and Poland. Many houses in country villages have special platforms built on their roofs to encourage the storks to nest there.

White storks may rear up to 5 young in a brood. Eggs take a month to hatch and fledglings remain in the nest for two months before taking their first flight.

While white storks (above) feed on frogs, fish and small animals, marabou storks (left) with their ugly reddish throat pouches feed on carrion. Marabou are residents on the African continent.

WHITE STORKS may pair for life. Male and female share in building the nest, incubating the eggs and feeding the young. Their voice boxes have lost their muscles, so storks have no call and communicate by clattering their bills to comfort each other. Pairs return to the same nest site every year, after winter migration to Africa. It is obvious why they are symbols of happy marriage and omens of good luck, as well as an unlikely explanation of the source of babies.

☞ *24 EGRET; 246 HERON.*

GIBBON DAY

The Malay name for the gibbon is 'wak-wak'. The unforgettable call that this ape makes carries for several kilometers – a series of rising whoops that get faster and faster. Gibbons live in small family troops, spending most of their lives in the jungle canopy. They are found only in eastern India, southern China and Southeast Asia.

A gibbon's arms are twice as long as the trunk of its body. Its fingers are slender and curved; the thumb and palm are separate almost to the base. On the ground or on a branch a gibbon walks upright using its arms to balance.

Gibbons rely on the strength of their arms and hands as well as the strength of the branch to hold their 6 kg / 13 lbs. as they land.

Getting from one tree to another may take a 20-m / 65-ft. leap.

MOVING ARM-OVER-ARM through branches is called brachiating. Try it on a jungle gym and you'll find it exhausting.

☛ *235 ORANGUTAN; 50 BABOON.*

MAGPIE DAY

The green magpie (Cissa chinensis) occurs from the Himalayas to Vietnam and south to Sumatra and Borneo.

Bold, noisy and aggressive, common magpies, (*Pica pica*, below), are members of the crow family. They feed on insects, carrion and refuse, and rob other birds' nests of fledglings and eggs. They have become common suburban birds in Britain and Scandinavia, with a reputation for stealing and hoarding bright but useless objects in their nests.

The azure-winged magpie (Cyanopica cyanus, top right) is widespread in eastern Asia and Japan, then reappears in the mountains of Spain and Portugal, a remarkable discontinuous distribution. The standard explanation is that the two populations are relics of a once widespread population, but introduction to Portugal by early explorers cannot be ruled out.

SCIENTIFIC NAMES of living things consist of two words and are italicized. The first, beginning with a capital, is the genus and the second the species. Closely related species are grouped together in genera (plural of genus). The Ceylon blue magpie is closely related to the green magpie so is also placed in *Cissa*; its full name is *Cissa ornata*. Bird and mammal taxonomists have tended to place many species alone in their own individual genus to emphasize differences between them, rather than highlight similarities by grouping them together.

☞ 209 BOWER-BIRD; 250 CUCKOO.   223

TOMATO DAY

The tomato is one of the few fruits from plants of the family Solanaceae that is edible. Poisonous deadly nightshade, henbane and thorn apple are in the same family. Tomatoes were popular in Spain and Italy for more than 200 years before people in northern Europe overcame their suspicions and realized that tomatoes were a delicious exception.

Tomatoes became accepted in Britain because eating them was believed to make people fall in love. Their original English name was 'love apple'.

Tomato seeds pass through the human body without damage and can survive for long periods. Abandoned sewage beds are often carpeted with a thicket of tomato plants.

Tomatoes were introduced into Europe from South America in the 1500s. In Mexico their name is 'tomatl', and they are now known all over the world by derivatives of this name.

MORE THAN 60 MILLION tons of tomatoes are consumed each year. They are eaten fresh or cooked, or turned into juice, soup, ketchup or paste. Fry a slice of tomato and examine the cut edge where it has been heated intensely. The golden brown color comes from sugar in the fruit, which is caramelized during cooking. Caramel tastes sweeter than sugar, which is why tomatoes taste sweeter after frying.

☛ 348 SQUASH; 238 MELON; 180–1 SEED DISPERSAL.

CHIMPANZEE DAY

Our closest relatives, chimpanzees show striking physical and mental similarities to us, and 99 percent of their genetic makeup is identical to ours. Chimps were the natural choice for the first rocket flights into outer space to assess whether humans could survive acceleration and weightlessness.

Up to 60 chimps may live together in a social group. Their habitat is the savannah woodland of equatorial Africa.

Chimpanzees cannot even imitate our speech. But several have been taught sign language and could make simple requests and answer questions.

A 40-kg/88-lbs. male chimpanzee can exert a pull of more than 300 kg/660 lbs., three times the capability of a man.

Like humans, chimps grow gray hair when they get old.

CHIMPS FORM HIGHLY ORGANIZED and sophisticated societies, making use of a wide repertoire of sounds, facial expressions and gestures, including kissing and hand-holding. Their diet is mixed, but they will ambush and kill colobus monkeys using complex teamwork. Chimps can make and adapt simple tools such as a saliva-soaked stick to fish for termites in a rotten log.

☛ *203 GORILLA.*

ELEPHANT DAY

Elephants are the largest land animals. There are two species, the African elephant, with large ears and with tusks in both sexes, and the Indian elephant, with small ears and tusks only in the male. Indian elephants are used in the timber industry in Burma and Thailand to lift and move logs. Most elephants, like most humans, are right-handed and use their right tusk preferentially, so it is usually shorter.

The elephant's trunk is its nose and the two holes at the end are nostrils. It does not drink through its trunk but sucks up water then squirts it into its mouth. The trunk is a multi-purpose organ, also used for dust bathing and scenting danger.

The little elephant shrew (below) weighs 100 g / 3.5 oz.; the African bull elephant weighs 60,000 times as much – 6 tons. The hyrax (below) and aardvark are the closest living relatives of the elephant.

THE ELEPHANT'S TUSKS are its upper incisor teeth; otherwise there is, at most, a pair of molars on each side of each jaw. These giant ridged teeth are used to crush and grind grass, leaves, twigs and branches. They are replaced by new teeth six times during the elephant's life. When the last molars wear away the elephant starves to death. Poachers have almost wiped out some elephant populations for their ivory. Elsewhere, overpopulation of elephants in game reserves has caused irreparable damage to vegetation. There seems to be no happy medium for the elephant.

☛ *46 AARDVARK; 277 SHREW.*

226

OAK DAY

At least 320 different insect species, including the oak hawk moth (below, right), either feed or breed in or on the wood, leaves, roots, buds and foliage of oak. Oak foliage is often infested by the galls of minute spangle gall wasps, which induce the leaf tissue to produce a protective wall around their larvae. Other species of gall wasp cause the familiar woody oak apples that develop on twigs.

Most temperate oak species are deciduous. Red oak foliage (below) turns fiery red in autumn. In winter, oak twigs are recognizable by their clusters of chestnut-colored buds (above).

Acorns are nuts that contain a large food store. This is exploited by the acorn weevil (above), whose larvae chew their way out when the acorn falls, and then pupate in the soil.

OAK'S DURABLE TIMBER has been used for building construction, furniture and shipbuilding for centuries, while its bark is used for the production of tiles, insulating material and bottle corks. Bark from cork oaks (below) is carefully harvested on a 7–8 year cycle, without damaging the living cells beneath that are vital to the tree's survival.

Cut a section through a young oak twig and identify the layers – corky bark on the outside, living cambial cells and phloem below and dead, woody, water-conducting xylem in the center.

☞ 169 BIRCH.

CUTTLEFISH AND SQUID DAY

Cuttlefish and squid are cephalopods (see 'Nautilus'). Squid are predators of the open sea, feeding on fish and crustaceans. Prey is captured by the two long tentacles, passed to one or more of the sucker-equipped arms, thence to the horny beak which can inject poison before the prey is chewed and swallowed.

Cuttlefish skin contains pigment cells of three colors which can be expanded or contracted at will, allowing the squid to make rapid kaleidoscopic color changes.

Cephalopod eyes, fully developed in a newly hatched squid (above), are like ours, giving them excellent vision.

Cuttlefish live close to the coast and rest or lurk half-buried in sand. Unlike squid they contain an internal shell, the cuttlefish 'bone' which provides buoyancy.

CEPHALOPODS ARE AN IMPORTANT source of food for humans. Common squid are fished in Southeast Asia by netting, often with lights at night to attract squid to the surface, or by jigging, fishing with a small lure of bright feathers. Squid are dried in the sun in open racks, smoked or frozen.

Cephalopods breed just once then die. Following the breeding season cuttlefish bones are washed ashore and can be found on many beaches. You can work out the breeding age of a cuttlefish because the bone surface shows annual growth rings analogous to the growth-rings on a tree stump.

☛ *192 PIGMENTATION.*

WATER LILY DAY

Water lilies were enormously popular in Victorian times. Crowds gathered to see the giant Amazonian water lily when it was first established at Kew Gardens. The heady scent of lotus became part of the romantic image of the East.

The giant Amazonian water lily, Victoria amazonica, *has leaves 2 m / 6 ft. in diameter which can support a small child.*

Nymphaea alba is the white water lily familiar in Europe. Its waxy leaves and unscented flowers float on the surface of the water.

The sacred lotus, Nelumbo nucifera, *is common in India and China. Its white and pink flowers emerge above the water and have a strong, sweet, hypnotic scent.*

Lotus seeds are a delicacy and can be eaten raw or roasted.

The tangle of vegetation formed by a bed of water lilies makes a safe haven for young fish and for amphibians.

WATER LILY LEAVES need protection against becoming waterlogged and against being eaten and this is afforded by their waxy surface or cuticle. A slit in the leaf allows rain to drain away but some tropical species rely on most of the heavy rain tipping off the leaf and the rest evaporating in the sun.

Cut two water lily leaves from paper and rub wax into the surfaces of one. Submerge both in water and let them float to the surface. Notice how the waxed leaf sheds water, while the unwaxed one becomes waterlogged.

☛ *92 WATER SURFACE.*

HERBS DAY

Rosemary contains pungent oils, which have found a use in cooking and cosmetics.

The first pharmacists must have been early hunter-gatherers, who learned by trial and error to use plant extracts to treat illnesses, to kill pests and to preserve and flavor food. This process of discovery would have been hazardous, because many plant products are toxic. Information that slowly accumulated must have first been handed down by word of mouth between 'medicine men.'

Hundreds of thyme varieties are grown, with scents and flavors ranging from lemon to caraway. Like many herbal extracts, thyme oil has antiseptic properties, making it a useful preservative; it is an ingredient of enbalming fluid.

Today sage leaves are best known as an ingredient of stuffings for meat, but in ancient times it had a reputation as a healing herb which conferred long life.

More than 600 varieties of mint are known. Besides the familiar peppermint form, lemon- and eau-de-Cologne-scented varieties are commonly grown, as well as many cultivars with varied leaf shapes. The most familiar culinary use is as mint jelly, eaten with lamb.

Camomile flowers are infused with hot water to make a sedative tea. The plants are also used to make lawns, which emit a sweet apple sent when they are walked on.

Nasturtium seeds are often pickled and the flowers make a colorful garnish for salads. The plant has a strong watercress-like flavor.

Borage leaves have a cool cucumber flavor and are added to drinks. The flowers make an edible, decorative garnish for salads and their seeds contain gamma-linolenic acid, which is used to treat patients with circulatory disorders.

Dried bergamot leaves give Earl Grey tea its distinctive taste. The plant originates from North America, where it was used as a medicinal tea by the Oswego Indian tribe.

VISIT AN HERB GARDEN and use your nose to explore the aromatic biochemistry of plants, by crushing and sniffing leaves.

☛ 44 TEA; 198 SPICE; 332–3 MEDICINAL PLANTS.

The pungent-leaved tansy, which is a member of the daisy family, was once given to farm animals to expel intestinal worms. The leaves were also placed between winding sheets of embalmed corpses, to keep worms at bay.

BOOBY DAY

Boobies are tropical representatives of the gannet family, comprising six of the nine species. They feed on schools of fish, mainly members of the herring family, by diving into the water from a height of 15 – 30 m/50–100 ft. and snatching a fish just below the water surface. But they can dive deeper, and have been trapped in fish nets at depths of 30 m/100 ft.

Brown boobies are the commonest tropical gannet, making sand-scrape nests on islands in the Indian, Pacific and Atlantic oceans.

Red-footed boobies build nests of twigs on the tops of low shrubs or trees on tropical islands.

Boobies form large breeding colonies – the blue-footed booby is responsible for large deposits of guano, mined as fertilizer, on many Peruvian islands.

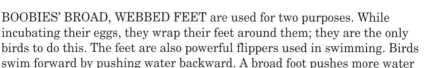

BOOBIES' BROAD, WEBBED FEET are used for two purposes. While incubating their eggs, they wrap their feet around them; they are the only birds to do this. The feet are also powerful flippers used in swimming. Birds swim forward by pushing water backward. A broad foot pushes more water back than a narrow one. See how much faster you can swim by wearing flippers, or try 'flippering' in the bathtub with two flat plastic tub-tops, one in each hand. With the tops you should feel a greater pushing force.

☛ *360 GANNET; 255 FRIGATE BIRD.*

MILLIPEDE DAY

Despite their name, millipedes ('thousand-legs') rarely have more than 200 legs (the record is alleged to be 752) and about a hundred is normal. They eat rotting vegetation, burrow, and help keep soil in good condition. Each segment of a millipede has two pairs of legs and is really two segments fused into one; in centipedes each segment has only one pair of legs.

Venom of Mexican blue millipedes was used for making poisoned arrows.

Mating (below) is a communal affair. Female millipedes make a 'nest' for their eggs and guard them until they hatch; the young (above) are almost colorless.

Pill millipedes (above) can roll into an almost perfect ball, presenting a predator with a slippery, armored problem with no obvious entrance.

Giant millipedes in Africa can be 20 cm long; similar millipedes in Malaysia, common on forest paths, can be 30 cm / 1 ft. long.

FIND MILLIPEDES by looking under stones or rotten logs (care!). Put a millipede on a flat surface and watch its leg movements as it walks. The legs lift in sequence and are moved forward with a very short stride. The lifting legs form a wave that moves from head to tail – in big millipedes there may be four or five groups of legs off the ground at any one time. Although millipedes cannot move quickly, the combined effort of all the legs can produce enormous pressure to shift obstacles and to burrow in hard ground.

☛ *352 LEAF LITTER.*

POPPY DAY

Meconopsis grandis *from west China.*

Californian poppy, Eschscholtzia californica, *is popular and easy to grow.*

Gardeners apply the name 'poppy' to a dozen genera of the poppy family, Papaveraceae, while botanists restrict it to the 70 or so species of *Papaver*. The field poppy, *Papaver rhoeas*, is a potent symbol of remembrance of those who died in war, chosen because it was the only flower to bloom in the mud and carnage of the battlefields of the Somme in 1916.

Papaver somniferum, *opium poppy, grows wild in Greece and the Orient.*

Field poppy, a common corn field weed until selective herbicides came into use, was believed in medieval times to be essential for good crops.

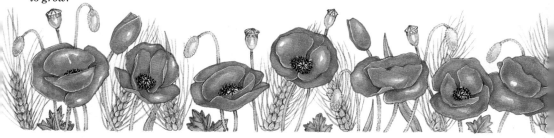

THE OPIUM POPPY was grown originally for its seeds which when eaten in quantity gave relief to the sleepless. The milky sap exuded from cuts made in half-ripe seed pods was used to make opium, a scourge in Victorian times and the cause of the Opium Wars between Britain and China. Now it is used to make morphine, an indispensable medical drug used in emergencies to combat extreme pain. Various morphine derivatives are used as milder sedatives and as painkillers during surgery. Unfortunately, it is also the raw material for heroin, a widely abused, highly addictive and ultimately lethal drug.

☛ 298 DRUG.

ORANGUTAN DAY

The doleful-looking orangutan is a native of Sumatra and Borneo. With the chimpanzee and gorilla it is one of the three apes most closely related to man. Its strange name is Malay – man ('orang') of the forest ('hutan') – although Malays now call it 'mawas' and only Europeans use the Malay name! Slow-moving orangs are too heavy to be acrobats like gibbons – a large male may weigh 100 kg/220 lbs.

Orangs climb slowly through the branches of the forest searching for fruit and young leaves. They build a nest of sticks to sleep in at night. Orangs are usually solitary but young ones stay with their mothers until they are five or six years old. They can live to be forty.

ALTHOUGH FULLY PROTECTED by law, mother orangutans are still shot by poachers who take the young to sell as pets or to unscrupulous zoos. Malaysian and Indonesian wildlife rangers and customs officers try to confiscate these young orangs to stop the trade. Confiscated orangs are taken to a special sanctuary at Sepilok in Sabah where they are given any necessary medical treatment and then released.

☞ *203 GORILLA; 225 CHIMPANZEE.*

235

GRAPE DAY

Grape seeds have been found in pre-historic tombs and vines were grown in Egypt during the reign of the pharaohs. Different varieties are grown as table grapes, for wine, for juice or canning, or for drying to make raisins or sultanas. The most obvious difference is between black grapes, like black Hamburg (table), and whites, such as riesling (wine).

The oldest wine ever drunk was from a wax-sealed Greek amphora recovered from a 2,500-year-old shipwreck in the Mediterranean. It was described as 'disgusting'.

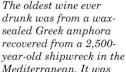

In the 1890s the vines of Europe began to die. Phylloxera, an aphid-like root pest, had been accidentally introduced from America and it spread like wildfire. It took French growers fifty years to replace their vines with new varieties grafted onto phylloxera-resistant American rootstocks.

RED WINE is colored by the skins of whole black grapes, while white wine is made from the juice of white or red varieties. The process of making red wine begins when slurry from crushed grapes is poured into an open tank. Yeast, a single-celled fungus, is added and fermentation begins. The yeast multiplies, converting sugar into alcohol and bubbles of carbon dioxide. After 2–3 weeks seeds and skins are separated and the yeast settles out, leaving wine whose fine sediment is allowed to settle in tanks before bottling.

☛ 237 EXOTIC FRUITS; 180–1 SEED DISPERSAL.

EXOTIC FRUIT DAY

To us, exotic fruits are those that are often unusual, expensive and come from tropical countries. To someone living in, say, Malaysia, these are familiar fruits that grow locally and it is our cherries, plums and pears that are exotic.

Passion fruit from South America have a tough, bitter skin, sweet-sharp pulp and hard black seeds.

Fresh South American guavas don't travel well, so are canned for export.

Mangosteen, the 'queen of fruits', is from Southeast Asia, as is rambutan and the closely related lychee.

Starfruit are grown in paper bags, to keep out fruit flies.

Rich in energy, avocados are often eaten with oil-and-vinegar dressing to add flavor.

Pawpaws, or papayas, come from fast-growing umbrella-shaped trees.

Mango (far left) is widely grown in India; pomegranates originated in Asia; and persimmon (right) is an important fruit in its native Japan and China.

THE MALAYSIAN DURIAN is the world's strongest-smelling fruit. Some Europeans are physically sickened by it but others love it. Annual durian festivals are held on Malaysia's east coast where people gather to tap, poke, measure and sniff the heavy, spiky durians and sample their rich and slippery white or yellow flesh. Durian trees are pollinated by bats and will only fruit where bats flourish.

Cut open and draw a tropical fruit and identify the seeds, skin and pulp. Then taste it and try and find words to describe the flavor.

☞ 272 CITRUS.

MELON DAY

Most melons grow in hot Mediterranean climates, but the watermelon needs humid tropical conditions close to the equator. Melons in European supermarkets are from North Africa, the Middle East, California or Mexico, and the melon bought in Sydney was probably grown in Queensland. Roasted melon seeds are sometimes sold as snacks.

Melons are monoecious – with separate male and female flowers on the same plant.

Muskmelons or cantaloupes are small. The flesh is pinky-orange and has a deliciously fragrant smell. Washed and dried, cantaloupe seeds are excellent food for birds.

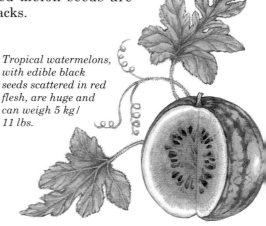

Tropical watermelons, with edible black seeds scattered in red flesh, are huge and can weigh 5 kg / 11 lbs.

Honeydew melons are large and may be green or yellow-skinned. They are only good when very ripe. Under-ripe they are tasteless and woody.

IN COLDER CLIMATES melons must be grown in a greenhouse. Seeds only germinate at 18°C/65°F or more. As the plant grows, train the main stem up a wire for 2 m/6 ft. then pinch off the top. Pinch off tips of side shoots once they reach 35 cm/14 in. Female flowers have a swollen base – the embryo melon. Remove the first few and wait until four open on the same day, then dab pollen from a male flower on the stigma of each. The tiny melons should begin to swell after a few days and will soon need supporting with net bags.

☛ *180–1 SEED DISPERSAL.*

238

KINGFISHER DAY

The ancient Greeks called the kingfishers 'halkyons' (sea-breeders), believing they bred on the surface of the ocean. They thought the gods calmed the seas during the birds' nesting period. The phrase 'halcyon days' has been with us ever since. There are 84 species of kingfishers across the world, 60 of them in tropical Asia and Australasia.

The common kingfisher sits motionless on a branch overhanging a stream, watching for prey, usually a minnow.

It plunges into the water head first, grabs the minnow in its bill, carries it back to its perch and bangs it on the branch to kill it.

The minnow is juggled in the kingfisher's bill until it is correctly oriented to be swallowed head first.

KINGFISHERS HAVE A PROBLEM in gauging the position of a fish in the water. As light rays pass between water and air they bend (refract). The fish is not actually where it appears to be when viewed from above the water – its image has been deflected. The kingfisher must compensate for this illusion as it dives, so as to hit the real fish, not the image.

Stick a model fish, cut from plastic, at the bottom of a bowl. Fix a stick to the bowl's edge and align it with the fish. Now fill the bowl with water. When you look along the stick again, the fish will appear to have moved.

☛ 246 HERON.

APPLE DAY

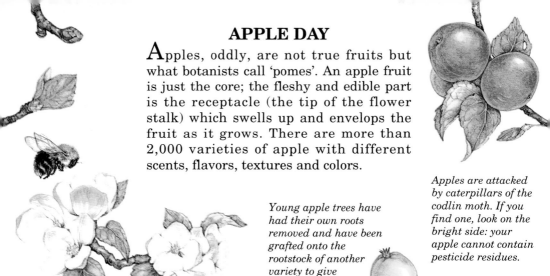

Apples, oddly, are not true fruits but what botanists call 'pomes'. An apple fruit is just the core; the fleshy and edible part is the receptacle (the tip of the flower stalk) which swells up and envelops the fruit as it grows. There are more than 2,000 varieties of apple with different scents, flavors, textures and colors.

Apples are attacked by caterpillars of the codlin moth. If you find one, look on the bright side: your apple cannot contain pesticide residues.

Young apple trees have had their own roots removed and have been grafted onto the rootstock of another variety to give particular growth characteristics.

Depending upon the variety, apples may be pollinated by themselves, by wind or by insects.

WE ENCOUNTER perhaps only five or six varieties of apples in our supermarkets. They have been chosen for ease of handling, uniform appearance and marketability. They are not the best of the apple varieties, many of which will become extinct unless people search out real apples. Good nurseries can still supply young trees of interesting, flavorsome varieties. Grafted on to dwarfing rootstock, they can be grown in the smallest garden. Varieties that are not self-fertilizing need another tree nearby to provide compatible pollen.

☞ 237 EXOTIC FRUITS; 38 WILD ROSE; 116 STRAWBERRY.

GIRAFFE DAY

A baby giraffe is born head-first and faces a 1.5-m/5-ft. drop to the ground as its introduction to life on the African plains. After spending over 14 months in the womb it can run with the herd within two hours of birth. If danger threatens, its mother protects it from predators with deadly blows from her heavy hooves.

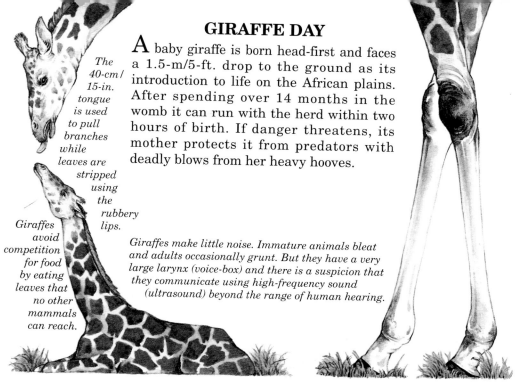

The 40-cm/15-in. tongue is used to pull branches while leaves are stripped using the rubbery lips.

Giraffes avoid competition for food by eating leaves that no other mammals can reach.

Giraffes make little noise. Immature animals bleat and adults occasionally grunt. But they have a very large larynx (voice-box) and there is a suspicion that they communicate using high-frequency sound (ultrasound) beyond the range of human hearing.

A GIRAFFE'S LONG NECK creates serious blood-flow problems. Its enormous heart pumps at three times the pressure of a human's to get blood to the brain. Lowering the head risks brain hemorrhage and raising it risks blacking out – too much and too little blood pressure respectively – so there are valves in the neck and brain blood vessels to control the flow.

Put a little water in a long, thin balloon, stretch it and turn it end-for-end to demonstrate the flow. Then mimic the action of valves by clamping clothes-pins along the balloon.

☛ *202 LONG NECK; 340 BIGGEST ANIMAL.*

OSTRICH DAY

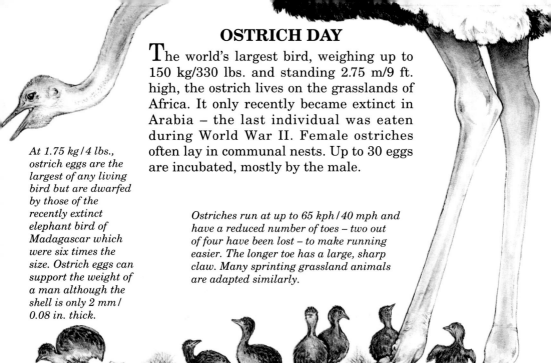

The world's largest bird, weighing up to 150 kg/330 lbs. and standing 2.75 m/9 ft. high, the ostrich lives on the grasslands of Africa. It only recently became extinct in Arabia – the last individual was eaten during World War II. Female ostriches often lay in communal nests. Up to 30 eggs are incubated, mostly by the male.

At 1.75 kg/4 lbs., ostrich eggs are the largest of any living bird but are dwarfed by those of the recently extinct elephant bird of Madagascar which were six times the size. Ostrich eggs can support the weight of a man although the shell is only 2 mm/ 0.08 in. thick.

Ostriches run at up to 65 kph/40 mph and have a reduced number of toes – two out of four have been lost – to make running easier. The longer toe has a large, sharp claw. Many sprinting grassland animals are adapted similarly.

OSTRICHES ARE FARMED for their plumes, meat, skin (which makes fine leather gloves) and eggs (which need to be boiled for 40 minutes).

Ostriches, together with kiwis, rheas, cassowaries and emus, are ratites – the most primitive group of living birds. Birds are actually highly specialized dinosaurs that probably evolved from lightly built coelurosaurs about 145 million years ago. So think of ratites as descendants of small, fast, carnivorous dinosaurs.

☛ *60 BIRD'S FEET; 202 LONG NECKS.*

242

ARCHERFISH DAY

Archerfish are the five species of the family Toxotidae, all members of the genus *Toxotes*. They normally live in brackish water at river mouths and in mangrove swamps from India eastward to northern Australia and the Pacific islands. Adults migrate out to sea to spawn in full-strength seawater around coral reefs, and the young return to brackish water when they are 1–2 cm/less than 1 in. long.

Archerfish are unique in being able to shoot insects off overhanging vegetation by spitting a jet of water. They eat the insect when it falls on the water surface.

Toxotes jaculator, pictured here, grows to 25 cm/10 in. It swims with its mouth at the water surface, takes a gulp of water, lines up on its prey, and spits a jet of water up to 1.5 m/5 ft.

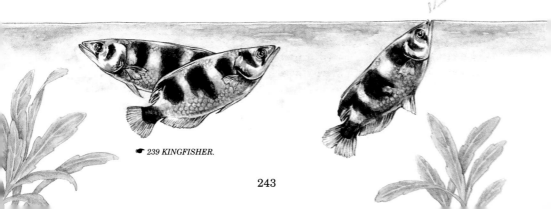

☛ *239 KINGFISHER.*

243

QUETZAL DAY

Quetzals are members of the trogon family – a group of 34 species that are solitary inhabitants of rainforests in the Old and New World. Trogons have zygodactyl feet but instead of the outer toe having moved to the back of the foot as in parrots, it is the inner (second) toe that has moved to give the two-forward-and-two-back arrangement.

Guatemala's national bird, the quetzal is also its unit of currency.

One of the world's showiest birds, the quetzal lives in dense rainforests from the highlands of southern Mexico to Costa Rica. From bill to tail tip the quetzal is 35 cm / 14 in. long, but the trailing plumes (regrowing after molting, left) overlying the tail add up to 60 cm / 24 in. to its length.

Trogons' skin has been described as having 'the consistency and strength of wet tissue paper'. They are the most difficult of all birds to skin and prepare as museum specimens.

AZTEC AND MAYAN civilizations worshiped the magnificent quetzals as gods of the air. Tail plumes were used in ceremonies. Birds were trapped, handled with great respect, their tail feathers plucked, and then they were carefully released so that their plumes could grow again. People took the name and the appearance of the quetzal and incorporated them into the name and into carved images of the Mayan plumed serpent god, Quetzalcoatl. Guatemalans now regard the quetzal as the spirit of freedom. They say that if caged, a quetzal dies of a broken heart.

☛ 356–7 RAINFOREST CANOPY.

MUSK-OX DAY

Not an ox at all, but one of the sheep and goat family, the musk-ox lives in one of the world's bleakest habitats – the Canadian tundra. Males, weighing at least 500 kg/ 1,100 lbs., begin to compete for females in July, butting and bellowing and becoming very aggressive. They even chase birds. Their name derives from the strong, un-pleasant musky smell the males give off.

Born in spring, young musk-oxen are prey to wolves; adults form a circle around the calves, horns pointing outward, to protect them. The mother suckles her calf through the next winter.

Horns are used in rutting and for defense against wolves. But they are no help in summer when the musk-ox molts and its bald patches are attacked by swarms of mosquitoes and blackflies.

Musk-oxen huddle together for warmth and protection in winter as chill Arctic winds blow at −20°C/−4°F.

RUTTING IS COMPETITION between males to gain and monopolize groups of females. It is common among animals that form herds – the Cervidae (deer) and Bovidae. The latter family of mammals includes the musk-ox, cattle, antelope, sheep and goats. The strong scent associated with rutting males is a chemical cue to the females to trigger them into breeding condition; it also triggers aggression in other males. By the end of rutting, the most powerful, dominant males have established their authority. Each has a group of females with which he mates.

☛ *59 DEER; 313 GOAT; 144 SHEEP; 19 WILD SHEEP.*

HERON DAY

Like most of the other 35 species of heron, the fish-eating gray heron shown here has special patches of continuously-growing feathers on its underside. These powder-down feathers crumble to dust which the bird spreads with its bill or wipes directly onto its head and neck. The dust absorbs grease, fish slime and dirt, and the heron combs it out using the claw on its middle toes.

The African black heron draws its wings over the water surface like a cloak, casting a shadow so that it can see fish below.

Vertebrae of unequal length allow the heron to fold its neck into an S-shape when flying.

Nankeen hight heron chicks beg incessantly for food, which is mainly composed of small green turtles regurgitated by parents.

Many heron species undergo striking color transformations in the breeding season. The green heron's eye changes from yellow to orange and its legs change from yellow to coral pink.

MANY POWDERS absorb liquids well. A variety of animals roll in the dust or take dust-baths to clean themselves. We use clays or fine muds in cosmetic face packs that draw grease and dirt from the skin.

Put a drop of cooking-oil on a plate and cover it with a teaspoon of flour. Stir it after a minute or two and you will find the oil has soaked into the flour to form lumps which can be 'combed' out with a fork. Try again with talcum powder: the result should be the same. Now rub some talc on your skin and see how it suddenly feels dry and clean.

☞ 24 EGRET; 60 BIRDS' FEET.

IMPALA DAY

When startled, members of a herd of impala leap in all directions. They jump as high as 3 m/10 ft., forward or straight up, and may turn in mid-air. This amazing display has evolved to confuse predators, such as leopards, which are unable to single out a target in the confusion.

A male impala has a pair of elegant ridged horns but the female has none.

In the dry season several hundred impala may form a herd but this breaks up in the rainy months into small groups of 20–30 females, each guarded by a single male. Left-over bachelor males form their own herds.

THE ARRANGEMENT by which several females pair up with a single dominant male is not unusual in the animal kingdom. By doing this, powerful and successful males can pass on these characteristics to a much larger number of offspring than if they were to mate with just a single female. Two kinds of skills help a young impala to survive. Instinctive behavior (which probably includes the leaping display) is inherited from its parents. Other skills are learned as it grows. Try to decide which of your behavior patterns are instinctive and inherited, and which you have learned.

☛ 59 DEER.

POISONOUS FUNGI DAY

Although several hundred species of wild mushroom and toadstool form part of the human diet, many species are poisonous. Fungal toxins act slowly and cannot have evolved as a defense mechanism, as they don't protect the fungus from being eaten; the toxic effects appear hours or days later, long after the deadly meal has been forgotten.

Panther cap causes muscarine poisoning, which is occasionally fatal.

The devil's boletus causes intense nausea, diarrhea and spasms.

The death cap is the most poisonous mushroom known.

Ink caps and the sickener (right) cause vomiting when eaten raw.

Brown roll-rim contains a cumulative poison which builds up over years.

Fly agaric and liberty caps contain hallucinogens – brain poisons – which cause delirium.

NEVER EAT WILD MUSHROOMS unless you're absolutely certain which species they are. There are plenty of good books on fungi, and a nature club may recommend someone who can give advice.

The mushroom is just a small part of a fungus, responsible for dispersing the spores from which new fungi will grow. The rest of the fungus is mycelium – thin threads ramifying through soil or rotting wood. Mycelium is difficult to see but you may be able to recognize it on a woodland floor if you move dead leaves and look at the soil surface.

☛ *162 POISONOUS PLANTS; 174 KILLER SNAKES; 4–5 FROG AND TOAD.*

PORCUPINE DAY

The porcupine's quills make it a dangerous animal to attack. It's a myth that they can be shot at a predator. When confronted, a porcupine will swivel about and charge backwards. The spines can be raised to make the porcupine look bigger, and clattered together to make a loud and disconcerting noise.

Spines break off when speared into an enemy, and the wound goes septic with serious consequences.

All porcupines can climb trees using their well-developed claws; South American species have prehensile tails and are arboreal.

Juvenile porcupines have soft, fur-like quills when they are very young.

FIND THREE OR FOUR 60 cm/2 ft. lengths of thin bamboo to make a porcupine tail. Cut the bamboo just beyond the "joint" or internode so the ends of the sticks are closed. Hold the bundle and clatter it. Now cut off the nodes so the sticks are open and rattle them together. The noise should be far more impressive. The tips of the porcupine's quills break off when they are fully grown so that the open-ended quills, like the bamboo sticks, make a much louder noise.

☛ 324 ESCAPE AND DEFENSE.

CUCKOO DAY

American cowbird –
a brood parasite like
the cuckoo.

The European or Common cuckoo lays its eggs in the nests of other, smaller birds. As soon as the egg hatches, the fledgling cuckoo pushes any other nestlings or eggs out of the nest so as to be able to take all the food brought by its foster parent.

Caterpillars form a large part of the cuckoo's diet. It is resistant to the irritant hairs of some caterpillars that make other birds vomit. The hairs lodge in the cuckoo's stomach lining which eventually peels away. The hairs are coughed up in a ball and the stomach lining grows again.

The 'cuckoo' call is made by males only – and with the beak closed.

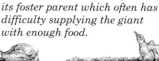

A young cuckoo soon outgrows its foster parent which often has difficulty supplying the giant with enough food.

CUCKOOS AREN'T THE ONLY BIRDS to be brood parasites – the American cowbirds use the same trick to have their young reared. All 42 species of true cuckoo (Cuculinae) are parasitic but only some of the other 85 species of the cuckoo family (which includes the roadrunner) behave this way.

The eggs of each individual female common cuckoo are the same, but different birds may lay very different eggs. A female will try and lay her eggs in the nest of a bird with similar eggs; a blue-egged female, for example, will try to lay in the nests of dunnocks.

☛ *325 PARASITE; 175 ROADRUNNER.*

BUTTERCUP DAY

The bulbous buttercup (*Ranunculus bulbosus*) shown here grows in drier grassland than the common and familiar meadow buttercup. It differs in having reflexed sepals, and the base of the plant has swollen bulb-like tubers. The flower is unspecialized and is thus a good example of a 'typical flower'.

Buttercups have five petals with, just below them, five sepals forming a calyx.

Yellow stamens above the tightly bunched green carpels have swollen tips (anthers) which produce pollen.

Pollen falling on the stigma at the tip of each carpel grows inward to fertilize the ovule ('egg') in the carpel.

Petals and stamens fall as the ovary (the old carpel base) matures. Each ovary becomes a seed with a tiny hook at its apex.

USE A RAZOR BLADE, scalpel or very sharp knife to slice a flower in half. Try to identify the different parts. The buttercup here has both male (anthers) and female (stigma and ovary) components, but some plants produce separate male and female flowers. Ovaries may be complex with many ovules served by a single stigma as in the poppy. Petals may not be true petals but modified sepals or leaves. Infinite variations occur. Pollen may be carried from anthers to stigma by insects, birds or bats, by the wind or by water. Some flowers are self-pollinating.

☛ 196 PARTS OF A FLOWER.

HOG DAY

The hog or pig family, the Suidae, contains a number of different species including our familiar domestic pig. All the hog species here use their snouts to turn over the soil, looking for fruits, seeds, roots and fungi. Wild hogs are pests in many parts of the world, and are hunted both for this reason and for food.

Misnamed, the African red river hog isn't a river dweller but it loves mud wallows as much as any other hog species.

Ugly African warthogs feed in small groups by day on grass roots. At night they wedge themselves into burrows made by porcupines or antbears.

Piglets of the wild pig are striped with brown – effective camouflage in shafts of sunlight.

THE HOG'S TUSKS are the incisor teeth of the lower jaw and, like rodents' incisors, they grow continuously. The ones in the upper jaw are smaller and grind against the bases of the lower ones. The tusks wear away as the pig rootles for food.

Tribespeople in Vanuatu used to remove the upper teeth from their pigs and feed them on soft food, so that their tusks eventually grew in a circle. Such pigs were highly prized and when they were eaten their tusks were made into bracelets or pendants and used in the headman's regalia.

☛ 3 PIG.

OWL DAY

The eagle owl is the biggest owl with a wingspan of 2 m/6.5 ft. Its 'ears' are tufts of feathers – the real ears are lower on its head.

A barn owl's feathers are specially thick and fluffy so that it flies silently as it swoops on its prey, mostly small rodents.

The nocturnal owl's eyes are huge, to capture as much light as possible, and there is no room to move them in their sockets. Instead, the owl turns its whole head sideways. In many owls one ear is bigger and higher than the other, more sensitive to low-pitched sound, while the smaller ear is 'tuned' to high-pitched noise. This allows owls to pinpoint a mouse by its faint sounds in pitch darkness.

Barn owl numbers have declined drastically in Britain and Europe, partly because of loss of nest sites. They prefer to breed in old barns.

In the Middle Ages barn owls were considered to be birds of ill omen: they should be welcomed, because they feed on vermin.

FAINT SOUNDS AND ECHOES even give us clues to our surroundings in the dark. Try finding a friend in a completely darkened room while moving about with your fingers in your ears. It's not easy. Take your fingers out and try again. Make your ears asymmetrical, like an owl's, by bending one ear-lobe. It should help.

☞ 104–5 NOCTURNAL ANIMALS.

A snowy owl lays up to 12 eggs which the female incubates.

PLANKTON DAY

Plankton is the name given to the thousands of different kinds of tiny plants and animals that float in oceans and lakes. Phytoplankton – minute plants – make their food from sunlight, water and carbon dioxide, a process called photosynthesis. Zooplankton – minute animals – feed on the phytoplankton and are eaten by fish, whales and basking sharks.

Zooplankton includes the larvae of many sea creatures such as crabs and sea-urchins.

In some tropical oceans the wake of a boat glows at night with the sparkles of luminous plankton called dinoflagellates. A single drop of water may contain 6,000 dinoflagellates.

Like land-plants, phytoplankton make oxygen as they photosynthesize.

TRAWL FOR PLANKTON by wading in the sea with a net made from fine nylon stocking on a hoop of wire. Turn the net inside out into a clear jar of sea water and examine what you've caught with a magnifying glass. If you have a microscope, place a drop of water on a slide and examine it.

If you can't visit the sea, trawl in a pond or lake.

Phytoplankton, algae, will be pale green. The green is chlorophyll, the substance that traps sunlight and uses it to react carbon dioxide and water to make sugars. Zooplankton are often transparent.

☛ 92 WATER SURFACE.

254

FRIGATE BIRD DAY

With a 1.8-m/6-ft. wingspan and a body weighing less than 2.25 kg/5 lbs., the frigate bird is an effortless glider but is clumsy on land. It scoops most of its food from the sea surface while in flight – fish, squid, jellyfish and young turtles. Pacific islanders once domesticated frigate birds, using them like carrier pigeons, as inter-island messengers.

Frigate birds breed on tropical islands and reefs. They have the longest chick-rearing period of any bird; the young begin to fly after six months but return to the nest to be fed by parents until they are a year old.

Females hunt for sticks while the male, throat puffed out, stakes out and guards the nest site, adding sticks that the female brings.

With their enormous wings and light weight, frigate birds have the lowest known avian wingloading.

The male's throat pouch turns from orange to bright red in the breeding season and can be blown out like a balloon.

FRIGATE BIRDS attack other birds in flight. Boobies lumbering home with a crop full of fish are favorite targets. The frigate bird grabs the booby by the tail, flicking its victim into a nosedive. The panicking booby regurgitates fish, which the frigate bird catches. Sometimes the booby hits the sea before regurgitating. Scientists call this piratical behavior 'kleptoparasitism', living by thieving.

☞ *232 BOOBY.*

BEETLES DAY

Some species of jewel beetles (Buprestidae) (above) may live as a larva and pupa for up to 40 years in the trunks of tropical hardwoods.

Beetles occur anywhere and everywhere, which is one of the reasons why there are so many species of beetles. We are surrounded and outnumbered by beetles but we rarely see them because we don't look in the right places. Look under stones and logs; pick apart dead fallen trees and look under pieces of loose and flaking bark.

Anal glands of bombardier beetles (above) spray a chemical that explodes upon contact with air – the noxious fumes are a defense against attackers.

Fearsome 'horns' of hercules beetles (left) and stag beetles (right) are all show – they can deliver only a gentle nip.

Nicrophorus beetles (left) bury small mammal corpses then lay eggs close to the body which is eaten by their larvae.

Some of the numerous, ingenious methods for catching beetles are described in this book. Pitfall traps are especially good for catching ground beetles (Carabidae) and rove beetles (Staphylinidae). Baiting pitfall traps with rotting meat or dung hung in a bag above the aperture will attract burying beetles (Necrophorus) and dung beetles (Geotrupes). Baited traps are a health hazard – use sensible safety precautions, observing scrupulous hygiene.

Ground beetles
(Carabidae) are
fast-running
predators. Some
tropical species
are arboreal.

Find beetles by 'beating' vegetation.
A stout stick and a pale-colored
umbrella are needed. Open the
umbrella and hold it under a bush.
Tap the vegetation sharply once or
twice and insects will fall into the
open umbrella. Don't thrash the
bush – any beetle that didn't let go
in the first few seconds is going to
cling on, whatever you do.

Larvae of chafer
beetles (above) eat
roots and are pests;
Colorado beetles
(below) are potato
pests.

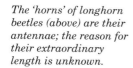

The 'horns' of longhorn
beetles (above) are their
antennae; the reason for
their extraordinary
length is unknown.

The pale greenish thoracic spots of
the firefly (left) are luminous
and can be flashed on and
off. A Malaysian species
congregates on riverside
trees and individuals
flash synchronously –
the tree looks as if it
is covered with
Christmas
lights.

FLIGHT INTERCEPTION traps work on beetles that fly and fall
when they hit an obstacle. Stretch a length (up to 3 m/10 ft.) of
very fine black meter-wide terylene netting vertically between
two poles so that the netting is taut and about 5 cm/2 in. above
the ground. Plastic trays are placed under the net and filled with
1 cm/0.4 in. of water with a little detergent added. Beetles hit
the net, fall into the soapy water, and are removed by filtering.

☛ 286 BIOLUMINESCENCE; 106 MAGNOLIA; 340 BIGGEST ANIMAL;359 ARMOUR;
285 EPIDEMIC; 347 BUG.

MEERKAT DAY

Meerkats, or suricates, are small mongooses that live in the dry sandy plains of southern Africa. They form tight-knit packs of perhaps 30 individuals, operating as a raiding party for food – insects, small rodents and occasionally snakes – and cooperating to maintain their communal burrows and to drive off predators. Unmated females even act as nursemaids to the pack's young.

Afrikaaners know meerkats as 'stokstertjes' – 'stick-tails'. The tail forms the third leg of a tripod as the meerkat stands upright basking in the sun or on lookout duty for enemies.

Meerkats are extremely agile and aggressive. Cornering a scorpion, one or two individuals will distract it while one bites off its sting before it is eaten.

RAIDING PARTIES of pocket-sized meerkats move as one, attacking and defending like small, high-speed footballers against other packs and even large predators such as jackals. Tails are held upright on the move, allowing gang members to spot each other quickly and maintain position in a formation. Scaring off another group, a pack will jump up and down in unison, call a shrill battle cry and scuff in the dust to produce a dust cloud to confuse the enemy and make the pack look bigger. If they win, they celebrate by scent-marking each other and surrounding stones and vegetation with secretions from their anal pouches.

☛ *215 MONGOOSE.*

LADYBUG DAY

Seven-spot ladybugs lay batches of yellow skittle-shaped eggs which become glued to a leaf.

There are more than 4,000 different species of ladybug in the world. Practically all are predators on aphids (greenfly and blackfly) and other small plant-sucking insects, such as scale insects, that are often pests. Ladybug adults and larvae are important pest controllers. Certain species have been introduced into countries where scale insects attack the crops.

The larvae feed ravenously on aphids and scale insects, piercing their bodies and sucking out the juices. As they grow, they shed their skin three or four times to allow them to increase their size.

Larvae hatch from the eggs after about a week and allow their skins to dry before going hunting.

Full-grown, the ladybug larva sheds its skin one last time, revealing the pupa beneath.

Although the adult's body is already visible through the pupa, a week's intensive change is needed to reorganize the larva into an adult. When the adult emerges it is pale and lacks spots, but its cuticle soon hardens and darkens and its pattern develops.

THE SPOT PATTERN on a ladybug's elytra is constant in some species but not in others. While the pattern of the seven-spot ladybug shown here is consistent, two-spot ladybugs are exceptionally variable. The variation is determined both genetically and environmentally. The form with two black spots on a red background is capable of surviving hibernation better than other forms; a black-suffused form has higher reproductive success. The balance of skills between the two forms ensures that the genes that control both color types persist.

☛ 256–7 BEETLE.

DANDELION DAY

Each yellow 'flower' of a dandelion is actually a cluster of more than a hundred tiny self-contained flowers (below, left) called ray florets. Each has a single petal, and a tube at the base encloses the stigma and anthers. The ovary at the base of the floret has a single ovule destined to become a seed.

Dandelions are visited by insects, especially beetles and hoverflies.

Once fertilized, the dandelion closes and the petals wither.

The dandelion head or 'clock' swells as the seeds develop. Each ovary produces a stalk topped with fluffy hairs.

Once the seeds are mature the clock opens and the seeds dry and loosen. They are blown away in the wind. Seeds germinate almost immediately on a suitable surface.

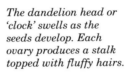

DANDELIONS ARE VERY SUCCESSFUL weeds, producing large numbers of wind-dispersed seeds that can travel great distances. They colonize waste ground, cracks in pavements and small bare patches of soil. Many weeds use the wind to carry their seeds to new habitats. Place a shallow tray of damp sterile potting compost on a windowsill or above the soil surface in the garden. See how long it takes for wind-blown seeds to land and germinate. Try and identify the weeds; grow a few to maturity and examine their flowers and seeds.

☛ *180–1 SEED DISPERSAL.*

TIGER DAY

Tigers usually hunt alone. They lie in ambush, relying on their striped camouflage to conceal them among the shadows in long grass, then leap and bring down their prey – often a wild pig or a deer. Old or disabled tigers may become man-eaters and are then ruthlessly hunted by marksmen, for they often become serial killers.

Sharp, pointed teeth are used to tear off and eat up to 25 kg/55 lbs of meat in a single meal.

Immensely powerful shoulder, neck and jaw muscles are used to kill prey as large as a buffalo – or gently carry a cub.

Porcupine quills may mean death by starvation for a tiger. One lodged in the jaw or paw means the tiger cannot hunt.

Tigers originated in Siberia. Indian tigers lie in the shade or even swim to keep cool in the heat of the day.

TIGERS STALK THEIR PREY very slowly, with no sharp or sudden movements, carefully placing their thickly padded feet. They retract their claws so that these cannot catch on twigs or stalks and make a noise.

Watch how a cat stalks and how it settles into a crouch before it leaps. The tiger's behavior is very similar to a cat's – they are close relatives. Like a tomcat, the male tiger marks his territory with urine which is rich in salt. The damp patches are very attractive to butterflies which congregate there to feed on the salt.

☞ 63 LIONESS.

CHAMELEON DAY

A chameleon is slow-moving and depends on its ability to change color to protect itself. Color change is caused by cells that contain particles of pigment contracting or expanding under the chameleon's transparent skin. A chameleon will go dark rapidly in the sun or when angered. When cold or frightened it turns pale.

Many of the 80 species of chameleon have spines or lumps on their skin. This Jackson's chameleon has horns on its face.

Chameleons live in trees (arboreal) and use their flexible tails to grasp shoots and branches.

A chameleon traps its prey by shooting out its sticky tongue up to a distance of 10 cm/4 in.

A CHAMELEON'S COLOR CELLS are like the dots that make up a newspaper photograph. Examine a printed photograph with a magnifying glass. Pale areas are made up of small dots of ink, like contracted pigment cells, and dark areas are composed of large dots, like expanded cells. Colors are made by mixtures of colored dots: red and yellow dots for orange, blue and red for purple, etc.

☛ *192 PIGMENTATION.*

CROWNED CRANE DAY

With its red wattles, topknot and gangling appearance the crowned crane is a faintly ridiculous bird. It lives in marshland and damp plains from the Nile valley southward through Africa. In the air it is elegant and powerful, flying in flocks in V-formation up to 2 km/1.25 mi. high and calling repeatedly with a resounding trumpet-like note.

Cranes have a mixed diet of berries, seeds and roots as well as small invertebrate animals, snakes, lizards and frogs.

All cranes have a distinctive windpipe that is coiled, convoluted and much longer than might be expected. This helps produce the loud call that travels for several miles.

The crowned crane's nest is an untidy pile of vegetation on the ground on which two pale blue eggs are laid.

LIKE A CRANE'S WINDPIPE, the tube of a trumpet creates sound of a particular note when air in it is vibrated. The trumpet player purses his lips and blows, creating vibration, and changes the note by pressing keys that vary the pipe length. A piece of tubing with a funnel stuck in one end will work like a trumpet. Like the crane, you cannot alter the pipe length so the notes you play will be limited. Experiment by tightening your lips to produce a higher note.

☞ *136 JAPANESE CRANE.*

CROCODILE DAY

Primitive but successful reptiles, crocodiles have lived on earth since the time of the dinosaurs. Large specimens of several of the thirteen species may reach 10 m/33 ft. in length. They occur throughout the tropics in shallow fresh or brackish water. The estuarine crocodile can survive far out at sea and has colonized the Pacific islands as far east as Fiji.

Newly hatched crocodiles slip though the gaps between the mother's teeth and are carried around in her mouth.

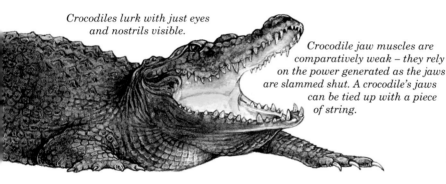

Crocodiles lurk with just eyes and nostrils visible.

Crocodile jaw muscles are comparatively weak – they rely on the power generated as the jaws are slammed shut. A crocodile's jaws can be tied up with a piece of string.

ESTUARINE CROCODILES may kill as many as 2,000 people a year. They drag their prey underwater to drown it, then store it wedged under a log until it has rotted. Because a crocodile's teeth are not adapted for cutting, its food has to be soft enough to be torn into chunks of a size to be swallowed.

In one night at the end of the World War II, crocodiles almost wiped out a Japanese infantry regiment cornered in a Burmese mangrove swamp. For years afterward, crocodiles caught in the area were found to have metal identity tags, coins and ammunition in their stomachs.

☛ *137 KOMODO DRAGON; 32 PIRANHA.*

CAMEL DAY

Domesticated, but still bad-tempered and needing great skill in their control, camels have been indispensable in allowing man to travel and survive in the desert. They are superbly adapted to life in very dry conditions, minimizing water loss and controlling body heat. They can walk up to 1,000 km/600 mi. without food or water.

Closable nostrils and two or three rows of thick eyelashes protect camels against sandstorms.

When fat stored in their humps is metabolized, it provides camels with energy and water. Camels lose heat at night and gain it by day, their temperature fluctuating by up to 6 degrees.

The African dromedary has one hump, the Central Asian bactrian camel has two.

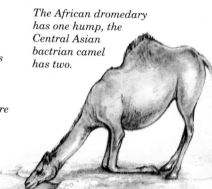

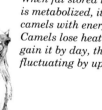

CAMELS SURVIVE hot, dry, sandy conditions in other ways, too. A thick web of skin between their two toes stops them sinking in sand. Their urine is very concentrated and their droppings are almost dry – camel drivers use them as fuel for their fires. They can lose 40 percent of their body weight in water before becoming distressed. Their red blood cells are oval, not round as in other mammals, to prevent them clumping as the blood concentrates as the camel gets drier.

☛ *78–9 DESERT.*

265

VULTURE DAY

The six vulture species of the Americas are not closely related to the fifteen species of the Old World, despite their similar appearance and habits. The two groups are placed in different families, the Old World species with the eagles and kites. Most vultures feed on carrion – often the decaying bodies of large mammals.

King vultures range from Mexico to northern Argentina. Their strangely patterned heads often feature in Indian art.

The bare faces and necks of most vultures make it easier for them to clean off the putrid mess after feeding.

Vultures circle on rising thermals of warm air looking for prey. They will congregate in the air above a dying animal or a lion kill. They may reach extraordinary heights – in 1973 a Ruppell's griffon vulture was hit by a passenger jet at 11,000 m / 37,000 ft.

THE UNPLEASANT HABITS of vultures know no bounds. Griffon vultures hunt burning ghats in India waiting for corpses not completely consumed by fire to be thrown into the river. The Egyptian vulture (below) is an indiscriminate feeder on carrion, garbage and excrement. It also picks up stones in its beak and uses them to break open ostrich and flamingo eggs.

☛ 270 EAGLE; 28–29 MOUNTAIN.

HORSESHOE CRAB DAY

Up to 60 cm/2 ft. long, slow-moving horseshoe crabs are marine and live in shallow water or on mud-flats and feed on worms and mollusks.

Horseshoe crabs are not true crabs. They are perhaps most closely related to the trilobites, extinct for 225 million years. They themselves have lived on Earth for 300 million years. Just four species survive – one in North America and three in Southeast Asia.

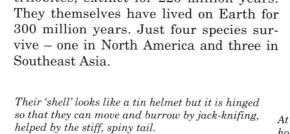

Their 'shell' looks like a tin helmet but it is hinged so that they can move and burrow by jack-knifing, helped by the stiff, spiny tail.

Underneath the shell, the mouth is surrounded by five pairs of legs and a pair of pincers. Feathery gills under the back of the shell absorb oxygen.

At spring tides horseshoe crabs gather on the shoreline in large numbers to breed. The eggs are buried in the sand. Larvae look like minute trilobites.

WHY HORSESHOE CRABS SURVIVE to the present day and trilobites became extinct is a mystery. Although related they were very different – trilobites were more like giant sea-living woodlice, well-armored and with good vision. They were successful, for we know of many hundreds of species from the fossils that have been found. They all died out in the Permian era when it was hot and dry – many shallow seas dried up and much of the dry land was desert. But the successful trilobite design lives on – 'copied' by horseshoe crab larvae, many other crustaceans and even some beetle larvae.

☞ *95 LIVING FOSSIL.*

MACAW DAY

Macaws are the largest members of the parrot family. Fifteen species live in the rainforests that stretch from Mexico to northern Argentina. Small groups fly screeching over the treetops searching for food – palm nuts, fruit and seeds – which they crack open with their powerful bills and muscular tongues.

Gold-and-blue macaws have been kept in captivity in Europe since the 16th century.

The Scarlet macaw (below) is a popular zoo bird more than 1 m / 3 ft. long.

The military macaw (right) has a bare face and blushes when it gets excited.

Macaws have zygodactyl feet – two toes forward and two back – useful for grasping branches and spherical fruits. They can use their feet almost as we use our hands, holding food and biting pieces off.

LIKE MANY PARROTS, macaws have been immensely popular as pets and as zoo and aviary birds. Unfortunately, the trade (much of it now illegal) in wild birds continues, and the populations of many parrots, already victims of habitat destruction, have declined to the point where they are endangered. Spix's macaw is now reduced in the wild to a single male: its extinction is assured unless the few birds held in captivity can be induced to breed sufficiently to reestablish a wild population.

☛ 280–1 PARROT.

LOBSTER DAY

Lobsters, like crabs and prawns, are decapod ('ten-leg') crustaceans with five pairs of walking legs. In true lobsters the first pair are claws, much larger in the male than the female. One claw is used for crushing, the other for picking and scraping. Spiny lobsters (crawfish) lack claws and their antennae are strongly spined as defense against predatory fish.

Spiny lobsters (below) make lengthy breeding migrations, traveling nose-to-tail in long chains.

True lobsters live in holes and crevices among rocks in shallow water, only venturing out to feed.

Lobsters eat small crabs, fish, worms and mollusks. They are particularly fond of dead fish which can be used to bait lobster pots, wickerwork basket traps with a funnel-shaped end.

The American lobster (bottom, left) is the heaviest crustacean, the record specimen weighing a little over 20 kg / 45 lbs.

EUROPEAN AND AMERICAN LOBSTERS (*Homarus vulgaris* and *H. americanus*) are dark blue when alive. Curiously, the pigment responsible is related to that of carrots. When a lobster is boiled the pigment breaks down and the color changes to bright red. Similar changes occur in several other crustacea, including prawns and crabs, when they are cooked. Lobsters are an expensive delicacy. The edible meat is the muscles that power the tail and legs, but the best part is the succulent claw muscle. Extracting it requires the use of pliers or a tool similar to a pair of nutcrackers.

☛ 308 CRAB; 139 SHRIMP.

EAGLE DAY

Unlike the closely related carrion-feeding vultures, eagles kill their own food or take freshly dead meat or fish. Being among the largest birds, their speed and power allow them to take prey sometimes much larger than themselves. A crowned eagle weighing about 4 kg/9 lbs. is known to have killed a 15 kg/35 lbs. bushbuck. Exceptional eyesight, grasping talons that puncture prey, and a powerful, sharp beak that tears the prey into pieces are the key to the eagle's hunting success.

Bateleur (French for 'tightrope walker') eagles eat mainly snakes.

The bald eagle (national emblem of the USA) eats fish and may rob other birds, especially ospreys, in the manner of a frigate bird.

The Philippine monkey-eating eagle (below) is one of the largest birds of prey. Fewer than 50 pairs survive in the wild.

Energy-efficiency allows eagles to eat little – a 3.5-kg / 8-lbs. golden eagle needs only 250 g / 9 oz. of meat a day. Eagles use wind currents and rising thermals of warm air for lift, moving their wings as little as possible.

IN SILHOUETTE, the eagle's primary feathers (longest and largest wing feathers) are plainly visible, as in the African fish eagle (below). Find a feather and identify the central rib (rachis) and the individual ribs (barbs). The barbs are zipped together by tiny hooks. Run your fingers down the feather to pull the barbs apart; stroke back toward the tip to relink the barles and make the feather surface intact again.

☞ 266 VULTURES; 350 KESTREL; 253 OWL.

BAT DAY

Bats or Chiroptera ('hand-wings') are the only flying mammals. Of 970 species, 170 are Megachiroptera – big fruitbats – and 800 are Microchiroptera – smaller insectivorous bats. A bat's wing is formed of fine double-layered skin stretched between the greatly lengthened fingers and forearm.

Microchiroptera are able to hunt insects in pitch darkness but flying foxes need some light to navigate safely.

Bats navigate by beaming blips of ultrasound – so high pitched we cannot hear it – at their surroundings. Grotesque facial features and large ears focus the echoes that tell a bat the shape and distance of objects nearby.

South American vampire bats use razor-sharp teeth to break the skin of sleeping cattle to suck their blood.

BATS ARE DECLINING in many areas, so carry out a survey in your area. Look for bats emerging from old buildings and church roofs at twilight and survey likely hunting grounds, like pond margins and woodland edges. Contact local wildlife organizations, which often survey local bat populations with electronic detectors.

Fruit bats (above) have large, flat-crowned grinding teeth and strong jaws. Fisherman bats (left) snatch fish from the surface of ponds and rivers in South America.

☛ *104–5 NOCTURNAL ANIMALS.*

CITRUS DAY

Lemons, oranges, limes, mandarins, kumquats, pomelos and grapefruit are all citrus fruits. Citric acid gives them all their characteristic sharp flavor. The Chinese first cultivated citrus 4,000 years ago. Now we consume 40 million tons of oranges each year, half of that total as orange juice.

Citrus fruits are rich in vitamin C. Americans nicknamed British sailors 'limeys' because they were given lime juice to combat scurvy, a disease caused by vitamin C deficiency.

Kumquats (top) are not strictly citrus but the closely related fortunella: they are often made into preserves, pickles, or kumquat liqueur.

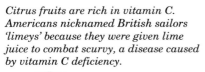

The zest or rind of a citrus fruit contains a spicy oil; that from the bergamot is widely used in perfume making.

MAKE YOUR OWN fresh orange juice. Slice two thin-skinned oranges. Put two or three neat slices to one side and put the rest into a food blender with two or three tablespoons of sugar and 750 ml/3 cups of water. Run the blender at maximum speed for 10–15 seconds. Strain the juice through a sieve and serve with ice in a glass decorated with an orange slice.

Lemonade can be made the same way, but use less fruit and more water. Too much rind and pith makes the drink bitter. It may be necessary to discard some or all of the lemon skin.

☛ 237 EXOTIC FRUIT.

LOCUST
(GRASSHOPPER) DAY

Grasshoppers belong to an order called the Orthoptera, a name derived from the Greek *orthos* (straight) and *pteron* (wing), describing the way in which the wings lie along the body at rest. The alternative name for their order is the Saltatoria, derived from the Latin *saltare* (to leap) and referring to their enlarged hind legs, modified for jumping.

Grasshoppers are herbivores, biting pieces from leaves with their large jaws (above). The migratory, swarming behavior of locusts (seen laying eggs below) has made them notorious destroyers of crops since Biblical times. Locust swarms are sometimes so large that they can be tracked with radar.

Some orthopterans are wingless, but in all species the wings develop gradually, enlarging every time the nymph molts.

ADULT GRASSHOPPERS communicate by sound, produced in a process called stridulation which involves rapidly dragging pegs on the hind legs over the horny forewings. Sound is detected in an ear, or tympanum, located on the abdomen just forward of the hind leg. Catch some grasshoppers, keep them in airy containers in a sunny place, and listen to their song. Each species has its own distinctive pattern of stridulation and females will respond only to calls of males of their own kind.

☞ 347 BUG.

DUCKBILLED PLATYPUS
DAY

The platypus's bill is soft, not hard as widely believed, and is very sensitive. It is used to probe for prey under stones in streams and rivers.

The Australian duckbilled platypus and echidna are the only mammals that lay eggs – they are monotremes. The platypus lives in a burrow near water. It swims well using its webbed feet and otter-like tail, catching crayfish, shellfish and insect larvae. Young platypus have teeth, which are lost as the bill develops.

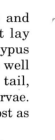

The female seals herself into her nest-burrow before laying and incubating two soft-shelled eggs. These hatch in ten days but it is six months before the young can look after themselves.

The eye and ear lie in a deep fold of skin which is closed while the platypus is under water. Males defend themselves with poisonous, horny spurs on their hind legs, so must be handled with thick gloves.

MAMMALS ARE DIVIDED into three groups – monotremes, marsupials (pouched mammals such as kangaroos) and placental mammals (the majority of mammals, including ourselves). All suckle their young, but placentals develop theirs internally to an advanced stage. Marsupials and monotremes rear their young, born or hatched as tiny embryos, in a pouch or held against the mammary glands by the mother's tail (as with the platypus).

☛ 305 MARSUPIAL.

NAUTILUS DAY

We use the name nautilus for two very different groups of cephalopod mollusks. Cephalopods include nautilus, cuttlefish, squid and octopus. Unlike other mollusks, cephalopods are highly mobile and sophisticated, with good vision, sense of smell and touch. They are the most intelligent invertebrates, with learning and memory capacity.

The paper nautilus or argonaut is not a true nautilus but a female octopus. Horny flaps on her rear arms form a shell that protects her and her eggs.

Pearly nautiluses are found in the Indian and Pacific oceans at depths down to 600 m / 2,000 ft. They never surface, and the first living examples were observed (by scuba divers off New Caledonia) only 25 years ago.

Air chambers provide the nautilus with buoyancy. The pores allow air to move in and out to compensate for changes in pressure with depth.

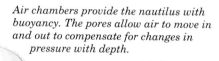

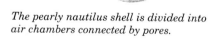

The pearly nautilus shell is divided into air chambers connected by pores.

THE PEARLY NAUTILUS is the last cephalopod with a permanent external shell. Nautiloids first appeared on earth at the end of the Cambrian period, 520 million years ago, and evolved numerous genera and species. They were soon overtaken by an even more successful cephalopod group, the ammonoids (ammonites), with several thousand species including some spectacularly large predators with shells more than 1 m/3 ft. across. Common as fossils, ammonoids became extinct 70 million years ago; a few nautiloids survived.

☛ *228 CUTTLEFISH AND SQUID; 30 OCTOPUS.*

BIRD OF PARADISE DAY

Ferdinand Magellan brought the first bird of paradise skins to Europe in 1522, but the first living specimens were brought to England in 1862, by Alfred Russel Wallace. By the 1890s 50,000 birds per year were killed for hat feathers, a slaughter that was only halted in the 1920s when trade in feathers and skins was prohibited.

The riflebird (below) has a call like a ricocheting rifle bullet.

THERE ARE 43 SPECIES of bird of paradise, ranging from New Guinea to northeastern Australia. Male courtship behavior is as extraordinary as their plumage. The magnificent bird of paradise (top left) strips leaves from shrubs in a 5 m/16 ft. radius before it begins its display. Raggiana's bird of paradise (right) congregate in leks and a tree full of displaying males is one of the most breathtaking sights in ornithology.

☛ 151 PEACOCK; 83 LYREBIRD; 209 BOWER-BIRD.

SHREW DAY

Shrews are very small and very active, needing enormous amounts of energy to keep going. The Etruscan or Savi's pygmy shrew is the smallest mammal, weighing 2 g/0.07 oz. Most shrews eat continuously, consuming more than their own weight of insects, worms and seeds each day. When food is in short supply, they sometimes become cannibals.

Shrews need to feed continuously. They rest for only brief periods and can starve to death in two hours.

Cats won't eat shrews because they smell bitter and contain venom. But owls manage them perfectly well.

Shrews are quarrelsome, squeaking loudly and fighting when they meet to gain territory for their all-important food supply. Most shrew confrontations involve squeaking rather than physical aggression.

Shrews are found everywhere except the polar regions, South America and Australasia.

THE SHREW'S PROBLEM is that it is so small. Small objects radiate heat faster than large ones, because they have proportionately more surface area relative to their volume. So small shrews needs proportionately more food to fuel their metabolism than larger mammals.

Fill a large and a small glass with hot water. See how long each takes to cool, by monitoring their temperatures with a thermometer. If you increase the surface area of a hot object, it cools more quickly – try the experiment with two scoops of hot mashed potato, by flattening one out. The flat one cools faster.

☛ 341 SMALLEST ANIMAL.

PELICAN DAY

The pelican's bill isn't used to store food but forms a scoop-net when it is fishing. The bones of the lower bill bow outwards and the great pouch beneath the bill instantly takes in up to 3 gallons (nearly 15 litres) of water. The pelican drains the water out of its bill and swallows any fish left behind. All seven species feed in fresh or salt water.

The Spanish for pelican is 'alcatraz' – the notorious prison in San Francisco Bay was named after the pelicans that used to breed on the island.

Brown pelicans are the only pelicans to fish by diving from the air – all the other five species fish while swimming.

The brown pelican (below) breeds on the American coasts and is the state bird of Louisiana. It often scavenges around fishing piers and boats.

WHITE PELICANS FISH in teams on the salty lakes of central Africa. They swim in crescent formation towards the shore, beating their wings on the water, and closing in to trap the fish. When the fish are encircled the pelicans race into the center and scoop up the fish.

Pelicans are among the heaviest flying birds, but are graceful once airborne, flying in long lines or V-formations.

☛ *93 BEAK.*

278

POLAR BEAR DAY

Polar bears are huge, powerful Arctic carnivores that range over most of the frozen Arctic Ocean, and they have been known to travel surprisingly far out to sea with the pack ice. In summer they may be found on dry land on the coasts of Alaska, Canada, Greenland and Russia.

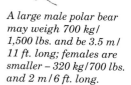

A large male polar bear may weigh 700 kg / 1,500 lbs. and be 3.5 m / 11 ft. long; females are smaller – 320 kg / 700 lbs. and 2 m / 6 ft. long.

The mother stays with the cubs in the den for 4–5 months, suckling them on rich milk, before breaking out of the den and taking them on their first hunt.

Cubs, usually twins, are born in midwinter in a den excavated in a snowdrift.

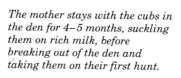

Bears ambush seals, the mainstay of their diet, at their breathing holes in the ice, scooping them from the water with a single bone-shattering blow from their paw.

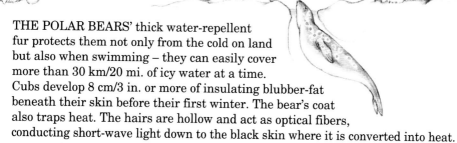

THE POLAR BEARS' thick water-repellent fur protects them not only from the cold on land but also when swimming – they can easily cover more than 30 km/20 mi. of icy water at a time. Cubs develop 8 cm/3 in. or more of insulating blubber-fat beneath their skin before their first winter. The bear's coat also traps heat. The hairs are hollow and act as optical fibers, conducting short-wave light down to the black skin where it is converted into heat.

➤ 89 BLACK-BEAR; 2 SEAL.

PARROT DAY

Members of the parrot family, Psittacidae, are found throughout the world's tropics, and include some of the gaudiest of birds. The group includes cockatoos, cockatiels, lories, lorikeets, macaws, lovebirds and parakeets. They all have large heads, short necks, strongly down-curved hooked bills and zygodactyl feet. The nocturnal kakapo of New Zealand is the only flightless species.

A 'galah' in Australian slang is a joker. It's also an acrobatic pink and gray parrot common around towns. Galahs for some unknown reason dislike pink objects and will selectively destroy all the pink plastic clothespins in a neighborhood leaving the other colors unmolested.

The New Zealand kea is a large, inquisitive and easily approached parrot which is attracted to human settlements. It has acquired a reputation, some say unjustly, for killing sheep by landing on their backs and digging out fat from around their kidneys. Its usual diet is plant material and carrion.

All 315 species of parrot lay very round, white glossy eggs. Most species nest in tree-holes but some Australian parrots dig a nest-hole in a termite mound. Argentinian gray-breasted parakeets build enormous colonial nests in the branches of a tree and add to it year after year. Eventually it gets too big and comes crashing down.

Lovebirds (extreme right) come from Africa and Madagascar. Caged birds really do seem to like each other's company, sitting snuggled up together. In the wild, lovebirds travel about in large flocks and can damage crops.

PARROTS AND THEIR RELATIVES are renowned for their ability to talk, but they themselves haven't the slightest idea what they are saying. They learn best when young, mimicking the sounds they hear most often. These may be phrases – 'Who's a pretty boy, then?', snatches of songs or, most unfortunately for the owner, the sound of a telephone, a power drill or a lavatory being flushed. Most parrots have a small repertoire, but the record holder had a 'vocabulary' of nearly 1,000 words.

☛ *268 MACAW.*

281

CAVE ANIMAL DAY

Caves provide a habitat for two classes of animals: those that live and breed there permanently, without ever venturing into the outside world, and those that shelter in caves but feed in the surrounding landscape. Many species that have become adapted to a permanently subterranean existence have lost the power of vision and rely on scent and touch to survive in the darkness.

In a world of complete darkness, where there is no vision, colors are redundant and cave salamanders are white, like many of the creatures that share their habitat.

The cave swiftlet uses caverns for shelter and as a nest site, but spends much of its life hawking for insects over the coconut groves and beaches of Southeast Asia. Its nest is constructed from coagulated saliva, glued to the wall of the cave, and is the basic ingredient of the famous bird's nest soup. In swiftlet breeding areas there is a carefully regulated industry, where teams of collectors ascend rickety bamboo scaffolding to harvest the nests from cave ceilings. The number that can be collected is controlled, to ensure the continuity of this valuable local resource.

The exceptionally long antennae of cave crickets allow them to form a tactile picture of the world around them.

CLIFFS are the natural nest site of swifts in temperate regions but they have adapted to cohabiting with man by building nests under the eaves of houses. In spring, watch the way that common swifts construct nests with straw, grass and feathers, cemented to the eaves with saliva.

☛ 145 CAVE; 349 SALAMANDER; 88 NEST; 192 PIGMENTATION.

DEEP-SEA DAY

Three kilometers/2 mi. below the ocean surface, where the great plates that form the Earth's crust collide, there are constant volcanic eruptions. While monitoring these boiling hydrothermal vents near the Galapagos Islands in 1977, the American deep-sea research ship *Alvin* found giant tube worms, large clams and blind crabs that were completely new to science.

Giant clams (above) and mussels (right) are filter feeders, which live on the bacterial 'soup' that develops in these hot, mineral-rich waters. Blind white crabs (above) are detritus feeders. They have infrared sensors that allow them to 'see' their surroundings in the inky blackness of the ocean floor.

Riftia pachyptila, *the giant tube worm (right), is 3.5 m / 11.5 ft. long and so different from any other known life form that biologists have had to invent a new phylum for it.*

DEEP-SEA HYDROTHERMAL vent communities are based on energy captured by sulphur-metabolizing bacteria, rather than energy harvested by plants from sunlight. Some biologists believe that life itself may have evolved in similar environments. The unique character of these deep-sea communities is typified by *Riftia*, which has no mouth or gut, but depends entirely for its nutrition on symbiotic bacteria which live within its tissues.

☛ 179 ABYSSAL FISH; 165 MARINE WORM.

MOLE DAY

Young are born in a nest tunnel lined with grass and leaves. The mother immobilizes worms by biting their heads and stores them, still alive, nearby.

Small but powerful, the 100-g/3.5-oz. European mole can move 4–5 kg/9–11 lbs. of earth in five minutes as it burrows just beneath the soil surface, throwing up molehills at it goes. Almost completely blind and deaf, it relies on its sensitive snout to detect vibration, especially that of a worm breaking into its tunnel.

Extra lobes enhance the sensitivity of the star-nosed mole's snout. This species has functional eyes and often hunts on the surface. It stores fat in its swollen tail.

Moles can lift 20 times their own weight of soil with their powerful front paws. Moles' soft fur can be brushed with equal ease in all directions, making it easy for them to move backward and forward along narrow tunnels.

EARTHWORMS are remarkably common and moles rarely go hungry. You can gauge the numbers of earthworms by marking out a measured area, say 1 m/1 yd. square, and driving the worms to the surface by the following method. Water the soil and vibrate it by stamping or by sticking in a pitch fork and rocking it from side to side. Keep adding water and vibrating the soil. Most worms will emerge within twenty minutes. Count them and then calculate the number of worms in the whole garden.

☛ 54–5 UNDERGROUND.

Earthworms form 90 percent of the mole's diet.

EPIDEMIC DAY

Epidemics occur when parasitic or pathogenic biological organisms spread rapidly in their hosts and victims, causing high levels of infection and death. The Irish potato famine of 1845–47 was caused by an epidemic of potato blight fungus, *Phytophthora infestans*, which destroyed the crop that was the staple food of the rural poor; as a result, about a million Irish people starved to death and over a million more emigrated to America.

Potato blight is still a major pest of the crop (left), but modern fungicides and varieties with some resistance to the disease now keep it in check. In the developed world synthetic agrochemicals now largely prevent epidemics of plant diseases like smut fungi on cereals (bottom left), but in poor countries pests and diseases still destroy crops on a large scale.

LOOK FOR THE CHARACTERISTIC tunnels of elm bark beetles under the flaking bark of dead elm trees. This insect transmits Dutch elm disease, one of the most spectacular plant epidemics of recent years. A mutant, virulent form of the fungus *Ceratocystis ulmi*, carried from tree to tree by the beetles, blocks the water-conducting tissue in trunks, so that foliage turns yellow and trees die within about three years. The epidemic has virtually wiped out hedgerow elms in Britain, changing the rural landscape.

☛ 49 LICE; 188 FLEA; 184 RAT.

285

BIOLUMINESCENCE DAY

Certain species of fungi, sponges, corals, algae, hydroids, marine worms, crustaceans, mollusks and insects emit light after dark – a phenomenon known as bioluminescence. Their eerie glows and pulsating flashes of light are produced when a chemical in their tissues called luciferin is broken down by an enzyme called luciferase.

The pulses of light emitted from below a firefly's tail are a mate recognition device, allowing the sexes to meet after dark. Each species has a unique signal code.

Many deep-sea fish emit light in the darkness of the abyss. Each species has a unique pattern of lights, suggesting that they might aid mate recognition.

Bioluminescent fungi have been known since the time of Aristotle and are most common in rotting logs.

Glowworms, like fireflies, are beetles. People once kept them in jars, so that they could read by their dim, greenish-yellow light.

THE BEST PLACES TO LOOK for bioluminescence are in meadows, on warm evenings in summer, when glowworms congregate, and along the seashore in summer, when thousands of planktonic bioluminescent protozoans and algae emit flashes of light when waves break on the shore.

You can use artificial luminescence to help investigate the nocturnal behavior of animals. Mark the shells of large snails with coded blobs of luminous paint, then follow them by looking for their glow after dark in the moonlight.

☞ 179 ABYSSAL FISH; 11 FUNGI; 256–7 BEETLES.

LEECH DAY

Leeches detect light, heat and movement using receptor organs looking like tiny black dots on either side of the head (above). Receptors on the body surface detect body odors and blood.

There are 650 species of marine, freshwater and land-dwelling leeches, but land leeches occur only in Southeast Asia and Australia where hikers in the jungle are only too aware of them. Leeches and their bites can rarely be felt, but after the leech has dropped off the wound continues to bleed. A spreading patch of blood on clothing is often the first indication that a victim has been bitten.

Alerted to the presence of prey, a leech stretches out, rears up, and waves from side to side, waiting for contact. Some species drop on their victims from overhanging foliage.

Leeches are segmented worms, related to earthworms. All have 34 segments and are hermaphrodites – both male and female. They move by looping, using the suckers on the tail and surrounding the mouth to hold onto a surface.

An Australian tiger leech can drink ten times its own weight of blood.

FOR HUNDREDS OF YEARS leeches have been used to treat a wide range of diseases, for it was thought that 'bad blood' was the cause of disease and that removing it assisted recovery. During the height of popularity of this treatment in the early 19th century, France imported 500 million leeches in 18 years, each selling for today's equivalent of about $25. Even in the 1920s boxers used leeches to reduce the swelling around black eyes. Now leeches are making a medical comeback. They are farmed for their saliva which contains a compound called hirudin that stops blood clotting.

☛ 325 PARASITE; 327 TAPEWORM; 271 BAT.

PLANTS THAT MOVE DAY

Plants are not as static as they might seem. If they are filmed by time-lapse photography, the resulting film shows that their leaves, flowers and stems are constantly moving and responding to their surroundings. Some movements are rapid. The leaves of the sensitive plant *Mimosa pudica* (right) collapse when they are touched. Electrical stimuli cause cells at the base of each leaflet to lose water, so the whole leaf seems to wilt suddenly.

Wood sorrel and many other Oxalis *species display sleep movements, where their leaves fold at night.* Oxalis *and* Impatiens *species (right) have exploding fruits, and will detonate at the slightest touch.*

Scarlet pimpernel (left) has flowers that close in dull or cold weather, which may protect the pollen.

THERE ARE THREE MAIN TYPES of plant movements. Growth is slow and the result of new cell formation and enlargement. Tropic movements are a quick response to a directional stimulus, like light. Put a pot of seedlings in a darkened box, where light can enter through a narrow slit, and they will all bend toward the light – positive phototropism. Coiling of bindweed stems (right) is a nastic movement, caused by faster cell growth in the part of the stem that is not in contact with its support.

☛ 186 CARNIVOROUS PLANTS.

CAMOUFLAGE DAY

Camouflage is a key factor in the interaction between predators and prey. The stripes of a stalking tiger (below left) conceal it in the light and shadow of long grass, while the spots on the coat of a young fawn (below right) hide it in dappled sunlight on the edge of woodlands.

Ptarmigans, and several other birds that live in cold climates, develop white winter plumage that makes them almost invisible in a frozen landscape.

PREDATORY CRAB SPIDERS (above) and bottom-living plaice (top left) change color to match their surroundings, making their camouflage more effective against varied backgrounds. Successful camouflage often depends on appropriate behavior patterns; the marbled frogmouth (left) aligns itself along branches, to resemble a broken branch. When watching wildlife, learn from nature: camouflage yourself with colors that blend into the natural surroundings and avoid revealing your silhouette against the skyline. Construct a hide so that you can watch wary animals without disturbing them.

☛ *330 CRYPSIS; 192 PIGMENTATION; 43 SNOW.*

289

MOTH DAY

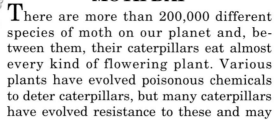

There are more than 200,000 different species of moth on our planet and, between them, their caterpillars eat almost every kind of flowering plant. Various plants have evolved poisonous chemicals to deter caterpillars, but many caterpillars have evolved resistance to these and may even recycle the chemicals.

The ermine moth (above) folds its wings at rest, but the feathery wings of the plume moth (right) are held at right angles to the body. Plume moths are weak fliers, and often settle on lighted windows at night.

Male footman moths (above) use plant poisons they ate as caterpillars as a perfume to attract females.

Burnet moths are day-flyers. Their bright colors warn birds not to attack them – they contain cyanide.

Night-flying tiger-moths can make high-pitched squeaks to 'jam' bats' radar.

MOTHS, LIKE BUTTERFLIES, can see ultraviolet light well but red poorly. Use a flashlight covered with red cellophane to watch moths feeding on flowers at night. Watch for the proboscis, or tongue, being unrolled to suck up nectar. Make a moth feeding station by mixing two large spoonfuls of molasses with one large spoonful of beer, painting the mixture as a stripe on a tree trunk. Choose dry summer weather and visit the bait after dark. Some moths will return to feed at the same time every night and become regular visitors.

☛ 306–7 BUTTERFLY.

RUBBER DAY

The discovery of the properties of the sap or latex of the Brazilian rubber tree *Hevea brasiliensis* roughly coincided with the invention of the pneumatic tire and the development of the internal combustion engine. Enormous demand for rubber for vehicle tires prompted its introduction as a plantation crop into many tropical countries. It was Malaya's major export commodity by 1940.

Rubber trees are grown in nurseries from rubber-nuts, shiny purple seeds with a squiggly pattern unique to each seed. Each fruit contains three nuts.

The tapper uses a curved knife to cut a broad, V-shaped slit in the bark. Latex runs down the cut and is channeled by a short metal gutter into a collecting cup strapped to the trunk.

Seedlings are planted out when about 1 m / 3 ft. tall. After 10 years the tree is mature enough to be tapped for the first time.

THE RUBBER INDUSTRY in the Far East owes much to Nathaniel Ward, inventor of a mini-greenhouse known as a Wardian Case (below). Rubber seeds have a short life span; only 2,800 of 70,000 rubber seeds sent to Kew Gardens from Brazil in 1877 survived the long sea journey. These had to be germinated before being sent on to Malaya by fast steamship inside Wardian Cases, safe from sudden temperature changes and salt spray.

☛ *44 TEA; 99 COFFEE; 309 SUGAR.*

OTTER DAY

Lively, energetic and playful, otters are perfectly adapted to aquatic life. Their underfur is short and waterproof, protected by longer guard-hairs. Their toes are webbed to assist in swimming and their ears are closable as they dive. They begin hunting at sunset for fish, amphibians and crayfish in the water, and for almost any small mammal or invertebrate on land.

Whiskers, sensitive to vibration, help otters to find their prey under water.

The unusual upright posture of the otter is its 'lookout' pose – like that of a prairie-dog. It is a secretive animal, and rarely seen, but its five-toed, webbed feet leave distinctive footprints.

A Californian sea-otter will pick up a stone, float on its back, and use the stone to smash open shellfish against its chest. This species was hunted to the brink of extinction in the late 19th century, but was saved by legal protection.

ALTHOUGH THE EURASIAN or common otter occurs all the way from Britain to Sumatra and Java, it is now rare in many places. Hunting and river pollution have caused its populations to decline. The wake of boats eroding the banks of waterways has made it impossible for the otter to build safe nest-burrows or holts on many rivers, as has the tidying and landscaping of river banks to make them more attractive for anglers.

Ring of Bright Water, by Gavin Maxwell, is a true story about otters and their lives, and how they took over the life of its author.

☛ 329 RIVERBANK.

MIMICRY DAY

The 1,000 species of clearwing moths all mimic bees or wasps. Sesia vespiformis is a mimic of hornets in Europe and can even flex its abdomen, as if about to sting.

Mimicry is found particularly frequently in insects and most commonly occurs when a harmless species evolves to look like a poisonous or well-defended species. In this way the harmless species benefits from the reputation of its model, the harmful species. Predators avoid the harmless and edible species in the belief that it is the harmful or poisonous species.

Harmless hover flies mimic bees and wasps in having black- and yellow-banded abdomens and a similar hovering flight.

Different forms of the African swallowtail butterfly Papilio dardanus *(left) mimic different species of danaid butterflies (right), which contain alkaloids poisonous to birds.*

MIMICRY WAS FIRST RECOGNIZED by the naturalist Henry Bates in the 1850s and typical mimicry, the harmless mimicking the harmful, is called Batesian mimicry. Later it was realized that there was also an advantage to harmful organisms in looking similar – predators had less to remember – and, indeed, there are numerous examples of this, termed Mullerian mimicry. In practice, the warning-colored stripes of bees and wasps (Mullerian mimicry) are often copied by Batesian mimics, like clearwing moths and hover flies.

☞ 289 CAMOUFLAGE.

PLANTS SURVIVING WINTER DAY

The freezing temperatures of winter kill foliage and damage the growing tips of plants, so most species have evolved strategies for winter survival. Most broad-leaved trees in temperate climates shed their leaves as the day length shortens in autumn and protect delicate growing points inside buds, that are sheathed in protective scales (left).

Parsely piert (right) is a winter annual, germinating in autumn and overwintering as a seedling, which makes rapid growth in spring. Most annuals overwinter as seeds.

*The perennial bluebell (right) stores starch in its bulb during spring, before the tree canopy shades its leaves.
The leaves die back in summer, leaving a bulb that lies dormant until the following spring.*

The evergreen trailing azalea (bottom left) produces a shrubby mat of tough leaves that are adapted to survive low temperatures in alpine regions.

MANY PLANTS have built-in dormancy mechanisms, which prevent their buds bursting in mild periods during the depths of winter. If you cut some beech twigs in midwinter and keep them in water in a warm place, they will not open. But cut some in early March and you will find that their buds will open indoors. A dormancy chemical, which must be destroyed by a prolonged series of winter frosts, prevents premature bud burst. Many seeds, like those of cowslips, have a similar dormancy mechanism.

☛ *154–5 HIBERNATION.*

294

EGGS DAY

Eggs are the key to the conquest of the land by the vertebrates – animals with backbones. The first vertebrates to venture onto dry land were the amphibians, but they had to return to water to breed for their eggs were like those of fish – protected by just a layer of jelly, and fertilized in water by the male swimming above the eggs and releasing sperm.

Reptiles' eggs (top right) are fertilized internally – while still in the female. They contain a food supply, and their shell resists desiccation.

Mammals fertilize their eggs internally, retain the young to an advanced stage of development before birth, then feed them after they are born.

Frogs and toads are typical amphibians, returning to fresh water to lay small eggs from which tadpoles hatch.

REPTILES WERE THE FIRST VERTEBRATES to escape from needing water to reproduce. By packaging their eggs in a waterproof protective shell with a food supply, they allow the young to develop to a stage where they can be independent and terrestrial as soon as they hatch. Thus the reptiles have a distinct advantage over the amphibians. But the eggs are vulnerable to desiccation and predation. Mammals have improved on this pattern, retaining the young internally and feeding them through a link to the mother's blood supply – the placenta. Then after birth, the young are suckled.

☛ 4–5 FROG AND TOAD; 152 MOUTHBROODING.

AUSTRALIAN PLANTS DAY

Australia is an enormous continent with a wide range of habitats, from alpine to desert and rainforest. Its long geographical isolation from the other continental land-masses and its extremes of habitat types have combined to give it a range of fascinating plants found nowhere else on Earth.

The grass tree Xanthorrhoea *is a fire-resistant member of the lily family that thrives in arid areas. Some species live for more than 350 years and do not flower until they are 200 years old.*

Banksias are named after Sir Joseph Banks, the botanist who explored Australia with Captain Cook. Aborigines eat banksia nectar and the flowers are pollinated by honey possums.

*Sturt's desert pea (*Clianthus formosus*) grows in arid parts of Western Australia. Its spectacular, claw-shaped flowers make it a popular ornamental plant.*

LIKE MANY ISLANDS, Australia has a large number of endemic species that occur nowhere else on Earth. Large tracts of the continent are arid and subject to bush fires. Several species are adapted to regular burning: the fruits of *Banksia ornata* only disperse their seeds after they have been scorched by flames, and *Xanthorrhoea* is stimulated to bloom by fire, often producing flower spikes from blackened stumps.

☛ 141 GUM TREE; 75 KOALA.

CAPYBARA DAY

Capybaras are the world's biggest rodents, the size of a sheep and weighing up to 65 kg/145 lbs. They live in groups of 10–20 individuals close to slow-flowing waterways in South America. At dawn and dusk they wallow in the water and feed on aquatic vegetation, rather like small hippopotamuses.

The characteristic deep muzzle of the capybara accommodates the continuously growing long cheek teeth used to grind tough vegetation. Overlapping incisor teeth grow continuously and grind against each other to maintain sharp cutting edges for gnawing.

Capybaras give birth to 2–8 young, which quickly become independent but stay within family groups.

LIKE THEIR CLOSE RELATIVE, the guinea pig, capybaras are good to eat and are hunted by country people in South America. Capybara-hunts are uncomfortable and can be dangerous – shooting and retrieving capybaras in treacherous swampy ground is bad enough, but a wounded capybara will head straight for the water where its blood attracts piranhas. Experienced capybara-hunters are often scarred by piranhas with which they have to fight for their catch.

☛ *32 PIRANHA; 184 RAT; 57 RABBIT.*

DRUG DAY

The narcotic properties of plants must have been discovered in prehistoric times, when people learned by trial and error to identify edible plants. Many species contain chemical compounds that affect the nervous system and brain. Tobacco (right) contains the alkaloid nicotine, a mild stimulant that has been smoked since the reign of James I, when it was first brought to Europe from North America. It is now known to be a major cause of lung cancer, and its toxic properties can be gauged from the fact that nicotine is an effective and widely used insecticide.

Thornapple has been used as a source of hallucinogens since the time of the Aztecs, but Mexican women leave their crying babies under its flowers, whose heady fragrance sends them to sleep.

THE ADDICTIVE PROPERTIES of narcotic plants have earned them a grim reputation, but some species have been grown for legitimate purposes at various times in history. Cannabis (top left) has stems which contain long, tough fibers and was once grown on a large scale for rope making. The rigging of most Elizabethan ships was made from cannabis hemp. Coca (left) the source of highly addictive cocaine, was an ingredient of soft drinks until the late 19th century, when its dangerous properties were recognized. It is still used as a local anaesthetic for dental surgery.

☛ 332–3 MEDICINAL PLANTS; 44 TEA; 99 COFFEE.

SWAN DAY

Five of the world's seven swan species are pure white birds of the Northern Hemisphere, breeding in the far north and migrating south for the winter. The black-necked swan is a native of southern South America while the black swan originated in Australia and Tasmania and has now been introduced into New Zealand.

Mute swans carry their chicks, or cygnets, on their backs when they are young.

Swans mate for life and return to the same nest site each year to build an enormous nest of dry vegetation in which the female lays 5–8 greenish white eggs.

The Dutch discovered Black swans in Western Australia in 1697 – the first specimens seen in Europe caused amazement.

Drooping heads are a symptom of partial paralysis, caused by ingesting lead shot discarded by anglers. Death soon follows.

MUTE SWANS IN BRITAIN have been the property of the Crown since the 12th century and are strictly protected. A royal licence is needed to hunt, capture or keep swans. But royal protection cannot help against everyday hazards. Swans weigh about 15 kg/33 lbs., and once airborne are not very maneuverable. Many die in collisions with overhead power lines. Swans feed on aquatic vegetation and are at risk from water pollution. Many died in Britain from ingesting lead fishing weights, which are now banned.

☛ 185 GOOSE; 336 DUCK.

PEPPER DAY

We use the word 'pepper' for two entirely different plants. Originally from South America, capsicum (left) is a member of the nightshade family, Solanaceae, and gives us sweet peppers (capsicums) and hot peppers (chilies). Originally Indian, piper (right) is a member of the Piperaceae and gives us black and white pepper (peppercorns).

Cayenne pepper is dried, powdered hot chili pepper (above and right).

Pepper is a climbing vine. The small green fruits turn red when ripe and are dried to make black peppercorns. If they are first soaked and the outer pulp removed, they become the milder white peppercorns.

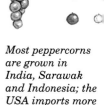

Most peppercorns are grown in India, Sarawak and Indonesia; the USA imports more than a third of the world's crop.

Sweet peppers are mild; dried and ground they become paprika, used in Hungarian cookery.

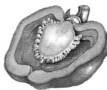

CENTURIES OF BREEDING by man has involved the deliberate selection of hot varieties of chili. Plants grown from seeds from one chili might have produced a few hotter-flavored offspring, so their seeds were used for the next crop. Crossbreeding and selecting like this, to obtain and enhance desirable characteristics, mimics natural selection and is the process that has given rise to most of the varieties of domestic animals and cultivated plants that we see today.

☛ 198 SPICES; 317 SCENT AND TASTE.

PENGUIN DAY

The fifteen species of the penguin family live on the fringes of the Antarctic Ocean and one species breeds as far north as the Galapagos Islands. Incapable of flight, their reduced wings and specially adapted feet are powerful flippers and they can swim at up to 35 kph/22 mph. But traces of their flying ancestors remain – the now useless keel on their breast-bone was once the attachment for flight muscles.

Juvenile emperors get fed only every ten days. They huddle together for warmth awaiting a parent's return with food from the sea.

Rockhopper penguins live on the Falklands and other subantarctic islands. Their name derives from their fearless jumping from rocks as they travel across rough terrain.

Emperor penguins live on Antarctica itself. They don't make nests; the 1.3-m / 4.25-ft. tall male incubates the egg on the top of his feet where they are covered by a thick fold of skin – the incubation pouch.

THE BREEDING of the emperor penguin is an epic of avian endurance. Females lay a single egg in May and pass it to their mate, before leaving for the sea to feed. He incubates the egg through the Antarctic winter, battered by 200-kph/125-mph winds and enduring temperatures of –30°C/–22°F for two months, with the egg balanced on his feet. The chick hatches just before the female returns and the starving male returns to the sea, 90 km/55 mi. away, to feed. Parents feed the chick until November, when it makes the long journey to the ocean, to dive for fish and squid during the brief Antarctic summer.

☛ *10 FLIGHTLESS BIRDS.*

COCONUT DAY

Coconut palms may be 30 m/100 ft. tall. The wood is used for building and the leaves for thatch and for weaving into mats and baskets. The fruit, the coconut, contains a refreshing liquid when green. Ripe, it yields the hard, sweet white meat. The fiber of the husk (coir) is used to make mats, ropes and brushes. A new use has recently been found for coir, as a horticultural compost, replacing peat.

Coconuts can float in the sea and germinate successfully when thrown ashore by storms.

Coconut meat can be eaten fresh. Dried, it becomes copra, a source of valuable vegetable oil.

Working inward, there are four layers to a coconut - rind, husk, shell and meat. Husk removed (below, left) the shell has three soft eyes at one end. Old husks and shells (below, right) are breeding pools for mosquitoes.

TAKE A COCONUT and get help to open it neatly. Use a hacksaw to saw a line around the circumference of the shell, then break it by laying a knife along the saw cut and tapping the back of the knife sharply with a hammer. Hang up the end of the nut with the eyes for the birds – blue tits love coconut. Eat the meat from the other half yourself then dry the half-shell. Sandpaper the inside and outside to a fine gloss. Be patient – it takes a long time as coconut shell is one of the hardest plant substances known. Polish with a little cooking oil to bring up the color of your traditional Polynesian drinking bowl.

☛ 322 PEAT BOGS; 157 SEEDLING.

YUCCA MOTH DAY

Yuccas and agaves (Agavaceae) are desert plants from North and Central America with rosettes of large, tough, sword-shaped leaves. They are unusual in having a specific pollinator, so specific that a particular yucca species is pollinated by usually only one pollinator species. The pollinators are small white, gray or spotted moths belonging to the family Prodoxidae, all 30 species of which pollinate Agavaceae.

The yucca moth, Tegeticula yuccasella, does not feed during its short life, and collects pollen only for pollinating the yucca flower.

Yuccas flower irregularly, producing a spectacularly tall flower-spike. Bats visit the flowers for nectar, and female moths collect pollen, rolling it into a ball beneath their tongues.

The female moth flies to another yucca flower, crawls to the bottom and pierces the ovary with its sharp ovipositor, laying several eggs. Then it climbs the stamen and presses the pollen ball onto the stigma.

THE RELATIONSHIP BETWEEN YUCCA MOTHS and the yucca is termed symbiosis. Both parties benefit and, indeed, are dependent upon the relationship. Yucca moth caterpillars can only eat yucca seeds, and yuccas are only pollinated by yucca moths, so the survival of one species is dependent on that of the other. Not all seeds are eaten by the caterpillars, so the yucca still reproduces.

☛ *346 ORCHID; 323 FLY-POLLINATED FLOWERS.*

FLAMINGO DAY

African lesser flamingos feed in very salty water. Excess salt is concentrated by glands in the upper bill and weeps out of their nostrils.

Flamingos wade in shallow and often brackish pools or lakes. They sweep their bills upside-down through the water, moving the upper and lower halves rapidly to pump water across ridges on the tongue and through slits in the upper bill, trapping small creatures such as shrimps and water-fleas.

The largest flamingo colony in East Africa numbered over a million pairs of birds.

Flamingos are panicked by aircraft. Colonies in the Bahamas became endangered when tourist flights became frequent, because parents deserted nests and young.

THE STRIKING PINK of the flamingo comes from the tiny shrimps that form a large part of its diet. Captive flamingos are fed carrot juice or artificial color to prevent their feathers fading to grey. Not many animals' or plants' colors are derived directly from their food.

Soluble dyes, like food coloring and ink, can be added to water in vases of flowers, producing weird colors in their petals. Wait a day or two for the flower to suck up the colored water. Spring flowers, such as daffodils, work particularly well because they transpire a lot of water.

☛ *192 PIGMENTATION.*

MARSUPIAL DAY

The name marsupial comes from 'marsupium', the ancient Greek word for a pouch. It is here that the tiny young, little more than embryos, climb when they are born and attach themselves to a nipple. Some marsupials suckle their young for many months while they grow large enough to be independent.

Virginia opossum – common in the USA.

Opossums occur in North and South America while possums are Australian. The two groups belong to different families.

The fat-tailed marsupial mouse stores fat at the base of its tail. In a drought the fat provides energy and water.

Australian long-tailed pygmy possum.

The slow, stocky Australian wombat trundles through the night feeding on grass and roots. If disturbed, it burrows rapidly and can be completely concealed in two minutes.

Star of airline advertisements, and model for cuddly toys, in real life the koala can be bad-tempered and vicious.

THE ONLY LARGE CARNIVORE to evolve in Australia was the thylacine, or Tasmanian tiger, which became extinct on the Australian mainland before Europeans arrived but survived in Tasmania until 1935. Marsupials declined when Europeans brought cats, rats, foxes, mice and intensive farming, which preyed on and competed with marsupials and destroyed their habitats. Tasmania and smaller Australian islands like King Island are free of foxes and are still havens for marsupials

☛ 135 KANGAROO; 75 KOALA.

305

BUTTERFLY DAY

The 'dust' on a butterfly's wings is tiny scales. These are hairs with flattened ends, shaped like table-tennis racquets. The microscopic structure of scales is complicated – they have ridges running lengthwise and much finer ridges running crossways. Scales are built up from several layers of cuticle and are hollow inside.

Millions of monarch butterflies (left) migrate 4,000 km/ 2,500 mi., from the USA to Mexico.

Many butterflies are sexually dimorphic – males are brightly colored but females are drab.

Butterflies rest with their wings folded. When they are suddenly opened the brilliant flash of color frightens predators.

Melanin, the pigment in human skin, causes black wing patterns.

Butterfly colors are produced either by pigments in the scales or by their physical structure. Find a dead butterfly (spider's webs in outhouses and sheds are a good source). Keep one of its wings in a dark place and leave the other on a sunlit windowsill. After a few weeks, compare the two; in sunlight the pigment color, due to solid chemical colors stored in the wing, will have faded.

In temperate climates many butterflies only survive for a matter of a few days – just long enough to mate and lay eggs. The rest of the life cycle is spent as an egg, caterpillar or pupa. The exceptions are species that hibernate as adults, like small tortoiseshell and peacock butterflies, that survive for up to eight months.

Some butterflies defend territory so aggressively that they will attack people.

Butterflies see ultraviolet light that we cannot see. The butterfly colors we see probably look quite different to another butterfly.

STRUCTURAL WING COLORS are produced by sandwich-layers of cuticle trapping or reflecting particular colors, or by very fine cross-ridges on the scale reflecting different colors at different angles, a process called interference. Demonstrate structural colors by blowing soap bubbles in bright sunshine; the thin skin of the bubble traps some colors and lets others reflect back. 'Newton's rings' – the violet, green, yellow, orange and red rainbow circles produced when damp microscope slides are pressed together – are also structural colors.

☛ 290 MOTH; 118 MIGRATION; 192 PIGMENTATION.

CRAB DAY

Crabs are members of the Decapoda order (Greek: 'deka', ten; 'podos', foot), crustaceans with a short abdomen and a broad carapace or shell. Because their leg joints are hinged so as to move in only one plane, it is easiest for crabs to move sideways. But many species can easily move forwards and backwards, too, as well as swim. Crabs' abdomens are folded under their bodies.

Mangrove crabs climb trees. They carry extra water to keep their gills wet while they're out of the sea.

Japanese spider crabs, up to 3 m / 10 ft. across, are the largest crustaceans. They are hermit crabs that have redeveloped their own body armor.

Ghost crabs are semi-transparent and run swiftly on tropical beaches. Their shadows are easier to see than they are.

Hermit crabs live in discarded seashells. Because they are protected, their abdomen has lost its armor and is longer than in other crabs.

COLLECT HERMIT CRABS from a rock pool at low tide. As they grow, these crabs must continually search for larger homes to accommodate their increased bulk. Large, empty gastropod mollusk shells are relatively uncommon, so as the hermit crabs increase in size they face stiffer competition for new homes. If you place several hermit crabs with different sized shells in a large dish of sea water, you will be able to watch their duels, fought with their pincers.

326 PARTNERSHIP; 269 LOBSTER; 139 SHRIMP.

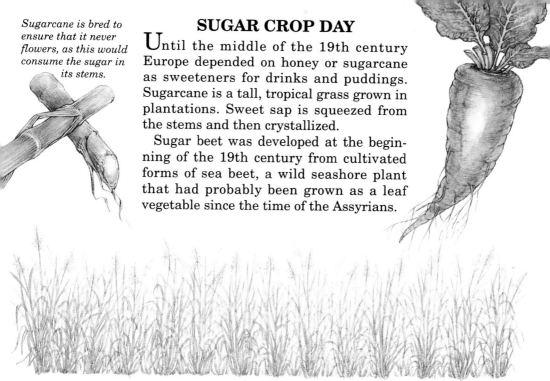

Sugarcane is bred to ensure that it never flowers, as this would consume the sugar in its stems.

SUGAR CROP DAY

Until the middle of the 19th century Europe depended on honey or sugarcane as sweeteners for drinks and puddings. Sugarcane is a tall, tropical grass grown in plantations. Sweet sap is squeezed from the stems and then crystallized.

Sugar beet was developed at the beginning of the 19th century from cultivated forms of sea beet, a wild seashore plant that had probably been grown as a leaf vegetable since the time of the Assyrians.

FIND A PLANT infested with greenfly and feel the leaves under the insects; they will be sticky. The aphids use hollow mouth parts called stylets to tap into the sugars and amino acids that are transported in the phloem cells of the stem and leaf veins. The sucrose content of the phloem is high but there are only minute quantities of essential amino acids. If you examine the aphids with a powerful hand lens, you will see minute droplets of excess sucrose drop from their tail ends. These dry to form the tacky coating on leaves.

☞ 87 CORN; 237 EXOTIC FRUITS.

RHINOCEROS DAY

There are five species of rhinoceros, living in Africa, India and Southeast Asia. All have one or two horns, made of tightly compacted horny fibers, which they use in fighting and in defence. Rhinos have poor eyesight, bad tempers, and excellent hearing and sense of smell. They never attack elephants, so tourists in national parks in India and Nepal view rhinos from elephant-back.

The African white rhino grazes grass by tearing off the shoots using its wide lips. The biggest rhinoceros, a large bull, can weigh 3,000 kg / 6,600 lbs.

African black rhinos are browsers, using their prehensile upper lips to grasp small branches and twigs.

Rare and endangered, the Sumatran rhinoceros is the only rhino with hair on its body. Populations survive in western Malaysia, Sumatra and Borneo.

RHINOCEROSES have been ruthlessly hunted for their horns, which are falsely believed by some Chinese to have powerful medicinal properties and which are also prized as dagger handles by rich Arab sheikhs. Habitat destruction has reduced rhino populations. The Javan rhino is probably extinct. Attempts to breed the Sumatran rhino in captivity have not been very successful, but recent reliable sightings in Sabah confirm that it still survives in Borneo, where it was thought to be extinct.

☛ 130–1 ENDANGERED ANIMALS.

310

CANE TOAD DAY

The marine or cane toad is the world's largest anuran, reaching a length of 25 cm/ 10 in. and weighing over 500 g/18 oz., with an appetite to match. It has been introduced from tropical America into Pacific and Caribbean Islands and Australia, to eat rats and insect pests in sugar-cane plantations, but has become a major pest in its own right.

Male midwife toads hobble around with strings of eggs wrapped around their back legs; when they are ready to hatch, they are transferred to a pond.

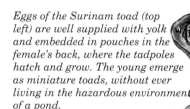

Eggs of the Surinam toad (top left) are well supplied with yolk and embedded in pouches in the female's back, where the tadpoles hatch and grow. The young emerge as miniature toads, without ever living in the hazardous environment of a pond.

THE INTRODUCTION OF CANE TOADS (above left) to Australia is a classic example of the danger of introducing alien predatory species into an isolated island fauna. They have done incalculable ecological damage by eating young birds, lizards and iguanas. Cane toads have a phenomenal rate of reproduction, laying 35,000 eggs each year, and defend themselves by squirting a powerful poison from the parotid glands. The cane toad population in Australia is now out of control.

☛ 4–5 FROG AND TOAD; 8 NEWT; 164 GIANT HOGWEED.

HOUSE MOUSE DAY

Our ability to build houses and store food has been exploited by house mice since the beginning of civilization. The house mouse originated in Central Asia, where it lives in fields and woods, but it has followed wherever man has spread. The animal is nocturnal, so the first hint of its presence is often the sound of scratching and rustling from pantries, kitchens and under floorboards at night.

The African climbing mouse has a prehensile tail, like a harvest mouse.

Litters of 6–7 naked, blind mice are produced every two months and begin breeding when they are six weeks old. Large infestations quickly build up in grain stores and other favorable habitats, contaminating food with their urine and droppings. Mice may live for 3 years in captivity, but have a short life span in the wild.

MOUSE-LIKE MAMMALS have a very wide distribution. The Malaysian tree-living mouse (top left) is an agile climber, while the striped or zebra mouse (above, left) is a ground-living species found over much of Africa. In Australia marsupial mice, or dunnarts, are fierce predators, living under logs and stones and eating more than their own weight in grasshoppers, lizards and grubs in a single night. They have also developed a taste for European house mice, which have become a major pest in Australia.

☛ 22 HARVEST MOUSE.

GOAT DAY

Children as young as nine or ten herd goats through the dry mountains of Iran and the Caucasus for three or four months at a time. Man's lifeline in these dry regions, domestic goats are descended from the truly wild goats of the Middle East and Central Asia. They can hybridize with other wild goat species such as the ibex and markhor, but not 'goat-antelopes' such as the chamois.

Goats provide meat, leather and milk that can be used by people allergic to cow's milk.

Agile chamois live in small herds high in the mountain ranges of Europe and Asia Minor.

The American mountain goat is distantly related to the chamois but is short-legged and lumbers along like a bear. It lives high among broken rock on snow-covered mountains, insulated by its thick coat.

Alpine ibex live high in the Alps and Pyrenees feeding on small plants and, in the winter, lichen.

GOATSKIN PROVIDES US with fine, hard-wearing leather. Books are often bound in Niger morocco, so-called because it is produced in Nigeria and is 'morocco' – goatskin. The leather is tanned to preserve it using a solution made from boiled bark and leaves of the sumac tree.

Visit a library and look at the different leather bindings. Morocco is often colored and has a pronounced grain. Calf is smooth and light brown.

☛ *144 SHEEP; 19 WILD SHEEP.*

313

REDWOOD DAY

California redwoods are confined to a narrow belt of coast from Oregon to south of Monterey. There is no reason, other than infection by disease or destruction by man, why these massive trees should not live forever; unlike most conifers, they produce suckers from their roots, so even when the adult tree dies a new shoot arises from its base to take its place. Their tall, straight trunks make them an ideal source of timber; as a result, many of the best specimens have been felled.

The world's tallest tree is a California redwood known as "Howard Libbey", which is 112 m / 367 ft. tall and about 500 years old. Other specimens are known which are 2,600 years old.

Felled conifers show a clear pattern of annual rings in their stumps, with broader rings corresponding to years when growth conditions were good.

Each male and female "flower" (known as a stobilus in conifers) is minute in proportion to the tree. The mature cones are only 2 cm / 0.8 in. across.

CALIFORNIA REDWOOD and its close relative, the Wellingtonia or giant sequoia, are the largest living organisms that have ever existed on Earth. Both species were introduced into Europe about 150 years ago. The best way to see and compare conifer species is to visit an arboretum – a collection of fine specimen trees that are given room to develop without close competition. Dense plantations conceal the true beauty of conifers.

☛ *318 PINE.*

ROCK POOL DAY

The commonest sea anemone on European rock pools is the beadlet anemone, which occurs in green and red forms. When it withdraws its tentacles it can survive for several hours out of water.

Rain can dilute sea water and sunshine evaporates it during the period when small rock pools are exposed, so the species that live in them often have to tolerate substantial fluctuations in salinity.

Edible crabs, with carapaces like a neatly crimped pie crust, live in rock pools on the lower zones of rocky shores.

Common starfish sometimes congregate in large numbers close to shore during the breeding season.

The snakelocks anemone, with long, waving tentacles, lives high on rocky shorelines, often in shallow pools that have low salinity.

Different species of winkle occur in zones down the shore. The smallest species live in the splash zone and are only briefly immersed in sea water. Common winkles graze on algae-covered rocks, while flat periwinkles live amongst the seaweeds, closer to the low water mark.

Seaweed species show a distinct zonation on the seashore, with the saw-toothed serrated wrack growing in the middle and lower reaches of the shore.

MAKE A ROCK POOL VIEWER, to explore marine life at the seashore. Instructions can be found at the end of the book.

☛ 94 STAR FISH; 308 CRAB; 117 SHELL; 339 SEA ANEMONE; 100 EDIBLE SEAWEED.

CHEETAH DAY

Speed, rather than stamina, is the key to the cheetah's hunting success. It can achieve at least 100 kph/60 mph in short sprints, but unless it catches its prey within 20 seconds it begins to tire and gives up the chase. During the frantic pursuit it generates so much heat that it must stop to cool down and catch its breath; if it has made a kill other scavengers use this recovery period as an opportunity to steal its victim.

Long, pointed canine teeth, used for killing, are a distinctive feature of carnivore dentition.

Learning to hunt is a slow process for young cheetahs and they are unable to feed themselves until they are over a year old. During the training period the mother catches gazelles without killing them, then releases the crippled animals for her cubs to chase and learn to kill.

The cheetah's speed and acceleration are achieved with the aid of a flexible backbone, which acts as a spring and helps to drive the long legs backward and forward. The unusually long tail is used to counterbalance the body during sudden swerves and turns.

IF YOU EXAMINE the paws of a domestic cat you will see that it can retract it's claws. Cheetahs are the only members of the cat family which cannot do this — a characteristic which makes it easy to follow their trails across the dry, dusty plains where they hunt. Recent studies of cheetah DNA revealed that they possess surprisingly little genetic variation. Biologists believe that they almost became extinct during the last Ice Age, with a few animals surviving as founders of today's populations.

☛ *63 LIONESS; 261 TIGER.*

SCENT AND TASTE DAY

Natural habitats are full of chemical signals that act as threats, lures and mating stimuli. Chemoreceptors of many animals are finely tuned to detect these, sampling the scent-laden air that enters their respiratory systems and tasting the chemical constituents of their food. The human nose and tongue are relatively crude scent and taste receptors compared with those of species that depend heavily on chemical detection systems for their survival.

The constantly flicking tongues of snakes and other reptiles detect volatile substances in the air, by drawing them onto a sensory structure in the roof of their mouths, called Jacobsen's organ.

Giraffes' tongues are long and prehensile – ideal for gripping tender young shoots of acacia trees.

The large, branched antennae of many male moths are ultra-sensitive detectors of mating pheromones, the chemical signals that are released by female moths. Some moths can detect minute traces of pheromones over a distance of 1 km / 0.6 mi.

TASTE BUDS are groups of receptor cells in the tongue which detect chemical stimulants in food and convey messages to the brain through the nervous system. Rabbits have over 17,000 taste buds on their tongues, but the pigeon (top right) is equipped with a paltry sixty. Trout and salmon (left) return from the sea to spawn in the river where they hatched from eggs, using an extraordinary ability to recognize the chemical composition of its soil, rocks and vegetation.

☛ *148 STRANGE NOSES; 120 HEARING; 345 EYES; 25 SALMON; 45 TROUT.*

317

PINE DAY

Conifer forests are mainly confined to the northern circumpolar regions, where summers are short. The conical form of the trees allows them to shed snow, which would otherwise break their branches.

Many pine-cones take several years to mature. Cones of the Scots pine are pollinated in their first year, grow in their second and ripen and shed seeds in their third season.

Pine forests are home to the capercaillie, a spectacular game bird.

Conifers are gymnosperms – a term which means 'naked ovule'. Their ovules, and later their seeds, are exposed on the surface of the whorl of bracts which constitute the cone. In flowering plants (angiosperms) the seeds are enclosed inside a folded, protective bract, called a carpel. Conifer cones range in length from 3 cm/1 in. in Italian cypress to over 30 cm/1 ft. in big-cone pine.

All conifers produce aromatic resins, which protect them from pests and diseases, but pine beauty moth larvae and large pine weevils are undeterred by these gooey substances and cause damage to conifer plantations.

The last strongholds of red squirrels in Britain are pine forests, where they feed on conifer shoots and seeds.

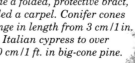

SCOTS PINE GROWS THROUGHOUT EUROPE, from Spain to Lapland and across to Siberia, but it is particularly associated with the old conifer forests of northern Britain, like the Black Wood of Rannoch and the last remnants of the ancient Caledonian Forest of Scotland. Bring some ripe cones of Scots pine into a warm room and watch how the scales open as they dry. When you tap them on a hard surface the winged seeds will drop out and rotate like helicopters as they fall. Most conifers have wind-dispersed seeds.

☛ 314 REDWOOD; 196 PARTS OF A FLOWER.

WOMBAT DAY

Australian wombats are, apart from the marsupial mole, the only burrowing marsupials. Common wombats are big – up to 1.2 m/4 ft. long – and weigh up to 35 kg/80 lbs. It is now accepted that there are just two species of wombat – the common wombat (below) from southeast Australia and Tasmania, and the hairy-nosed wombat (right).

Wombats' strong stubby feet are adapted to allow them to dig rapidly. Their main living tunnels are about 20 m / 65 ft. long with several escape holes. Wombats keep out intruders by arching their powerful backs to block the tunnel completely.

Like the koala, probably its closest relative, the female wombat's pouch points backward. She can dig without filling the pouch with soil.

Hairy-nosed wombats are found in the savanna grasslands of South Australia and southern Queensland.

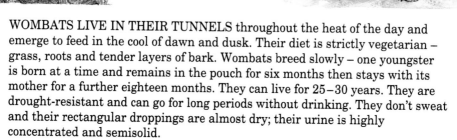

WOMBATS LIVE IN THEIR TUNNELS throughout the heat of the day and emerge to feed in the cool of dawn and dusk. Their diet is strictly vegetarian – grass, roots and tender layers of bark. Wombats breed slowly – one youngster is born at a time and remains in the pouch for six months then stays with its mother for a further eighteen months. They can live for 25–30 years. They are drought-resistant and can go for long periods without drinking. They don't sweat and their rectangular droppings are almost dry; their urine is highly concentrated and semisolid.

☞ 54–55 UNDERGROUND; 135 KANGAROO; 75 KOALA.

HORSETAIL DAY

Horsetails are the last survivors of a group of plants that dominated large areas of the earth's surface over 200 million years ago. Modern-day horsetails all belong to the genus *Equisetum* and are virtually identical to fossils that can be found in 300 million year old Devonian rocks, suggesting that this is the oldest surviving genus of plants on Earth.

Horsetail stems have hollow centers and a ring of air canals, allowing oxygen to reach their roots, which often grow in stagnant mud.

Horsetails can accumulate gold but extracting the metal would be uneconomic – 4,000 kg / 8,800 lbs. of plant would yield 1 kg / 2.2 lbs. of gold.

The distinctive whorls of leaves and stems contain dense silica deposits and were often used by frontier settlers to scour pots and pans, earning horsetails the alternative name of 'scouring rush'.

Equisetum giganteum *is the largest of the 29 surviving horsetail species, with trailing stems that are up to 13 m / 43 ft. long. This would have been dwarfed by the* Carboniferous Calamites, *a tree horsetail that was 18 m / 60 ft. tall. Prehistoric horsetails left excellent fossils in coal deposits.*

THE SILICA in living horsetails – which is technically a form of opal – can be collected by drying some stems and burning them in a metal pan. The powder that remains is an abrasive, that was once used for polishing soft metals, like pewter.

☛ *170 PRIMITIVE PLANTS; 114 FERN; 62 MOSS.*

DODOS AND EXTINCTION DAY

The dodos or solitaires were gigantic pigeons that evolved from a flighted ancestor on the isolated islands of Mauritius, Reunion and Rodriguez in the Indian Ocean. Isolated and without predators, they lost the power of flight, increased in size to about 25 kg/55 lbs., and evolved the habit of nesting on the ground.

Like the dodo, the flightless greak auk was easy to catch and kill. The last bird was slaughtered in Iceland in 1844.

The last passenger pigeon died in the Cincinnati Zoo in 1914.

European sailors discovered the dodo's sanctuary in the 16th century. Many birds were killed for food, and introduced monkeys, pigs and rats destroyed eggs and chicks. By 1680 every Mauritius dodo was dead.

ALL THAT IS LEFT of the solitaires is two heads and two feet in European museums, a small number of skeletons from the 17th century, and some further bones recently excavated on Mauritius. Extinction is for ever.

The dodo is one of the most famous examples of extinction in historic times, well known as it was a large and spectacular species. But other cases raise little attention and most are not even noticed.

Species extinctions are now occurring more rapidly than at any time in Earth's history, due to pollution and habitat destruction.

☛ 35 PIGEON; 130–1 ENDANGERED ANIMALS; 356–7 RAINFOREST CANOPY; 10 FLIGHTLESS BIRDS.

PEAT BOG DAY

Peat bogs form from the slow decay of layers of sphagnum moss, compressed under the weight of new growth. Sphagnum retains large volumes of water in a network of dead leaf cells, so bogs behave like a living sponge and support a unique assemblage of plants and animals that thrive in permanently wet conditions.

Carnivorous sundews obtain essential nitrogen by trapping and digesting insects.

The high water table in bogs provides a fine habitat for frogs and wading birds.

Insect life is particularly abundant in peat bogs, which offer a range of feeding and breeding sites. Caterpillars of the large heath butterfly feed on sedges and cotton grass.

Bog bean creeps around the edges of shallow pools, rooting from leaf nodes.

Find a plant of sphagnum moss and examine its unique leaves under a microscope. A network of narrow, green, living cells surrounds glassy, dead cells that store water.

Curlews probe for insects and other invertebrates around shallow pools. Moorland raptors, including hen harriers, often hunt over bogs.

CONSTANT WATER PERCOLATION means that soluble minerals are quickly washed out of peat lands. *Narthecium ossifragum* (above), the bog asphodel, was so called (*ossifragum* means 'bone breaker') because cattle that grazed on the plant were thought to develop brittle bones, a symptom that was really caused by the low mineral content of bog-land vegetation. Overexploitation of peat, for horticultural use and as fuel, threatens peat bogs and plants like bog bean (right) that thrive in them.

☛ *56 POND.*

FLY-POLLINATED FLOWERS
DAY

Many fly-pollinated flowers depend on deception to attract pollinating insects. They frequently have the color and texture of dead flesh, with an aroma to match, and these carrion flowers attract flies that would normally lay their eggs in decaying carcasses or excreta.

Rafflesia arnoldii is the world's largest flower. It is parasitic on jungle lianas in the forest of Sumatra and has no leaves or roots, drawing nutrients instead through fine threads that permeate its host. The lurid flower, over 50 cm / 20 in. in diameter, smells of carrion.

Aristolochia elegans is one of a group of species known as Dutchmen's pipes, which imprison insects. It has a strongly scented, purple and brown flower with a light window in its center. When flies crawl through this they are prevented from retreating by backward pointed hairs, which only wilt and unblock the entrance after the flies have pollinated the stigmas in a hidden chamber.

IN SPRING, search for flowers of *Arum maculatum* (left), commonly known as cuckoo pint, lords-and-ladies, or wild arum. This plant captures insects in much the same way as *Aristolochia*, but with an additional adaptation – the club-like spadix generates heat and gives off a musky odor, luring flies into its floral prison. Larger tropical aroids generate overpowering stenches of rotting fish and corpses.

☛ *196 PARTS OF A FLOWER.*

323

ESCAPE AND DEFENSE DAY

All wild animals are part of a natural food chain. Those in the lower echelons must either defend themselves or develop a means of escape from carnivorous predators.

Porcupine fish inflate themselves to deter predators.

Fire-bellied toads (right) and coral snakes (top right) exhibit warning coloration. Red is an almost universal threat or warning color in the animal kingdom, signifying that the organism is either poisonous or unpleasant to eat.

A hedgehog rolls itself into a spiny ball when attacked, protecting its soft underparts. Badgers, however, are undeterred and are skilled at unrolling and skinning them.

Lizards' tails are shed when they are grabbed by a predator – a phenomenon known as autotomy. The tail continues to wriggle while its owner escapes. Sometimes two new tails are regenerated after such encounters.

Armadillos (bottom right) roll into an armored ball when attacked.

OPOSSUMS HAVE PERFECTED the technique of pretending to be dead when they are threatened, lying limply on their side with their tongue hanging out until their assailant loses interest and moves away. 'Playing possum' has become a common expression for feigning death when in mortal danger. Search a nettle patch or hazel bush for weevils that live on the leaves, and notice how they too 'play possum' when captured.

☛ 173 PLANT DEFENSE; 162 POISONOUS PLANTS; 289 CAMOUFLAGE; 293 MIMICRY.

PARASITES DAY

The perfect strategy for a parasite is to use its host as a source of food and protection, without killing it. Many parasitic organisms infect more than one species of host and require a vector to carry them from one host to the next.

The stems of dodder, a flowering plant parasite, look like a mass of threads. It is a complete parasite, with reduced leaves and no green chlorophyll, and so relies on its hosts, which include nettles, gorse and alfalfa, for all its nutrient requirements. Dodder seedlings germinate in soil, but then twine around any plants that they touch and clamp on to their xylem and phloem with a haustorium.

Mistletoe seeds, dispersed by birds, germinate in crevices between branches of apple and poplar and produce a special tissue called a haustorium, which taps the host's water and nutrient supply.

Nematode worms parasitise many invertebrates, including spiders.

Leeches are bloodsucking parasites and were once used by doctors to treat various illnesses. This practice still continues in some areas, where leeches are used to remove blood from bruised tissues.

TSETSE FLIES are one of the most devastating vectors of human parasites. These bloodsucking insects transmit the trypanosome parasites that cause fatal sleeping sickness in man and cattle. When they suck blood they transfer the microscopic parasites into the host's bloodstream. Antelope are the alternative host for the sleeping sickness trypanosome and do not appear to be harmed by it. Killing the tsetse fly vector is the best method for controlling the disease.

☛ *287 LEECH; 188 FLEA; 49 LICE; 327 TAPEWORM.*

PARTNERSHIP DAY

Biologists recognize several forms of symbiosis, where two different organisms live together in a close relationship. This interaction can include parasitism (where one species exploits the other), mutualism (where both organisms benefit) and commensalism (where only one species benefits while the other is neither benefited nor harmed). The bacteria in a cow's gut, which break down cellulose in grass, represent an example of mutualism, since both organisms benefit.

The wet fur of tree sloths provides a comfortable habitat for a moth which lay its eggs in the sloth dung which is deposited in a regularly used midden. The sloth's coat offers a mating site and free transport for the adult moths.

Hermit crabs place stinging sea anemones on their shells as camouflage and as a deterrent.

Buffaloes benefit from parasite-hunting oxpeckers that rid them of fly larvae.

The birds that peck food scraps from the jaws of crocodiles are protected by their fearsome host, who benefits from their dental-care services.

GROUPERS (below) visit cleaning stations on coral reefs, where cleaner wrasses remove parasites and dead skin from their gills and mouths.

Watch the way that garden robins dash forward to collect soil animals disturbed by a gardener's spade, in the same way that cattle egrets catch insects disturbed by the hooves of grazing animals; both are examples of commensalism.

☛ 24 EGRET; 138 LICHEN; 71 ROBIN; 325 PARASITE.

TAPEWORM DAY

Tapeworms are the largest parasites to infest humans, living in the gut and reaching a length of 10 m/33 ft. or more. They have a body which is divided into a chain of 2,000 or more reproductive units, called proglottids. These resemble segments and each produces eggs which are shed in the feces. The whole animal is anchored to the gut lining by a scolex, or head of hooks and suckers.

Over 1,000 species of tapeworm infest vertebrates that range from sharks to humans. The commonest human parasite is the beef tapeworm, which is contracted by eating undercooked beef, where the larvae live in muscle tissue.

HUMANS CAN ALSO ACT as a host for tapeworms that spend part of their life cycles in pigs, fish and dogs. Pig and dog tapeworm larvae invade human muscle and various organs, including eyes, brain, heart, liver and lungs, and are dangerous parasites. Dog tapeworms, which can be contracted from infected pets, form cysts that can grow in the liver for 20 years and reach the size of a football, requiring surgery for their removal.

☛ *325 PARASITE; 214 EARTHWORM; 165 MARINE WORM.*

THYLACINE DAY

The Tasmanian wolf, Tasmanian tiger or thylacine is (or was) the largest carnivorous marsupial. Fossil thylacines have been found in mainland Australia and New Guinea. The size of a large dog and weighing up to 35 kg/77 lbs., the thylacine has distinctive tiger-like stripes and a backward-pointing pouch like a wombat's.

Tasmanian devils are the largest remaining predatory marsupials in Australia.

Only discovered in 1805, by 1835 thylacines had become notorious as sheep killers and the Tasmanian government offered a bounty for each dead one. By 1900 more than 3,000 had been killed.

The thylacine's legs are proportionately shorter than in many other large carnivores. Note how the back slopes downward very slightly.

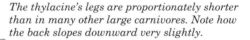

IN THE EARLY 1900s the thylacine population crashed and it became very rare. One was snared in 1933 and given to Hobart Zoo where it died on September 7, 1936. It was the last Tasmanian tiger ever seen alive. Despite warnings in the 1900s, the thylacine was never protected. Even in 1928 opposition from sheep farmers prevented its legal protection, yet the last specimen to be killed in the wild was shot only two years later. Occasional sightings of thylacines have been reported in recent years, but have not been authenticated.

☛ *321 DODOS AND EXTINCTION; 130–1 ENDANGERED ANIMALS.*

RIVERBANK DAY

Rivers begin as fast-flowing streams in upland watersheds, but by the time they reach lowland plains they are broad, slow-flowing stretches of water. Dippers (left) are large relatives of the wren and use rocks in shallow, upland rivers as perches, periodically diving into the water to catch small invertebrates on the riverbed. Kingfishers (right) dig nesting tunnels in riverbanks.

The large red damselfly is one of many invertebrates whose aquatic larval or nymphal stages develop on the riverbed and depend on unpolluted, well-oxygenated water.

Flowering rush grows on the edge of muddy rivers, and has razor-sharp leaves.

Water voles (left) are herbivores that make extensive burrow systems on the muddy banks of slow-flowing rivers. When alarmed they dive into the water with a distinctive 'plop', leaving a trail of bubbles as they escape underwater. Otters (right) have declined, through loss of habitat and river pollution. Their staple diet is fish like roach (below), which in turn depend on invertebrate animals. The presence of otters is a sign of a healthy river.

VISIT DIFFERENT HABITATS along the course of your local river, to see how the variety of wildlife changes the nearer it gets to the sea. Most animal life can be seen soon after dawn.

A riverbank at sunrise on a summer morning is a magical place. Few authors have succeeded in describing it as well as Kenneth Graham in *The Wind in the Willows*, his classic tale for children.

☛ 292 OTTER; 239 KINGFISHER; 56 POND; 92 WATER SURFACE; 229 WATER-LILY.

CRYPSIS (CONCEALMENT) DAY

Crypsis is the development of color patterns or shape to blend with the surroundings of the environment. Very many animals use camouflage, either to protect themselves from predators or, if they are predators, to conceal themselves from their prey until it is too late. Camouflage patterns may have evolved and be fixed in an animal's genetic make-up, or the animal may be able to change color to match its background.

When concealment fails, larvae of some hawkmoths scare predators by wriggling like snakes, inflating their front segments and displaying threatening false eyes.

Wing cases of thorn bugs are modified to resemble plant thorns. Successful camouflage also depends on appropriate behavior patterns; thorn bugs line up along twigs, like real thorns.

Larvae of some moths in the family Geometridae are shaped and coloured like dead twigs. Their disguise depends on them remaining absolutely still.

TROPICAL FLOWER MANTIDS (below) ambush other insects that mistake them for a flower, grabbing prey with a lightning strike of their spiny forelegs. Search for crab spiders, which use the same strategy, hiding in flowers and catching visiting butterflies. Crab spiders change color to match their floral background.

☛ *289 CAMOUFLAGE; 293 MIMICRY; 351 POISONOUS FISH.*

SEA CUCUMBER DAY

Holothurians, or sea cucumbers, are close relatives of star fish and sea urchins; all three groups of animals are members of the phylum Echinodermata. Unlike sea urchins, sea cucumbers have an external skeleton made of loosely connected plates that are embedded on a leathery body wall. This allows their bodies to change shape, aiding their movements with hydraulic tube feet which resemble those of other echinoderms.

Under extreme threat, some species eject their internal organs through their body wall and anus. The lost structures are then regenerated.

Some sea cucumbers defend themselves by discharging a mass of sticky, toxic white threads from structures called Cuvierian organs.

Holothurians feed on particulate matter in sea water, using mucus-covered tentacles around their mouths to trap food. The tentacles are bent over into the mouth, one by one, to remove the food particles.

SEA CUCUMBERS usually live in deep water but if you search eel grass beds on the lower shore at extreme low tide you may find the cotton spinner, a species that reaches a length of 20 cm/8 in. Its name derives from the sticky threads it discharges as a defense. Most holothurians live in the mud and sand on the sea bottom, moving through the sediments by sending waves of muscular contraction along their bodies, allowing them to creep like large worms. In Japan sea cucumbers are considered a culinary delicacy.

☛ 94 STAR FISH; 361 SEA URCHIN.

MEDICINAL PLANTS DAY

Plants are the traditional source of medicines for tribal cultures on every inhabited continent, but it is only recently that people in developed countries have been reawakened to their value as a source of life-saving drugs. About 40 percent of proprietary medicines available without prescription in your local chemist contain natural plant extracts.

Atropine, extracted from deadly nightshade, is used to dilate pupils before eye examinations.

Quinine, which comes from the bark of the cinchona tree of the Andes, is still widely used as an anti-malaria drug. Jesuits from Peru first brought ground cinchona bark back to Europe in the 17th century. Until this drug became widely available malaria killed 2 million people each year and made 200 million severely ill in India, Africa and Southeast Asia.

Like many medicinal plants, castor-oil plant also produces deadly toxins and ricin, the protein in its seeds, is one of the most dangerous plant products. The oil, squeezed from the same seeds, has been used as a purgative since the time of the ancient Egyptians and is used today in products ranging from ointments to eye drops.

Arnica is an alpine herb which contains arnicine, which is used for treating bruises.

Some plant species which produce ginseng are now endangered, because of the great demand for their roots, which are taken in various forms as a protection against disease and the deterioration of bodily faculties during old age. Ginseng is central to Chinese medicine, which emphasizes prevention rather than cure.

Witch hazel is a winter-flowering shrub whose bark yields an extract which reduces inflammation when it is applied to bruises.

Aspirin was only synthesized as a drug at the beginning of the 20th century. Before that time headaches were cured by using boiled extracts of meadowsweet or willow bark. Both contain salicylic acid, the active ingredient of aspirin.

Senna has been used for centuries as a powerful laxative, to relieve constipation. It has been a source of medicine in Arabia since at least the 8th century AD.

AFTER DECADES of uncontrolled destruction, the value of rainforests as a source of medicines is now widely recognized. The accumulated wisdom of cultures that use folk medicine can aid the search for plant medicines and some countries, like Costa Rica, have signed agreements with multinational drug companies to extract, test and market medicines from local plants.

☛ *298 DRUGS; 230–1 HERBS; 13 AROMATIC PLANTS; 84 FOXGLOVE.*

SILK MOTH (SILKWORM)
DAY

Silk is made from the cocoon of the silk moth, *Bombyx mori*. Although there are several million species of insect, only the silk moth and honeybee have been completely domesticated; wild populations of *B. mori* no longer exist and domesticated silk moths have lost the power of flight.

Eggs hatch into small black caterpillars which turn white when they feed on white mulberry leaves.

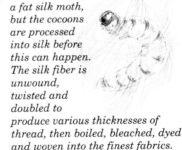

The caterpillar spins a silk cocoon, using spinnerets on its tail, after 45 days of continuous eating. Each cocoon contains 900 m / 1,000 yds. of double silk thread. The pupa inside would eventually hatch as a fat silk moth, but the cocoons are processed into silk before this can happen. The silk fiber is unwound, twisted and doubled to produce various thicknesses of thread, then boiled, bleached, dyed and woven into the finest fabrics.

ACCORDING TO ANCIENT LEGEND, silk production, or sericulture, began in China in 2640 BC. Silk was exported from China but the secrets of its manufacture were closely guarded until silk-moth eggs were smuggled to Constantinople in AD 550. From there, silk production spread to Spain, Italy and Sicily. Sericulture reached England in 1685 but failed because black mulberry leaves, which silk worms will not eat, were cultivated as food.

Silk moths can be fed on lettuce as an alternative to mulberry.

☛ 82 BUMBLEBEE; 290 MOTH; 144 SHEEP.

BARNACLE DAY

Barnacles have volcano-shaped shells, the vent of the volcano closed by a trap-door of four plates. Common on rocky shores between the high and low tide levels, they may also colonize pieces of driftwood or other flotsam that has been in the water a long time. Despite looking like limpets, barnacles aren't mollusks but a group of arthropods ('joint-legged animals') called Cirripedia, related to shrimps.

Prawn-like barnacle larvae are free-swimming. They find a suitable surface, glue themselves back-downward to it, then secrete their shell.

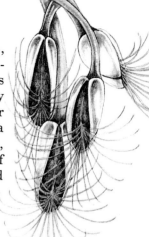

Barnacles are permanently glued to rocks and cannot move closer to mate. Instead, each hermaphrodite animal is equipped with an unusually long penis, which it uses to fertilize its neighbor.

Stalked goose barnacles are often washed ashore attached to driftwood.

BARNACLES HAVE CONQUERED one of the roughest habitats on Earth – rock surfaces subject to the full power of an ocean storm.

If you take a piece of rock with barnacles attached and place it in a bucket of sea water the barnacles will open and extrude feathery legs which they wave, filtering plankton and other tiny fragments of food from the water.

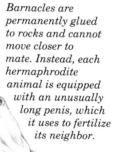

☛ *308 CRAB; 269 LOBSTER; 139 SHRIMP.*

DUCK DAY

Ducks, geese and swans are collectively known as waterfowl and are classified in the order Anseriformes. They were among the first birds to be domesticated, over 4,500 years ago.

Many ducks, like the Chinese Mandarin and Carolina wood duck, are noted for their spectacular breeding plumage, which is usually much more colorful in the males. Courtship involves elaborate rituals of posturing to display the feathers to best advantage, forging a link with a female that is maintained through the breeding season.

Steamer ducks, from the coastal waters and rivers of South America and the Falkland Islands, are almost all flightless and move by flailing their wings over the surface. Early-19th-century travelers called them steamer ducks because they resembled paddle steamers, as they trundled over the water surface.

The four species of eider duck live in Arctic and subarctic seas. The down from their chests, which they use as a nest material, has the best thermal insulation properties of any natural substance and is still collected in Iceland to make eiderdown comforters.

South American torrent ducks have outsized feet for swimming in fast currents and soft bills for picking stoneflies from the river bed.

VISIT A WILDFOWL PARK in early spring to watch the courtship rituals of waterfowl. Notice that quacking is just a small part of the duck vocal repertoire; whistles and grunts are equally common. Notice too that different species use a variety of feeding methods; dabbling ducks, like mallards, up-end and feed in shallow water, while diving ducks (like tufted duck) exploit deeper food sources.

☛ *299 SWAN; 151 PEACOCK; 364 PHEASANT.*

TRACKING DAY

Wild animals are naturally secretive and difficult to watch, but often leave characteristic signs of their presence. Birds of prey regurgitate pellets (left) containing the fur and bones of the small mammals that they eat.

Squirrels shred pinecones to reach the nutritious seeds between the scales.

Wood mice gnaw a hole in hazelnuts to reach the kernel, squirrels split them in half and nuthatches wedge them in a bark crevice and peck a jagged hole.

Many animals leave characteristic droppings that are sometimes used to mark the edge of their territory. Rabbit droppings are pea-sized. Fox droppings are sausage-shaped, with a spirally twisted point.

After heavy snow, when no other food is available, rabbits, hares and deer strip bark from young trees, sometimes killing them.

CHOOSE AN AREA of woodland or hedgerow and survey it for signs of animals, to build up a picture of the wildlife that lives and feeds there.

☛ 73 SQUIRREL; 60 BIRD'S FEET.

Birds of prey leave characteristic wing and tail prints in soft snow when they drop onto mice.

Many mammals leave distinctive tracks. Badger footprints show clear claw and toe pad impressions above a central main pad. Badgers often follow regular routes.

ALBATROSS DAY

The biggest albatross is the wandering albatross with a wingspan of more than 3.5 m/11.5 ft. Turbulence close to the wave crests of the Southern Ocean helps keep albatrosses gliding for days on end. The Wandering albatross can travel up to 950 km/600 mi. in a day. Albatrosses may be the longest-lived birds, with a life span of up to 80 years.

The chick of the gray-headed albatross defends itself by vomiting partially digested squid over an intruder.

The wandering albatross feeds far out to sea on squid and surface-dwelling fish. Dozing on the wing at night, its non-stop feeding journeys may cover more than 7,000 km/4,500 mi.

Wandering albatross nestlings weigh up to 16 kg/35 lbs., five times more than a newborn human. Wing exercises before their first flight consume a third of their weight.

WITH LONG TAPERED WINGS held almost straight out, the albatross resembles a glider. Tiny movements of its wingtips swing it to the next wave crest, where it surfs down the upcurrent of wind. Find upcurrents of air over a low hedge or wall and fly a toy glider down the upcurrent, just like an albatross.

☛ 65 GULL.

SEA ANEMONE DAY

Sea anemones have a single body opening, so their mouth also serves as an anus. They are the simplest animals with organized body tissues and are diploblastic, with a body wall composed of outer ectoderm and inner endoderm cells, separated by gelatinous mesoglea. The latter is replaced in all higher animals by a cellular mesoderm.

The stinging tentacles of the orange ball anemone end in small spheres.

The dahlia anemone is one of the larger species found in temperate waters.

Plumose anemones possess long muscular columns and a dense head of tentacles.

Most sea anemones attach themselves to rocks and shells with their pedal disk and can use its muscular contractions to glide slowly over the surface; some burrow in sand, so just their mouths and tentacles protrude.

THE SEA ANEMONES belong to a class known as the Anthozoa, a term that means 'flower animal'. Their delicate, floral appearence is deceptive; they are all armed with lethal stinging organs, called cnidoblasts, which discharge paralyzing threads called nematocysts when fish brush against them. If you brush your finger over the tentacles of a sea anemone they feel sticky, because the minute barbed nematocysts hook into your thick skin but cannot penetrate it.

☛ 219 JELLYFISH; 254 PLANKTON; 326 PARTNERSHIP; 37 FISH PARTNERSHIP.

BIGGEST ANIMAL DAY

At 5.5 m / 18 ft. the giraffe is the tallest living mammal, by virtue of its elongated neck that allows it to browse high branches.

Although large size may allow animals relative security from predators, it also confers several disadvantages. Large herbivores must spend much of their time feeding to satisfy their dietary requirements and there are additional penalties of extended gestation periods and slow reproduction rates in some species.

The largest flying insects are the birdwing butterflies, from New Guinea and surrounding islands. African goliath beetles are the largest coleopterans, and reach a length of over 10 cm / 4 in.

The African elephant is the heaviest land vertebrate, tipping the scales at a portly six tons. The extinct dinosaurs were much larger, with brachiosaurus weighing a massive 190 tons. The largest living reptile is the Komodo dragon, which weighs in at a svelte 60 kg / 130 lbs. The heaviest flying bird is the kori bustard, weighing about 12 kg / 26 lbs. – larger, flightless birds, like ostriches, are unable to generate sufficient muscle power to offset additional weight of larger flight muscles.

THERE ARE WIDE, genetically controlled size variations within species. Visit a pet show and compare dwarf Dutch rabbits with Flemish giants, which are ten times larger. These represent opposite ends of the size spectrum within the species, artificially selected by rabbit breeders.

☛ 341 SMALLEST ANIMAL.

SMALLEST ANIMAL DAY

As animals become smaller their surface area increases in relation to their volume, so they lose heat faster. For this reason small bird and mammal species are common in warm climates and are less frequent in colder polar and alpine regions.

Tiny pygmy gliders fly using membranes of skin between their legs.

Ingram's possum weighs 25 g/ 1 oz. or less; Savi's pigmy shrew, weighing just 2 g/0.07 oz., is the smallest mammal.

Sizes of antelope range from the giant eland, weighing a ton, to the 3-kg/7-lbs. royal antelope, which stands 25 cm/10 in. tall at the shoulder – about twice the height of the eland's hoof.

Hummingbirds are the largest birds that can hover continuously in still air; larger, heavier species are unable to generate enough lift to support their increased weight in hovering flight.

Ingram's planigale, at 4 g/ 0.15 oz., is the smallest marsupial and nests in cracks in dried mud.

The pigmy marmoset, at 125 g/ 4.5 oz., is the world's smallest monkey and lives in the Amazon rainforest, feeding on tree sap and gum that it gouges from tree bark with its teeth.

Thread snakes are the shortest snakes – just 10 cm/4 in. long – and come from Martinique.

PROTISTS ARE A KINGDOM of minute, single-celled organisms with many animal characteristics. Collect some by scraping slime from rotting stems and leaves in a pond, then examine this under a microscope. At high magnification you should find creeping *Amoeba*, fast-swimming *Paramecium* and rotifers with whirling heads of cilia.

☛ *340 BIGGEST ANIMAL.*

FUNGI DAY

Two major divisions of the fungal kingdom are the basidiomycetes and ascomycetes. In the former, spores are produced on large cells called basidia, which are embedded in the fine tubes or gills under the toadstool cap. In the latter, spores are fired from vase-shaped containers (asci) embedded in the toadstool surface.

Tinder fungus is a basidiomycete that was once used to kindle fires.

Horn of plenty (top) and bird's nest fungus (above) are basidiomycetes.

Ceps are highly prized edible toadstools in the basidiomycete genus Boletus.

Jelly babies are ascomycete toadstools with gelatinous caps.

Summer truffles are the most prized of all edible ascomycetes. They grow underground.

Morels are prized by fungus gourmets and appear in spring. Spores are shot from asci that are embedded in their conical caps.

Candlesnuff fungus has microscopic asci hidden in its blackened tips.

Brightly colored russulas are basidiomycete species that need careful identification. Some are edible but others, like the red-capped Russula emetica, *are poisonous.*

COLLECT AN ASCOMYCETE FUNGUS, like jelly babies fungus (below, left), and bring it into a warm room. Watch its upper surface through a hand lens as it dries out: you should see 'puffs' of ejected ascospores, like volcanic eruptions.

11 FUNGI; 354 FUNGUS FORAY; 248 POISONOUS FUNGI; 14 FUNGI AND MOLD.

SLUG DAY

The best time to watch slugs is by flashlight in late evening, when they emerge from their daytime refuges to feed, leaving glistening slime trails over paths and leaves. Slime acts as a deterrent to predators, lubricates their muscular foot as it glides over the soil surface and helps to prevent water loss. Throughout the day they burrow or shelter under stones, to escape desiccation.

Slugs are hermaphrodites, with both male and female reproductive organs, but exchange sperm before laying glistening white eggs (bottom left).

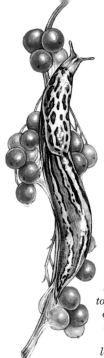

Great gray slugs climb into vegetation to breed, become entwined in a spiral during courtship, then hang from a long mucus thread while they mate.

The common large slug has several color forms along its geographical range, with black forms in northern England, brown forms in the south and orange individuals in France.

SLUGS ARE EASY ANIMALS TO KEEP in vivaria, where their behavior can be studied. Slugs are particularly fond of the white pith inside grapefruit; you can trap them by placing inverted, hollowed-out grapefruit rinds in flower borders. If you poke a large black slug it adopts an aggressive posture, withdrawing its antennae, contracting so that its back forms a large hump and gently rocking from side to side, as if in silent fury.

☛ 355 SNAIL; 117 SHELL.

ALOE DAY

The avoidance of constipation is a human preoccupation that dates back to the time of the ancient Egyptians; extracts of *Aloe ferox*, known as bitter aloes, have a long history of usage as a purgative, to promote regular bowel movements. The genus also yields more benign natural products, including extracts of *Aloe vera* that are used in shampoos and cosmetics.

Aloe dichotoma, *the kokerboom tree (below), grows in arid parts of Namibia and is the largest aloe species.*

Most aloe flowers are red, a color that attracts pollinating birds.

ALOES ARE SUCCULENT PLANTS that grow in desert regions of tropical Africa and Arabia. Most aloes have structural adaptations for water conservation that are similar to those of true cacti from the New World. This superficial resemblance is due to both groups of plants evolving independently in a similar way to the same environmental stresses – water shortage and high temperatures. This process, known as convergent evolution, accounts for many similarities between distantly related living organisms.

☛ *78–9 DESERTS; 149 CACTUS.*

EYE DAY

Frogs have large eyes and acute vision, but are color blind.

Compound eyes of invertebrates like dragonflies (left) are composed of many facets, known as ommatidia, each with a separate lens. Objects crossing the field of view flicker across the ommatidia, so compound eyes are effective for detecting movement.

Vertebrate eyes work on the camera principle, with a single lens that focuses an image on a light-sensitive retina at the back of the eyeball.

The large pupils of the South American night monkey open fully after dark, giving excellent night vision.

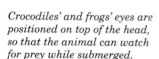

Crocodiles' and frogs' eyes are positioned on top of the head, so that the animal can watch for prey while submerged.

Eyelids clean the eye surface. In birds, like the Asiatic fishing owl, a third eyelid sweeps across the eye.

Pottos have layers of guanine crystals in their retinas, increasing the sensitivity of their night vision.

IN ORDER TO UNDERSTAND animal behavior, it is important to learn how other creatures see the world around them. Honeybees can detect ultraviolet light, beyond the range of human vision, so colors look quite different to them. Find out what colors bees prefer by placing dishes of sugar solution on artificial flowers, made of red, green and blue card. Count the bee visits to each color.

☛ *104–5 NOCTURNAL ANIMALS; 120 HEARING; 317 SCENT AND TASTE.*

ORCHID DAY

The Orchidaceae are one of the largest plant families, with over 17,500 species. Many are noted for their exotic flowers, which are almost all intricately adapted to accommodate particular species of insect pollinator. Bee orchids (below) mimic female bees, with an outline that resembles a furry body and outspread wings.

The exotic blooms of tropical orchids last for several weeks and are popular cut flowers. Several wild species are threatened with extinction, due to excessive collection by unscrupulous orchid fanatics.

Most orchids, like Dactylorhiza *species (right), produce dust-like seeds that must form a symbiotic association with a fungus before they will grow.*

ONE OF THE MOST EXTRAORDINARY orchids is the Madagascan *Angraecum sesquipedale*, whose flower has a 30-cm/12-in. nectar spur. It is pollinated by a nectar-drinking moth, *Xanthopan morgani-praedicta*, with a proboscis length to match. Charles Darwin predicted the existence of the insect from the flower structure, forty years before it was actually discovered. Orchids transfer their pollen with detachable stamens, called pollinia, which stick to the head and proboscis of insect visitors. Pollinia can be removed by poking a pencil point into their base.

☛ 190 AFRICAN PLANTS; 323 FLY-POLLINATED FLOWERS; 196 PARTS OF A FLOWER.

BUG DAY

Although the name 'bug' is often used as a general term for an insect, it is applied correctly only to Hemiptera. In these insects the jaws are modified to form a sharp-tipped sucking tube which is used to pierce the stems and leaves of plants and to suck sap containing sugars and amino acids, the building-blocks of protein, manufactured by the plant.

More than 50,000 species of bug have evolved and almost all are sap-feeders. But a few have adapted to sucking fluid from animals – pentatomid or assassin bugs drain the juices of caterpillars.

Bedbugs are a member of a group that has adapted to feeding on birds and mammals. A nocturnal bloodsucker, the bedbug is a pest in many parts of the world.

MANY BUGS spend much of their lives plugged into the phloem of a plant – the tubular cells that carry food manufactured by the plant. Find a plant that is infested with pale-colored aphids and cut off a shoot carefully without disturbing them. Stand the shoot in a jar of water with red food coloring added to it. The red coloring will travel up the shoot in the xylem (the 'water-pipes' of the plant), then into the phloem. At this point the aphids should start to turn pink.

☛ 256–7 BEETLES; 356–7 RAINFOREST CANOPY.

SQUASH DAY

Squashes, gourds and pumpkins have been cultivated for thousands of years in the Americas and formed part of an ancient agricultural system based on squashes, beans and maize.

Numerous pumpkin cultivars exist and specimens weighing over 300 kg / 650 lbs. are common.

Most squashes are grown for their edible fruit pulp and seeds, but the hard, dried skins of bottle gourds are also used as containers. They are native to sub-Saharan Africa, but gourds dating from 7000 BC have been found in South America. They may have drifted there on ocean currents, since experiments show that seeds remain viable inside gourds that have floated for 220 days in sea water. Courgettes, which are known as zucchini in the United States, are immature forms of edible marrow, which can weigh up to 50 kg / 110 lbs. when fully grown.

TRY GROWING MARROWS from seeds, which will germinate faster if they are soaked in water overnight. Scratch your name on the skin of a young zucchini with a pin, then watch the letters expand as it grows into a full-sized marrow.
☛ *238 MELON.*

Many members of the gourd family produce separate male and female flowers on the same plant, but varieties are often deliberately bred that are all female. These develop seedless fruits, which are less bitter than seeded varieties.

348

SALAMANDER DAY

Recent research has shown that Siberian salamanders can survive temperatures of –50°C/–58°F, and can revive after being frozen at –15°C/–5°F for several years. Their blood contains an antifreeze chemical that replaces water in cells and prevents damage from ice crystals in their bodies.

Salamanders are closely related to newts and different species exhibit a range of adaptations to life in the water and on land. Some produce eggs that develop into aquatic larvae and then into terrestrial adults with lungs. Terrestrial forms produce eggs in grape-like clusters under logs and guard these until they hatch into miniature salamanders, without going through an aquatic stage.

Some salamander species can detect the orientation of Earth's magnetic field.

The European fire salamander (below) is terrestrial but returns to the water to breed.

SOME FORMS OF SALAMANDER, known as axolotls, reach sexual maturity while they still retain larval characters, such as external gills. This phenomenon is known as paedomorphosis, a word derived from Greek which means 'child form'. Mexican axolotls metamorphose into adult forms with lungs if their ponds dry up, setting out in search of new ponds for breeding. They can also be induced to metamorphose by adding iodine to their aquaria; this stimulates their thyroid gland to produce thyroxine, a hormone that is essential for amphibian metamorphosis.

☛ *8 NEWT.*

KESTREL DAY

A small feather, called an alula, on the leading edge of the joint in each wing of this raptor gives it an outstanding ability to hover above its prey in preparation for making a kill. The alula breaks up the airflow over the upper wing surface, preventing the wing from stalling while the bird remains almost stationary.

Kestrels occur on every continent except Antarctica.

European and North American kestrels have adapted well to modern urban living and sometimes nest on ledges on high buildings and in industrial installations.

Large numbers of European kestrels were poisoned by pesticides in the 1950s and 1960s but their numbers have recovered. They are now one of the commonest birds of prey.

Kestrels lay 4–5 eggs but breeding success rates depend on food supply. In all raptors the chicks from the last eggs to hatch have difficulty in competing for food with larger nestlings that hatched first.

The endangered Mauritius kestrel is one of the world's rarest birds.

EUROPEAN KESTRELS regularly hunt alongside highways, where the grassy borders provide an excellent habitat for the small mammals that form a major part of their diet. Long car journies offer good opportunities to watch their technique for hovering and hunting. Notice how they hunt in wide, sweeping circles, then descend into a series of stationary hovers before dropping onto their prey. They carry their victim away in their talons.

☛ 270 EAGLE; 253 OWL.

POISONOUS FISH DAY

More people are killed by poisonous fish every year than are eaten by sharks. Tourists who wade along reefs and shorelines in warm seas should always wear shoes, in case a venomous fish lies hidden in the sand. Venomous weaver fish are quite common along some parts of British and European coasts.

The distinctive stripes of a young eeltail catfish warn that it has poisonous glands on its dorsal and pectoral fins. This coloration fades to a uniform brown in adult fish.

Soapfish are covered with a poisonous mucus.

Pufferfish (blowfish) can swallow water rapidly and inflate their bodies as a defensive precaution, but they are also very poisonous. Nevertheless, they are eaten in Japan in a dish called 'fugu', which is prepared by highly trained cooks. One small mistake in following the recipe, with incorrect cooking of the fish, can prove fatal for diners.

The fearsome appearance and striped pattern of a lionfish, with an outline disrupted by many spines, act as camouflage. The spines have poison glands in grooves along their length and inflict painful wounds.

Stingrays lash out with their tails when attacked, inflicting severe wounds with a thorny, poisonous spine.

STONEFISH ARE ONE of the most feared poisonous fish in the oceans. They are superbly camouflaged and hide in shallow water. When walked on, their dorsal spine injects a venom that can kill a man within two hours. The pain is said to be so intense that victims beg to be put out of their agony.

 66 BARRACUDA.

351

Most snails are herbivores and many species feed on dead vegetation.

LEAF LITTER DAY

The floors of forests are giant compost heaps. In the tropics and in evergreen conifer woodlands there is a slow, constant rain of dead leaves, but in temperate latitudes they all fall at once, in autumn. Fungi and the tens of thousands of species of invertebrates on the forest floors are living garbage-disposal systems, breaking down the dead leaves and recycling their nutrients through the soil. Without them, the world's forests would quickly become submerged in stagnant, wet mats of leaves.

Woodlice (sow bugs) are herbivorous crustaceans that nibble dead plants and the fungi that grow on their surface. They need permanently moist conditions.

The woodland floor offers rich pickings for carnivores. Ground beetles specialize in a wide range of prey items and some hunt snails. Centipedes impale their prey in curved, poisonous jaws.

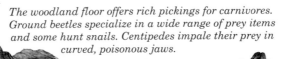

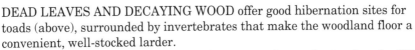

DEAD LEAVES AND DECAYING WOOD offer good hibernation sites for toads (above), surrounded by invertebrates that make the woodland floor a convenient, well-stocked larder.

Use a Tullgren funnel (see page 375) to extract invertebrates from leaf litter. Compare the populations from deciduous and coniferous woodlands – you should find the deciduous woodland litter is much richer in species. Build a compost heap to investigate the changing fauna of decaying vegetation.

☛ 355 SNAIL; 233 MILLIPEDE; 4–5 FROGS AND TOADS.

HAWKMOTH DAY

Hawkmoths, Sphingidae, or sphinx moths are among the largest, most powerful and most sophisticated of moths. There are 1,150 species distributed worldwide. Their large larvae feed on a wide range of host-plants and are characterized by a single erect horn on the end of the body – some of the caterpillars which are agricultural pests are known as hornworms.

The skull marking in the thorax of harmless death's head hawkmoths, and the fact that they squeak when touched, has made them the object of superstition. They are fond of honey, and raid beehives. Their caterpillars eat potato leaves.

Rhagasta olicacea *uses its long proboscis to drink tears, nasal secretions and saliva from cattle and humans in Thailand.*

Hawkmoths are common in warm climates, but make long migratory flights. Convolvulus hawkmoths from the Mediterranean sometimes reach Scotland and Iceland, a 1,500-km/950-mi. journey that they make in just a few days.

Most hawkmoths have a long proboscis for feeding on nectar in flowers. Hummingbird hawkmoths visit epilobium flowers by day.

HAWKMOTH LARVAE are easy to rear through to adulthood. See the end of the book for information on this. When the larvae stop feeding and their color darkens they are about to pupate, so line the bottom of the container with crumpled tissue paper for them to pupate in. Do not handle the delicate pupa; it may emerge in a few weeks but some species need to be left over winter in a cool, dry place.

☛ *290 MOTH; 334 SILK MOTH.*

FUNGI DAY

Fungi are so different from other organisms that taxonomists place them in a kingdom of their own. For most of their lives they grow as a mass of creeping threads, or hyphae, until these aggregate and develop into the fruiting bodies, with many bizarre forms.

Witches' butter is a gelatinous species that grows on decaying wood.

The common stinkhorn is covered with an evil-smelling brown jelly.

Earth stars grow on humus-rich soil in woodlands, opening into distinctive flower-shaped structures.

King Alfred's cakes, or cramp balls, grow on dead beech and ash trees.

Beefsteak fungus taints wood of infected oak trees with a dark brown hue.

Mycena species and the amethyst fungus both grow on decaying wood on the forest floor.

Edible horse mushrooms occur in grasslands on rich, organic soils.

The giant puffball is found in pastures and could be mistaken for a small sheep at a distance. The fruit body may be almost 1 m/ 3 ft. across and releases an estimated 7 trillion spores when it ripens.

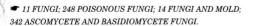
☞ *11 FUNGI; 248 POISONOUS FUNGI; 14 FUNGI AND MOLD; 342 ASCOMYCETE AND BASIDIOMYCETE FUNGI.*

SNAIL DAY

The shell of a snail, which protects it from desiccation and predators, is secreted by a ridge of specialized tissue along the side of its owner's body. Turns of the spiral are added to keep pace with the snail's growth.

Snails are common in areas with calcareous rock strata, since they need calcium carbonate to build their shells. Slugs tend to predominate in acid soils.

Edible snails (Helix pomatia) are a culinary delicacy in some areas, cooked in garlic butter, and are raised in large numbers in snail farms.

Giant African land snails (Achantia) have shells that can reach a length of 20 cm / 8 in. As destructive grazers, they have done great damage to native vegetation of countries like Hawaii, where they have been introduced as a food source. Their eggs have a tough, calcified shell and may be as large as the egg of a small songbird.

Most snails are herbivores, but the introduction of carnivorous snails to Hawaii has led to the destruction of native Partula species. Captive breeding programs in London Zoo have saved these endangered mollusks from extinction.

ALLOW A SNAIL TO CRAWL over a piece of glass and watch the waves of muscular contraction sweep across its foot. The mouth can be seen on the underside of its muscular foot; the animal feeds by rasping at the surface as it crawls, using a file-like tongue (or radula), covered in minute teeth. Garden snails often hibernate in outbuildings and similar sheltered places during winter. Mark their shells with small spots of paint, so that you can follow their movements in spring and investigate the size of their feeding territory.

☛ 343 SLUG; 117 SHELL.

RAINFOREST CANOPY DAY

A walk through a tropical rainforest during daytime can be a disappointing experience. Many of the animals that live on the forest floor are nocturnal and during the day most of the activity is confined to the canopy of branches, high above. The leaves and branches provide food, shelter, and breeding sites for the most diverse array of animal species on Earth.

Scores of tree frog species thrive in the high humidity of the forest canopy.

The overlapping tree branches provide perfect hunting territory for snakes like the emerald tree boa, which can glide silently through the foliage, catching frogs and robbing birds' nests. The tangle of branches provides an aerial highway and a perfect background to hide the camouflaged predator.

Oropendolas often choose to build their hanging nests near to nests of aggressive bees and wasps, which deter predatory opossums, toucans and snakes.

The harpy eagles of the South American rainforest nest in the crowns of trees and hunt over the canopy, swooping onto monkeys. Tree sloths are favorite prey. Eagles occupy large territories, and quickly disappear once commercial logging operations begin. When rainforests are destroyed, the top predators are the first animals to suffer.

There are many climbing fig species in rainforests and these are an important food source for birds like the double-eyed fig parrot. The enormous range of tree species and constant flowering season in equatorial rainforests means that there is a continuous supply of flowers and fruit throughout the year.

When danger threatens, the howler monkeys in the treetops scream hysterically, alerting every animal in the neighborhood to the potential threat. They also howl at night, to defend their territories against other members of their species. Their vocal duels can be heard up to 3 km / 2 mi. away.

The forest canopy foliage is also the feeding ground for caterpillars of butterflies and moths, which have a dazzling array of adaptations to protect them from birds. Many are toxic, some are covered in threatening spines and can inflate their bodies, and others rely on camouflage to escape the attentions of hungry predators.

STUDYING RAINFOREST CANOPY LIFE presents biologists with major problems. Long, straight tree trunks and the swarms of ants and other biting insects that cover them make tree climbing a difficult and painful exercise. Much remains to be discovered about the life history and habits of the vast array of insects in the canopy, which is particularly rich in shield bug species (above, right). Bats (above left) play a major role in rainforest ecology, with fruit bats dispersing seeds and other species pollinating flowers, but their nocturnal habits and the inaccessibility of the canopy hampers study of their activities.

☛ 271 BAT; 163 SNAKE; 4–5 FROG AND TOAD.

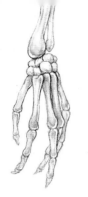

SKELETON DAY

The exoskeletons of invertebrates protect their internal organs but impose severe limitations on their growth, unless they are regularly shed and replaced. Animals with backbones – the vertebrates – have avoided this problem by evolving an internal skeleton, whose constant growth keeps pace with the rest of the body.

Hinge joints allow wrists, knees and fingers to articulate. Ligaments join bone to bone, while tendons join bone to muscle.

Ball-and-socket joints in the hips and shoulders allow free movement of arms and legs.

MUCH CAN BE LEARNED about an animal from its skeleton: large eye sockets suggest good eyesight; long limb bones are found in animals that run fast, like hares. You can collect clean skeletons of dead animals, provided that you soak the bones in concentrated washing soda overnight and then treat them with bleach for two hours. These chemicals are dangerous, so ask an adult for help. See the end of the book for further advice.

☛ 359 ARMOR.

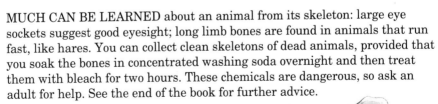

ARMOR DAY

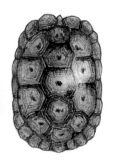

It is the destiny of most small animals to become a meal for larger ones, and a hard, armored surface can help to increase their chances of survival. It can range from the heavy carapace of a tortoise, composed of keratin and fused to its ribs, to the exoskeleton of a scorpion, which combines strength with lightness.

The spectacular success of insects can be attributed, at least in part, to the evolution of a rigid exoskeleton made of chitin, which combines with a protein to form sclerotin, a tough, light material. The sclerotized jaws of some beetles can bite through thin metal. The light but strong properties of sclerotin are essential for insects that fly, where their aerodynamic design must be balanced by the need for an armored skin.

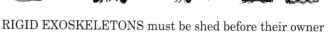

RIGID EXOSKELETONS must be shed before their owner can grow. Crab shells are composed of chitin which contains calcium, salts and protein. The process of shedding and renewing this armor dominates much of the animal's life and leaves it temporarily defenseless, until a new exoskeleton hardens.

In grasshoppers the tough exoskeleton provides a means of communication when hard pegs on their legs are rubbed rhythmically against their wings to generate a characteristic chirp.

☞ *358 SKELETON.*

GANNET DAY

A visit to a gannetry during the breeding season is one of the most memorable experiences in ornithology. Up to 60,000 birds may nest together, spaced just far enough apart to avoid conflict, and the whole colony is a constant scene of activity, with the air permanently filled with birds. The sound of calling birds is deafening and yet, in the midst of the confusion, individuals easily locate their nests and mates.

Nests, built of heaps of seaweed and feathers, are often sited on narrow rocky ledges, where a single egg is laid. Its tapered shape helps to prevent it rolling over the precipice.

Gannets catch fish by plunge diving, folding their wings and dropping almost vertically from up to 30 m / 100 ft. onto shoals of surface-swimming fish. Their long bills are perfectly adapted for grasping their prey, as they swim back to the surface and take to the air again.

WITH LONG, THIN WINGS, gannets are superb fliers, capable of hanging motionless in updrafts at the top of cliffs or gliding in long, effortless swoops. The best time to visit a gannetry is early in the breeding season, when the birds go through a complex pair-bonding ritual. Birds face each other, extend their necks, then point their beaks upwards and rub them together. This greeting ceremony is repeated between mates throughout the breeding season.

☞ 278 PELICAN; 232 BOOBY; 255 FRIGATE BIRD.

SEA URCHIN DAY

The rigid internal skeleton of a sea urchin, known as a test, is made up of ten double rows of plates, armed with movable spines carried on 'ball and socket' joints. The spines also help in locomotion, working in concert with five rows of hydraulic tube feet. Small, venomous appendages amongst the spines, called pedicellariae, seize any small animals that may venture too close.

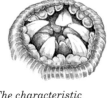

The characteristic feeding organ of a sea urchin – a mouth ringed with five chewing teeth that are moved up and down by ten pairs of muscles – is known as Aristotle's lantern.

The pencil urchins, like the sea mine, carry larger, thicker spines and some species brood their young in depressions between these.

Pencil urchin spines have occasionally been used as slate pencils.

Fertilized urchin eggs develop into microscopic, transparent larvae that remain planktonic for several months.

THE FRAGILE TESTS of burrowing sea urchins are often washed up along the tide line of sandy beaches. If you cannot find these, visit seaside gift shops, where larger tests are often sold as ornaments. Notice the five radiating rows of holes, where the tube feet protruded through the test surface, and look for the bases of the spines, mounted on the test plates.

☛ *94 STAR FISH; 331 SEA CUCUMBER.*

361

EEL DAY

Eels are snake-shaped bony fishes which lack pelvic fins. They are marine fish but some are catadromous, moving between salt and fresh water. The dorsal and caudal fins are continuous and very long so that the eel presents a ribbon-like surface to the water so as to maximize the power of each swimming stroke.

Snipe-eels are from great depths – 500 m / 1,600 ft. to 2,000 m / 6,500 ft. – in the central Atlantic, and grow up to 1.5 m / 5 ft. long.

The European eel, below, has probably the most peculiar life history of any fish.

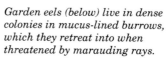

Garden eels (below) live in dense colonies in mucus-lined burrows, which they retreat into when threatened by marauding rays.

Fiercely predatory conger and moray eels are exclusively marine fish.

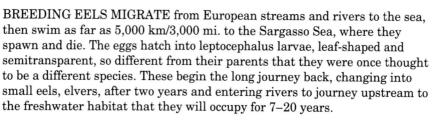

BREEDING EELS MIGRATE from European streams and rivers to the sea, then swim as far as 5,000 km/3,000 mi. to the Sargasso Sea, where they spawn and die. The eggs hatch into leptocephalus larvae, leaf-shaped and semitransparent, so different from their parents that they were once thought to be a different species. These begin the long journey back, changing into small eels, elvers, after two years and entering rivers to journey upstream to the freshwater habitat that they will occupy for 7–20 years.

☛ 118 MIGRATION.

BADGER DAY

Badgers are stocky members of the weasel family, Mustelidae. Here are two species, the African honey badger or ratel (left) and the European badger, below. The ratel is not just African – its range extends through Asia as far as eastern India. Both are burrow dwellers but their behavior is quite different.

The ratel is a ferocious animal that eats almost anything and will attack intruders close to its burrow. It weighs up to 12 kg/26 lbs., but will take on a buffalo, attacking and hanging on like a bulldog.

Look for black-and-white hairs on fences, scratched trees and dung neatly deposited in hollows as signs of a badger's presence.

The shy European badger is nocturnal and eats mainly worms. Fastidious, it takes its dry grass bedding out of its burrow and spreads it out to air during the night while it is out foraging.

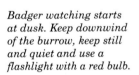

Badger watching starts at dusk. Keep downwind of the burrow, keep still and quiet and use a flashlight with a red bulb.

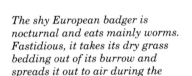

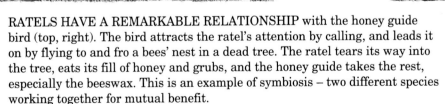

RATELS HAVE A REMARKABLE RELATIONSHIP with the honey guide bird (top, right). The bird attracts the ratel's attention by calling, and leads it on by flying to and fro a bees' nest in a dead tree. The ratel tears its way into the tree, eats its fill of honey and grubs, and the honey guide takes the rest, especially the beeswax. This is an example of symbiosis – two different species working together for mutual benefit.

Honey guides are brood parasites, like cuckoos. They lay their eggs in other birds' nests so their honey-guiding behavior is absolutely instinctive.

☛ 105 NOCTURNAL ANIMALS; 54–5 UNDERGROUND.

PHEASANT DAY

The common pheasant originated in Asia but has been introduced into Britain as a game bird on shooting estates, where it is reared under the watchful eye of game-keepers. As a ground-nesting bird, its eggs and chicks are at the mercy of stoats, weasels, foxes and birds of prey, and ruthless extermination of these predators was once a feature of all large country estates.

Pheasants are reluctant fliers and only take to the air when disturbed.

Pheasants belong to the galliformes, a bird family that includes peacocks, jungle fowl and tragopans (right), all of which are noted for their brilliant breeding plumage. Lady Amherst's pheasant (below) is often kept as an ornamental fowl in stately homes and sometimes escapes and breeds in the wild.

LEGEND HAS IT that the Romans brought pheasants to Britain, but the first authentic records are of introductions from the Caucasus in the Middle Ages. If you look closely you will notice that male pheasants have two different forms of plumage. Descendants of 16th-century Caucasian birds do not have white neck plumage, unlike late-18th-century introductions from China which have a white ring below their green collar. Survey the cock pheasants in your area, to determine whether they are of Caucasian or Chinese extraction.

☛ *151 PEACOCK; 81 CHICKEN.*

364

MUDSKIPPER DAY

Fish were the first animals with backbones to colonize land, and watching today's mudskippers must be very like returning to the first moments in terrestrial vertebrate evolution. Tropical mudskippers are related to the rock-pool gobies of temperate coasts, but they use the muscular stumps of their pectoral fins as crutches. They also leap by arching and suddenly straightening their bodies, making 60-cm/2-ft. jumps that give them their name.

Mudskippers sit on mud flats with their mouths gaping, absorbing oxygen into blood vessels in the mouth and pharynx. Oxygen also diffuses through the skin and into the gills, from water which they carry in their gill chambers and regularly renew from puddles.

Adult mudskippers are territorial and defend the area around their burrows. Juveniles without territories must climb out of the water on to mangrove roots to escape predatory fish that swim in with the tide. Their pelvic fins, which are fused to form an adhesive sucker, allow them to cling on until the tide recedes.

VISION IS A PROBLEM FOR FISH when they leave water, because eyes that work perfectly underwater are shortsighted on land. To overcome this mudskippers change the shape of the lens and cornea, a system that works well enough for them to catch flying insects. Try making a variable-shaped lens by filling a small plastic bag with water and focusing images through it.

☛ *4–5 FROG AND TOAD; 8 NEWT; 154–5 HIBERNATION.*

The naming of living organisms has always been problematic, and biologists throughout history have had to deal with two major difficulties.

Firstly, the human species has evolved into large numbers of nationalities, each with its own language. They all have different names for the same animal. The problem is made worse because even different regional groups within a nation often use distinct and obscure dialect words. In Britain, for example, there are sixty-five different regional names for a sow bug. Scientists throughout the world need a classification system for the world's flora and fauna that is based on a single language that they all understand.

Latin, with "Latinized" versions of words, has been established as the international language for scientific communication for several hundred years. Species are always given Latin names and, when they are first discovered, they are described in detail in Latin too. So the common sow bug is known to scientists throughout the world by its Latin name, *Oniscus asellus*.

The second major problem is that there are enormous numbers of species, many of which look similar to one another. Until the beginning of the 18th century it was customary to describe each in a long Latin phrase or sentence. This was a hopelessly cumbersome system, which was finally simplified at a stroke by a Swedish botanist called Carl von Linne (1707–78), who is usually referred to by the Latinized form of his name, Carolus Linnaeus.

Linnaeus shortened all the lengthy Latin descriptions to just the first two words of each, creating the binomial system that is used to this day. The first part of the name is referred to as the genus (which always begins with a capital letter), the second part is the species (which always begins with a lower-case letter). This system of using a Latin name of just two words is simple, precise and is understood by every scientist, everywhere.

But there is much more to taxonomy than merely giving every organism a name. Biological scientists strive to classify the living world in a way which reflects the natural evolutionary relationships between organisms. It is relatively easy to do this for living species within a genus; close comparisons show that *Ranunculus bulbosus* (bulbous buttercup) and *Ranunculus repens* (creeping buttercup) are obviously two closely related species within the same genus, *Ranunculus*. But deciding how buttercups might be related to ferns is much more difficult. The two groups of plants evolved from a common ancestor in the distant geological past, probably over 150 million years ago, and most of the intermediate forms have become extinct and have left few fossil remains. So taxonomists – the biologists who have the task of classifying and naming the natural world – must try to reconstruct such distant evolutionary relationships as best they can, by comparing common characteristics and key differences in living organisms and by gleaning fragments of information from an incomplete fossil record.

They place different groups of living organisms in a taxonomic hierarchy, beginning with kingdoms and ending with species. Five kingdoms are commonly recognized – Plantae (plants), Animalia (animals), Fungi (fungi), the Monera (blue-green algae and bacteria) and the Protista (algae, protozoa and slime molds). Classification can be controversial, even at this stage. Slime molds, for example, have some fungal characteristics and some animal features. Sponges are classified as animals, but they share some unusual features with plants. Some modern biologists would like to split the bacteria into more than one kingdom, based on new discoveries of bacteria that have a metabolism based on methane and can thrive at extraordinarily high temperatures. At present, we know very little about the majority of these microscopic organisms but it seems likely that lumping them all together in one kingdom will eventually prove unsatisfactory.

The next level of classification is the phylum, which groups together organisms within a kingdom that possess common characteristics. The best way to understand the classificatory system is to use an example. Sea squirts, frogs, tigers, and humans are all placed in the kingdom Animalia, phylum Chordata, because they all possess a backbone (of sorts) at some stage in their development. This system of classification, of grouping together organisms with common features and separating out those that are distinct, continues downward through the hierarchy. So, at the next level (the subphylum) the sea squirt is separated out into the subphylum Urochordata, because, unlike the others in the group, it does not possess a skull, but does have a simple backbone and nerve cord in its larval stage.

At the succeeding level (the class), frogs are separated into their own group (class Amphibia) because they are cold-blooded, while tigers and humans are warm-blooded. This system of sieving continues through two further categories; from here onward we will just follow the classificatory pathway of the tiger.

At the level of order the tiger is classified into the order Carnivora, based on its general anatomy and flesh-eating tendencies, along with 245 other species of dogs, cats, wolves, bears and weasels that share similar characteristics. At the next level of taxonomy, tigers are classified into the family Felidae, along with all the other cats like lions, panthers, cheetahs, lynx and domestic cats, that share its general features.

This brings us to the penultimate level of classification, the genus, where all the separate species of tiger-like animals are grouped. All tigers belong to the genus *Panthera* and there are just five species: *Panthera tigris*, the tiger (the largest of all cats); *Panthera leo*, the lion; *Panthera pardus*, the African leopard; *Panthera uncia*, the snow leopard; and *Panthera onca*, the jaguar.

And so, by a constant process of comparison, at progressively finer levels, and by separation into smaller and smaller groups of related organisms, tigers, and all the other organisms in the living world, are classified. It is the dream of every taxonomist to produce classifications that reflect the evolutionary history of life on earth, grouping organisms that have common ancestors at each level in the hierarchy. Such systems are usually represented as trees, rooted in some distant ancestral microorganism that evolved about 3,500 million years ago and extending into fine branches that represent the species that live on our planet today. Much of the trunk and many of the major branches of the tree are missing, lost in the great waves of mass extinctions that engulfed the Earth in the geological past. Many of the extinct organisms have left no fossil traces, so the tree will always be incomplete; we can only be sure about the relationships of living organisms, that lie on the twigs at the extremities of this imaginary structure.

Remember too that so far we have only managed to describe and classify about 1,400,000 species. Biologists estimate that we share the planet with at least 30,000,000 species. In the future, we should be able to describe more of the fine detail at the ends of the branches of the evolutionary tree and perhaps modify the overall shape of the tree itself, as organisms are reclassified in the light of new knowledge. The science of taxonomy is conducted according to certain ground rules, but its decisions are not set in stone and classifications change as taxonomic techniques improve. Such changes might seem confusing but, in truth, they reflect the real excitement of biological science – a relentless, exhilarating process of discovery and increase in understanding of the world around us.

The taxonomic hierarchy

Kingdom

    Phylum

        Subphylum

            Class

                Order

                    Family

                        Genus

                            Species

SAFETY

Advice on using dangerous chemicals
Some of the practical experiments suggested in this book involve the use of several toxic or corrosive chemicals. These should always be used under the supervision of an adult and be handled according to the manufacturer's instructions, which you will find marked on the bottles and packets.

For the following substances, we would advise wearing rubber gloves.
- caustic soda – causes burns to skin and eyes
- washing soda – injurious to skin and eyes

- copper sulphate – toxic by accumulation in the body
- dry cleaning fluid – inflammable, harmful vapor
- household bleach – harmful vapor, injurious to skin and eyes

You should protect your eyes from splashes with glasses of some kind – use sunglasses if no others are available.

Handling dead animal tissues and bones

Dead and decaying animal tissues are contaminated with microorganisms which can cause serious illnesses. Scrupulous hygiene is essential. Never bring animal remains into any area where food will be prepared. Always wash your hands, and all surfaces and instruments that come into contact with animal tissues, with a dilute disinfectant solution. As a precaution, it is wise to wear rubber gloves when handling hazardous or unpleasant materials, except when you are handling anything hot which may melt the rubber. Any cuts or abrasions to your skin should be washed thoroughly and treated with antiseptic.

You should ensure that you have been vaccinated against tetanus before you carry out any field work.

How to carry out an experiment

The best sets of experiment begin with simple tests for simple questions, examining one factor at a time. You could test your sow bugs in a chamber where one side was cool and wet and the other side was hot and dry, but if they did express a preference you would not know whether it was temperature or moisture that governed their behavior. Most experiments do not give simple answers, but their results usually suggest further experiments that you could perform to learn more about the organism under investigation.

Experiments should always be repeated several times. Scientists call this process replication; it ensures that they don't draw a conclusion from a single experiment where an unexpected factor may have confused the issue.

It pays to repeat an experiment several times to take account of natural variation. Repeat your experiments several times and take an average of all of your results to give a more accurate estimate of their true meaning.

You should always record your experiments as clearly and as precisely as you can. You should do this in four parts: an introduction, which explains why you carried out the experiment (your hypothesis); your experimental set-up and methods, so that someone else could repeat your experiment exactly and test your work; your results, clearly displayed in tables and graphs; and a discussion of what you think your results mean, and what new questions they pose. Remember that you should always try to identify the organisms that you study accurately; there are hundreds of species of sow bug worldwide, and they may not all behave in the same way.

If you follow this pattern for your experiments you will be well on the way to becoming a professional scientist.

Aquarium

When choosing an aquarium, buy the biggest that you can afford. This will allow you to create a wide variety of mini-habitats and stock them with a diverse range of animals. Line the bottom with gravel at one end, graded through sand into silt at the other. Add a few rocks and perhaps a clay flowerpot as a shelter, and plant oxygenating water-plants. If you plan to keep frog, toad or newt tadpoles, it is vital that you provide a floating log or some other surface that young amphibians can climb out on; if you don't, they will drown.

Fill the tank slowly, to avoid disturbing the bottom materials. Try to use water from a natural pond, rather than tap water, which may have been treated with fluoride. Then stock the tank with pond life. Try to achieve a natural balance, with herbivores and detritus feeders and perhaps a few carnivores. Remember that fish will eat all the invertebrates, and the voracious larvae of great diving beetles will soon consume all your tadpoles, so don't include these if you want to maintain variety.

The key to success with an aquarium is to keep the water clean and well oxygenated. Pond snails are essential – they graze algae from the glass sides of the tank. It is well worth investing in an aquarium pump, to maintain high dissolved oxygen levels.

Seawater aquaria are much harder to maintain than their freshwater equivalents and it is not worth keeping one unless you have access to regular supplies of fresh seawater and can aerate the water with an aquarium pump. Many coastal animals are adapted to the daily cycle of tides and these are difficult (but not impossible) to simulate in an aquarium.

Freshwater aquarium, with a varierty of depths and waterplants. The cover should be fine mesh, to let in air but to prevent insects escaping after hatching.

Emergent rock, for young frogs and hatching insects

Variety of oxygenating water plants

Coarser gravel

Finer silt

Breeding cages for insects

Insect breeding cages can be as simple as a cylinder of fine wire mesh closed by circular tin lids at either end. The golden rules for successfully raising butterflies, moths and any other insects from eggs or caterpillars are to avoid overcrowding, provide a constant fresh supply of their food plant and remove all droppings before they can go moldy and foul the cage. A layer of dry sand on the cage floor will help to keep it clean. If your food plants are placed in a jar of water, seal the neck of the jar with a cardboard ring, so that your caterpillars do not fall in and drown.

Once insects pupate they need to be transferred to a cage with dry sand on the bottom. Check daily to see if your pupae have hatched. With luck, you may be able to watch the moment of metamorphosis, when the dry chrysalis splits to reveal a brilliant butterfly.

If you collect caterpillars from the wild you will find that many are parasitized by ichneumon wasps. These usually either form a cluster of cocoons on the outside of dead caterpillars or emerge as tiny, metallic-colored wasps from pupae. They are fascinating animals, and worthy of close study under a hand lens or microscope.

Building a pond

A pond will attract a wide range of animals in the garden and it should incorporate the following features:

- Shallow margins, where plants can root in mud and send shoots out into the water. This marginal vegetation will allow birds to drink, amphibians to emerge and dragonflies and damselflies to lay eggs. When plants like brooklime (speedwell), bog bean and monkey flower bloom they attract many insects that will lay eggs and breed in the marginal zone
- A wide variety of oxygenating plants
- A healthy population of snails, to keep algal growth under control
- Deeper water in the center – at least 1 m/3 ft. – so that it does not freeze solid in winter
- Shelves built into the sloping sides, where pots of partially submerged plants, like yellow flag iris and reeds, can be placed

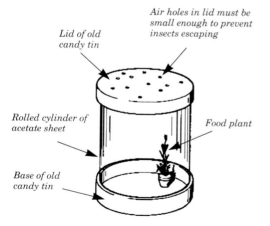

Air holes in lid must be small enough to prevent insects escaping

Lid of old candy tin

Rolled cylinder of acetate sheet

Food plant

Base of old candy tin

• A surrounding area of grass which is only cut once or twice each year and planted with wild flowers, to create a haymeadow flora that will give your pool a natural appearence. The longer vegetation will be ideal for frogs and toads to roam in after dusk, hunting slugs. Provide a pile of logs near the edge, where amphibians can hibernate in winter.

New ponds take some time to become clear and algal blooms may form in their early years. Minimise these by making sure that no nitrogen fertilizers are fed to the pond plants. If possible, use poor-quality, nitrogen-depleted soil for planting in ponds. Once you have established a variety of plants and animals the ecosystem will stabilize, the water will clear and you should be able to study the life cycles of its inhabitants at close quarters. Don't add fish to a small pond, as they will eat most of the interesting invertebrates and reduce their diversity.

Ponds need regular maintenance. Remove and compost excessive weed growth after first washing out pond animals in a bucket of water and returning them to the pond. In particular, control the growth of duckweeds and water fern, which can blanket the whole surface and exclude light. In autumn, cover your pond with a net, to prevent it becoming clogged with dead leaves.

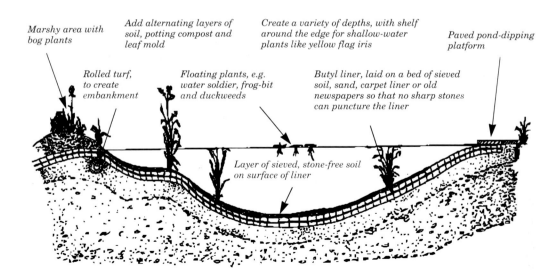

Marshy area with bog plants

Add alternating layers of soil, potting compost and leaf mold

Create a variety of depths, with shelf around the edge for shallow-water plants like yellow flag iris

Paved pond-dipping platform

Rolled turf, to create embankment

Floating plants, e.g. water soldier, frog-bit and duckweeds

Butyl liner, laid on a bed of sieved soil, sand, carpet liner or old newspapers so that no sharp stones can puncture the liner

Layer of sieved, stone-free soil on surface of liner

Collecting

Collections have an important place in natural history, as dead reference specimens are needed in laboratories and museums for identification purposes; but there is little point in assembling collections otherwise. Capturing and killing living organisms merely to arrange them in drawers and cabinets is a preoccupation that is rooted in the past. Natural populations of wildlife are under enough pressure from environmental destruction, without the added hazard of collectors removing the largest and rarest specimens from ecosystems. No one should collect any living organisms without first familiarizing themselves with the relevant national conservation laws. The penalties for ignoring these are usually hefty fines, or worse.

Animals and plants are far more interesting when they are alive than when they are dead, and by watching and recording their natural processes and habits there is a good chance that you can make original discoveries, even in countries where the flora and fauna has been intensively studied. So, if you feel the urge to collect, become proficient in the use of still and video cameras, and record your prey in their natural habitats. There is no greater thrill to be had in natural history than approaching an animal and recording its behavior on film, without it being aware of your presence. This also allows you to share your experience with others, and helps to spread the conservation message.

Compost heaps

Every garden should have at least one. A well-constructed compost heap will provide a constant supply of invertebrates for you to watch and experiment with. You need to aim for a heap which is well aerated, with alternating layers of soft plant material, like grass clippings and weeds, and tougher stems that will let air penetrate. Animal dung, like the sweepings from a rabbit's cage, makes an excellent compost accelerator, which will encourage the microbial action that will reduce the dead plant material to a fine, fibrous compost. As this happens, scores of animals will invade this temporary habitat. Brandling worms, slugs, snails, springtails, spiders, ground beetles, centipedes, millipedes and sow bugs will take

Lightweight, portable blind ideal for bird watching and bird photography

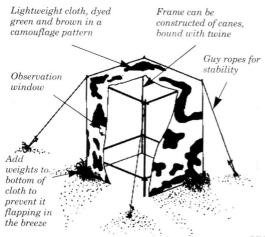

Lightweight cloth, dyed green and brown in a camouflage pattern

Frame can be constructed of canes, bound with twine

Guy ropes for stability

Observation window

Add weights to bottom of cloth to prevent it flapping in the breeze

up residence. Birds will come to feed on them. In autumn the rich food supply and the warmth generated by the decaying vegetation will attract hibernating hedgehogs, slow-worms and even grass snakes – so be careful how you dig into a compost heap in winter and spring.

and it is full of questions, like "Why did blue tits strip all the paint off my house windowframes in 1989?" and, "Why do thousands of jellyfish become stranded on the seashore near my home every year?" Someday, I'll get around to trying to answer these questions, but for now it's

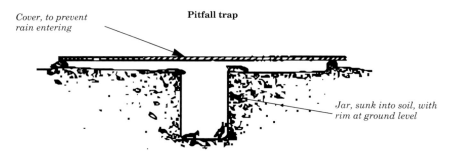

Cover, to prevent rain entering

Pitfall trap

Jar, sunk into soil, with rim at ground level

Explore your compost heap as it matures, armed with a set of collecting tubes and a magnifying lens or microscope; the variety of interesting animals and fungi is immense, and constantly changes as the heap matures.

Diaries and notebooks

All great scientific discoveries begin when an individual makes an observation. A nature diary or notebook full of observations acts as a source book for questions about the living world, as well as a record of your most memorable experiences in natural history. You don't need to record everything you see slavishly every day – just keep a record of those things that are especially interesting. I have kept such a diary, on and off, for thirty-three years

good to know that they're there, safely recorded, ready to conjure up vivid memories.

Get into the habit of keeping records of all your observations, preferably in a loose-leaf folder, so that you can add photographs and sketches. If you have access to a computer you could type up your observations neatly, using a word processing programme. If is often difficult to recover useful pieces of information from books written in diary form, but if you use a word-processing programme you will probably find that it will allow you to index your work, page by page, as you go along. This is an enormous advantage when you keep diaries for many years and want to check through them for important records.

Plankton nets

Make a plankton net either from a nylon stocking or a piece of fine nylon net curtain fixed to a strong wire ring. Attach a plastic bottle to the end, to collect the catch, and attach two closed, empty plastic bottles to the top of the mouth of the net to act as floats that will keep it just below the surface. The best way to trawl for plankton is behind a slowly moving boat, but you can land excellent catches by wading through the water on a sandy beach as the tide comes in.

Decant your catch into a transparent container and allow it to settle. Many planktonic animals are as transparent as glass, but after a while your eyes will become adjusted to their jerky movements and you will find that the water is full of crab, coelenterate, mollusk and worm larvae and, with luck, the beautiful ctenophores or sea goose-berries, with their rhythmically lashing combs of cilia.

Don't forget that there are planktonic larvae in freshwater too.

Tullgren funnel

The Tullgren funnel (illustrated) is the perfect instrument for extracting small invertebrates from soil, leaf litter and

Lamp

Soil

Kitchen sieve, placed on top of a kitchen funnel. The mesh size will determine what size of animals drop into the jar

compost heaps. Place your sample in the sieve, turn on the lamp and collect your specimens in a vial as they tumble out from the base of the funnel. Identifying many of these mini-beasts can be a challenge, because the soil has such a rich population of minute inhabitants, but you can start by classifying them according to their numbers of legs: if there are six, it's an insect; eight, a spider or spider mite; more than eight, an isopod (sow bug), centipede or millipede. If it jumps, it's probably a springtail; if it wriggles it could be a worm. These are the easy first

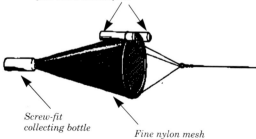

Two plastic bottles act as floats, keeping the net just below the surface

Screw-fit collecting bottle

Fine nylon mesh

steps; visit your library for more detailed information.

Sowing seeds

Simple rules for success:

- Sow seeds on a germinating medium. Excellent and inexpensive germinating mediums are widely available.
- Sow seeds at a depth that is equal to twice their diameter. Very fine seeds should be sown on the surface and watered from below, by lowering the seed tray into a pan of water and letting water rise to the surface of the medium by capillary action.
- Sow seeds thinly – overcrowding encourages disease. Keep the seedlings well aerated. If you use a plastic bag or propagator cover to speed germination, remember that warm stagnant air and condensation encourage fungal diseases.
- Always keep the medium well watered, but not saturated.
- Most seeds germinate well at a constant temperature between 68° and 75°F (20° and 25°C). A heated propagator is very useful for germinating seeds.
- Pot seedlings individually as soon as they develop two true leaves. Grow them in good light, but not where they can be scorched by direct sunlight.
- Be philosophical about your failures. If your seedlings all succumb to a mystery fungus, examine them under the microscope. Many fungi have fascinating spore-producing structures.

Microscopes

A microscope, although expensive, is probably the most useful scientific instrument that a natural historian can possess. Even a simple hand lens will open up a new world for investigation, because most of the world's wildlife is small, at or beyond the limits of normal human vision.

Simple, hand-held portable microscopes will allow you to appreciate the intricate design of an insect's eye or the fine structure of a moss capsule. More advanced compound microscopes, with magnifications of up to 1000x, will take you into the world of the protozoans, like amoeba, that swarm in thousands in every pond.

Moth trap

A moth trap, as illustrated here, will lure some of the most beautiful of all insects within easy reach. Remember that safety with electricity is vital. You should never use the moth trap outside when it might rain and should always connect it to the mains via a circuit breaker, so that you

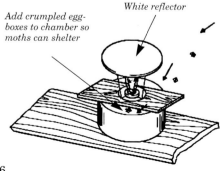

White reflector

Add crumpled egg-boxes to chamber so moths can shelter

cannot electrocute yourself. When you open the trap, be careful not to touch the hot bulb and be prepared to capture your moths quickly, in plastic vials, before they fly away.

Pond or rockpool viewers

Water surfaces reflect light, making it difficult to watch what is going on below. The solution is to take a deep plastic flower pot, cut a circle out of the base, and superglue a circle of transparent, rigid plastic in its place. Make sure the joint is watertight, lower it into the water and watch the life below through your underwater viewer. If the light is dim, or if you want to investigate nocturnal underwater life, fix a miniature flashlight inside, as a submersible searchlight. You may find it useful to make two or three different-sized viewers, for ponds and rockpools of varying sizes.

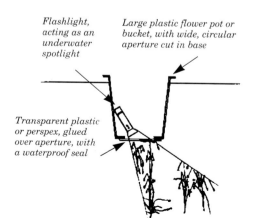

Flashlight, acting as an underwater spotlight

Large plastic flower pot or bucket, with wide, circular aperture cut in base

Transparent plastic or perspex, glued over aperture, with a waterproof seal

Pooters

A pooter is the entomologist's favorite tool for picking up small insects and other invertebrates. It consists of a sealed jar with two tubes inserted through the lid. One is held in the mouth, the other has a tapered end that is pointed at the insect. A sharp intake of breath is usually sufficient to suck the surprised insect into the jar. There is one essential precaution that you must observe: make sure the end of the mouth tube in the jar is covered with

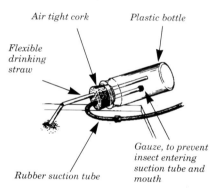

Air tight cork

Plastic bottle

Flexible drinking straw

Rubber suction tube

Gauze, to prevent insect entering suction tube and mouth

fine gauze, or you may find that your prey ends up in your mouth.

Vivarium

A vivarium is merely an aquarium without water, designed to house invertebrates, amphibians, reptiles and small mammals. You can create a habitat to suit each class of animal: soil, stones and rotting logs for invertebrates; moist moss and shelter for amphibians; dry shelter and warmth for reptiles; and straw bedding and shelter for small mammals. Adequate food and water are essentials, and you should only keep animals in captivity long enough for you to satisfy your curiosity about their behavior, without causing them to suffer. When you release them, choose a suitable habitat where they can acclimatize themselves to life in the wild again.

Wormery

This consists of a wooden frame holding two vertical sheets of glass, with a 5-cm/2-in. gap between them. The gap is filled with layers of different textures of moist soil and sand and a layer of leaves is added to the top (see illustration). When worms are added they can be watched as they mix the soil layers, and draw leaves down into their burrows. This activity is of immense agricultural importance, turning over and aerating the soil and adding organic humus.

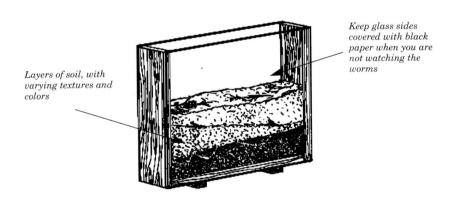

Layers of soil, with varying textures and colors

Keep glass sides covered with black paper when you are not watching the worms

381

giraffe 121, 202, 241, 317
Glaucomys volans (flying squirrel) 73
Glomeris marginata (pill millipede) 233
Glossinia sp. (tsetse fly) 177, 325
glowworm 105, 286
gnu (wildebeest) 115, 118
goat 28, 313
goldfish 150
Goliathus goliathus (goliath beetle) 340
goose 185
Gopherus agassizii (American desert
  tortoise) 79
Gorgasia sillneri (garden eel) 362
Gorgon taurinus (gnu) 115, 118
gorilla 130, 192, 203
Gorilla gorilla (gorilla) 130, 192, 203
Goura cristata (crowned pigeon) 35
gourami 48
grape 236
Graphosoma italicum (striped bug) 347
grass 85, 147
  see also cereals
grasshopper 273, 359
grizzly bear 25
ground squirrel 28, 54, 73, 85, 154
grouper 326
Grus japonensis (Japanese crane) 136
guava 237
gull 65
gulpers 179
gum tree 75, 141
Gymnobelideus leadbeateri (Leadbeater's
  possum) 131
Gyrinus natator (whirligig beetle) 92

habitats **see** caves; cold habitats; desert;
  peat bogs; plains; rainforest;
  underground; water habitat; yard
hagfishes 64
hair (and fur) 43, 167
Halcyon leucocephala (gray headed
  kingfisher) 239
Haliaeetus leucocephalus (bald eagle) 270
Haliaeetus vocifer (African fish eagle) 270
Hamamellis mollis (witch hazel) 332
hamster 154
Hapalochlaena lunulata (blue-ringed
  octopus) 30
hares 28, 43, 55, 120, 121, 182, 337
Harpia harpyja (harpy eagle) 356
harvest mouse 22
Hawaiian goose 185
hawkmoth 227, 330, 353
hawthorn 173

hearing and sound 23, 120
hedgehog 78, 324
Helianthus annuus (sunflower) 33
Helianthus tuberosus (Jerusalem
  artichoke) 70
Heliophorus epicles (butterfly) 307
Helix pomatia (edible snail) 355
Helogale parvula (dwarf mongoose) 215
Helostoma temmincki (kissing gourami) 48
henbane 162
Henopchus acuminatus (butterfly fish) 134
Heracleum mantegazzianum (giant
  hogweed) 164
herbs 44, 230-1
hermaphrodites **see** worms
heron 24, 246
Herpestes auropunctatus (small Indian
  mongoose) 215
Herpestes mungo (Indian gray mongoose)
  215
Heterocephalus glaber (naked mole rat) 55
Hevea braziliensis (rubber) 291
hibernation 154-5, 352
Hieraaetus morphnoides (little eagle) 270
Hieraaetus spilogaster (hawk eagle) 270
hinny 27
Hippocampus sp. (seahorse) 108
hippopotamus 131, 146
Hippopotamus amphibius (hippopotamus)
  146
Hirudinea (leeches) 287
Hirudo sp. (leech) 325
Hirudo medicinalis (medicinal leech) 177,
  287
hoatzin 95
hog 252
  see also pig
hogweed, giant 164
Homarus gammarus (common lobster) 269
Homo sapiens (man) 358
honey possum 105
honey-badger (ratel) 363
honey-guide bird 363
honeysuckle 196
Hordeum vulgare (barley) 166
hornbill 216
horns and antlers 59, 193, 245, 310
horse chestnut 158
horse family 27, 208
horseshoe crab 267
horsetail 320
house mouse 210, 312
house sparrow 15
hoverfly 293

howler monkey 357
hummingbird 205, 341
Hyacinthoides non-scripta (bluebell) 294
hyena 12
Hyaena hyaena (hyena) 12
hybrid 27
hydra 92, 176
Hydra sp. 92
Hydra viridis (green hydra) 176
Hydrochoerus hydrochoeris (capybara) 297
hydrothermal vent 283
Hyla cinerea (tree frog) 4, 356
Hylobates hoolock (gibbon) 222
Hylobates pileatus (pileated gibbon) 222
Hylobius abietis (pine weevil) 318
Hyoscyamus niger (henbane) 162
Hypnum cupressiforme (cypress-leaved
  feather moss) 62
Hypsignathus monstrosus (hammer-
  headed bat) 148
hyrax 226
Hystrix cristata (common porcupine) 249

ibex 313
iguana, marine 53
Illicium verum (star anise) 198
impala 121, 247
Impatiens sp. (touch-me-not) 288
Inachis io (peacock butterfly) 307
Indicator indicator (honey guide) 363
indri 130, 211
Indris brevicaudata (indri) 130, 211
insects
  ant 201
  aphids 309, 347
  armor 359
  beetle **see** beetles
  bioluminescence 286
  bloodsuckers 92, 177, 188, 194, 302, 347
  bog 322
  bug 330, 347
  bumblebee 82, 84, 345
  camouflage and crypsis 20, 330
  cave 282
  cicada 107
  cockroach 101
  desert 79
  and disease 49, 184, 188, 194
  dragonfly 72
  flea 184, 188
  garden 178
  grasshopper 273, 359
  hibernation 154-5
  lacewing 36

mountains 28-9, 122, 313
mouse
    harvest 22
    house 210, 312
    marsupial 305
    speed 121
    tail 22
    wood 337
mouthbrooding 152
moving plants 288
mudskipper 365
mulberry 334
mule 27
Muraena helena (moray eel) 17
Muraena sp. (moray eel) 362
Mus musculus (house mouse) 210
Musa sp. (banana) 125
Musca domestica (housefly) 210
mushroom **see** fungus
mushrooms **see** fungi
musk ox 245
mussel 153
Mya arenaria (sand gaper) 153
Mycena sp. (fairy bonnet toadstool) 354
Mygalomorpha (bird-eating spiders) 206
Myotis lucifugus (mouse-eared or little
    brown bat) 145, 155
Myrmecocystus sp (honeypot ant) 201
Myrmecophaga jubata (giant anteater) 41,
    148
Myrrhis odorata (sweet cicely) 13
Mytilus edulis (mussel) 153
Myxine sp. (hagfish) 64

Naja hannah (king cobra) 174
naming **see** scientific names
Nasalis larvatus (proboscis monkey) 148
Nathecium ossifragum (bog asphodel)
    322
nautilus 275
Nautilus macromphalus (nautilus.) 275
necks, long 202, 241
Nectarinia sp. (sunbird) 93
Necturus maculosus (eastern mud
    salamander) 349
needlefish 102
Nelumbo nucifera (sacred lotus) 180, 229
Nemichthyidae (snipe eels) 362
Neophron percnopterus (Egyptian vulture)
    266
Neotragus pygmaeus (royal antelope) 341
Nepa cinerea (water scorpion) 56
Nepenthes sp. (pitcher plant) 186
Nephelium lappaceum (rambutan) 237

Nephila sp. (spider) 206
Nereis diversicolor (ragworm) 165
nest 88
Nestor notabilis (kea) 280
netting **see** trapping
nettle 173, 196
Neuroterus sp. (spangle galls) 227
newt 8
    see also salamander
Nicotiana sp. (tobacco) 298
nicotine 298
Nicrophorus sp. (burying beetles) 256
`nits' 49
Noctilio leporinus (fisherman bat) 271
nocturnal animals 58, 91, 101, 104-5, 178,
    363
    see also bats; owls
noses **see** smell; strange noses
Notophthalmus viridescens (red-spotted
    newt or red eft) 8
nudibranch 34
Numenius arquata (curlew) 322
nuts 96, 157, 158, 227, 302
    see also fruit
Nyctea scandiaca (snowy owl) 43, 253
Nyctereutes procyonoides (raccoon-dog) 160
Nycticorax leuconotus (nankeen heron) 246
Nymphaea alba (white water lily) 229

oak 227
oats 166
oceans **see** water habitat
octopus 30
Octopus vulgaris (common octopus) 30
Ocypode sp. (ghost crab) 308
Odobenus rosmarus (walrus) 26, 168
oil-bearing plants
    castor 332
    corn 87
    eucalyptus 141
    nuts 157, 302
    olive 68
    peanut 96
    sunflower 33
Olea europea (olive) 68
olive 68
onion 183
Oniscus asellus (common sow bug) 210
Onymacris unguicularis (Namib beetle) 79
Ophiothrix sp. (brittle star) 94
Ophrys sp. (bee orchid) 346
Opisthocomus hoazin (hoatzin) 95
opium poppy 234
Opopsitta diophthalma (double-eyed fig

    parrot) 357
opossum/possum 305, 324, 341
Opuntia sp. (Galapagos prickly pear) 149
Opuntia lindheimeri (prickly pear) 111
Opuntia macrophila (prickly pear) 111
orangutan 131, 235
orchid 346
Orcinus orca (killer whale) 119
Oreamnos americanus (American
    mountain goat) 313
Ornithoptera alexandrae (Queen
    Alexandra's birdwing butterfly) 340
Ornithoptera paradisea (birdwing
    butterfly) 306
Ornithorhynchus anatinus (duckbilled
    platypus) 274
Orthotomus sutorius (Indian tailor bird) 88
Orycteropus afer (aardvark) 46
Oryctolagus cuniculus (rabbit) 57, 337
Oryza sativa (rice) 161
osprey 98
Ostrea edulis (oyster) 153
ostrich 10, 60, 121, 202, 242
otter 292, 329
Ovibos moschatus (musk-ox) 245
Ovis canadensis (Rocky mountain sheep)
    19
Ovis musimon (mufflon) 144
Ovis sp. (sheep) 144
owl monkey 104
owls 43, 54, 105, 120, 187, 253
Oxalis acetosella (wood sorrel) 288
Oxalis tuberosum (oca) 70
oyster 153

paddlefish 102
Pagurus bernhardus (hermit crab) 326
Pagurus sp. (hermit crab) 308
palms 125, 143, 302
Palomena prasina (green shield bug) 347
Palurius sp. (American spiny lobster) 269
Pan satyrus (chimpanzee) 225
Panax pseudoginseng (ginseng) 333
panda 67, 131
Pandion haliaetus (osprey) 98
pangolin 103, 109
Panolis flammea (pine beauty moth) 318
Panthera leo (lion) 63, 103
Panthera onca (jaguar) 131
Panthera pardus (leopard) 167
Panthera tigris (tiger) 103, 131, 261, 289
Pantodon buchholtzi (freshwater butterfly
    fish) 171
Papaver rhoeas (corn poppy) 234

393

Answer to piranha question:

It would take 6.25 minutes for the piranhas to reduce the whole human body to a skeleton.